GENDER

GEN
IVAN

DER

ILLICH

PANTHEON BOOKS NEW YORK

Library of Congress Cataloging in Publication Data
Illich, Ivan, 1926–
Gender.
Bibliography: p.
1. Women—Employment.   2. Women—Economic con-
ditions.   3. Sex discrimination against women.
4. Sex role.   I. Title.
5. Gender in History
6. Gender-specific tasks and tools
7. Sexism, modern—vs. traditional
patriarchy
HD6053.I38   1983   305.4′2   82–47893
ISBN 0–394–71587–X   AACR2
Manufactured in the United States of America
Book design by Camilla Filancia
First Pantheon paperback edition

Contents

Contents

Guide to Titled Footnotes

The footnotes have been composed for my students in a course at Berkeley in Fall 1982, and for those who want to use the text as a guide for independent study. Each *titled footnote* is meant as a reading assignment, as a tangent to the text, as a doorway to further research. Generally, I selected books I would like to discuss with my students, and starred a few that are of more general interest. Some items I included mainly because of the bibliography they contain, or for the guidance they provide to the history, the present status of research, and the controversy on the issue. These footnotes are not meant to prove but to illustrate and qualify my arguments; they are marginal glosses written in counterpoint to the text, outlines of my lectures to students who have prepared themselves by reading this book. The notes relate to the text as formerly *quesiones disputatae* related to the *summa*.

Acknowledgments

The break with the past, which has been described by others as the transition to a capitalist mode of production, I describe here as the transition from the aegis of gender to the regime of sex. In this book I sum up the position I reached in a conversation with Barbara Duden, and which grew out of a controversy between us. Originally, the issue was the economic and anthropological status of nineteenth-century housework. I have dealt with this in *Shadow Work*.[1] I consider this present essay one more step toward a *History of Scarcity* I want to write. In the case of Barbara Duden, I cannot recall who led whom into a new insight while remaining critical of the other's

1 VERNACULAR VALUES

Under the title *Shadow Work* (Boston and London: Marion Boyars, Inc., 1981, US Distributor: 99 Main Street, Salem, NH 03079) I have published five essays, of which the second and the third deal with the contrast between vernacular language and taught mother tongue. These essays are the result of long conversations with Professor D. P. Pattanayak, while I was studying under his guidance at the Central Institute of Indian Languages, Manasagangotri, Mysore 570006, India. For background, see Devi Prassad Pattanayak, *Aspects of Applied Linguistics* (New York: Asia Publishing House, 1981). For further research on this distinction, request the proceedings of the International Seminar "In Search of Terminology" (January 1982) from the above address. My two papers will become chapters of a book to be called *Vernacular Values*, which will appear in 1983 (Pantheon, New York) as a further contribution toward a history of scarcity. (On the term "vernacular," see FN 51.)

Acknowledgments

perspective. My collaboration with Lee Hoinacki was of a different kind. As at other times during the last two decades, we met to report to each other on what we had learned during the past year. We spent two weeks on his homestead and he reviewed my draft. While discussing and writing with him there and, later on, in Berlin, my text took on a new shape. Our conversations were frequently interrupted by laughter and the expressed desire that the reader come to share the pleasure we found in writing. I cannot say who finally turned any given phrase the way it now stands. Without his collaboration, I certainly would not have written *this* text.

In this book I have taken up the substance of several lectures that were part of my course on the social history of the twelfth century when I was a guest professor at the University of Kassel (1979–1981). I remember with gratitude Ernst Ulrich von Weizsäcker, Heinrich Dauber, and my students for their patient and courageous criticism.

I especially want to thank several people for what they have contributed through their conversations with me. Norma Swenson made me recognize the main weakness of *Medical Nemesis*, published in 1975: its *unisex perspective*. The reflections of Claudia von Werlhof on the *blind* angle of *economic perception* led me to distinguish its two faces, the shadow economy and the vernacular domain, both equally neglected but not equally denied. The distinction between *vernacular and industrial topology* on which I build I owe to Sigmar Groeneveld. Conversations with Ludolf Kuchenbuch have led me to new insights on the history of the *conjugal couple*. I have received invaluable encouragement from my old friends Ruth and Lenz Kriss-Rettenbeck (both ethnographers and art historians), with whom I share several teachers in the period between Hugo of St. Victor and Gustav Künstler. Part of my research was done while a fellow at the Institute for Advanced Studies in Berlin. Susan Hunt worked with me on this manuscript while preparing her reader on gender and sex, now available from Rt. 3, Box 650, Dexter, ME 04930.

I dedicate this book to Joseph Fitzpatrick, S.J., on his seventieth birthday. For thirty years he has tried to teach me sociology.

Cuernavaca, 1982

G*rateful acknowledgment is made to the following for permission to reprint previously published material:*

American Journal of Economics and Sociology: Excerpt from "The Monetary Value of a Housewife: A Replacement Cost Approach" by Harvey S. Rosen, January 1974. Copyright © 1974 by the American Journal of Economics and Sociology, Inc. Reprinted by permission of the *American Journal of Economics and Sociology*.

Catholic University of America Press: Excerpt from "The Position of Women: Appearance and Reality" by Ernestine Friedl, *Anthropological Quarterly* 40:3 (July 1967). Reprinted by permission of Catholic University of America Press.

The University of Chicago Press: Excerpts from the A. Leibowitz section and the Frank Stafford section of *Economics of the Family: Marriage, Children, Human Capital*, T. N. Schultz, ed. Copyright © 1974 by the University of Chicago. Reprinted by permission of the University of Chicago Press.

GENDER

I. Sexism and Economic Growth

Industrial society creates two myths: one about the sexual ancestry of this society and the other about its movement toward equality. Both myths are unmasked as lies of *humans* who belong to the "second sex." In my analysis, I begin with women's experience and try to construct categories that allow me to speak about the present and the past in a way that is more satisfactory to me.

I oppose the regime of scarcity to the reign of gender. I argue that the loss of vernacular gender is the decisive condition for the rise of capitalism and a life-style that depends on industrially produced commodities. Gender in modern English means ". . . one of three grammatical kinds, corresponding more or less to distinctions of sex (or the absence of sex) into which nouns are discriminated according to the nature of the modifications they require in words syntactically associated with them." (*OED*, 1932.) English nouns belong to masculine, feminine, or neuter gender. I have adopted this term to designate a distinction in behavior, a distinction universal in vernacular cultures. It distinguishes places, times, tools, tasks, forms of speech, gestures, and perceptions that are associated with men from those associated with women. This association constitutes *social* gender because it is specific to a time and place. I call it vernacular gender because this set of associations is as peculiar to a traditional people (in Latin, a *gens*) as is their vernacular speech.

I use gender, then, in a new way to designate a duality that in the past was too obvious even to be named, and is so far removed from us today that it is often confused with sex. By "sex" I mean the result of a polarization in those common characteristics that, starting with the late eighteenth century, are attributed to all human beings. Unlike vernacular gender, which always reflects an association between a dual, local, material culture and the men and women who live under its rule, *social sex* is "catholic"; it polarizes the human labor force, libido, character or intelligence, and is the result of a diagnosis (in Greek, "discrimination") of deviations from the abstract genderless norm of "the human." Sex can be discussed in the unambiguous language of science. Gender bespeaks a complementarity that is enigmatic and asymmetrical. Only metaphor can reach for it.

The transition from the dominance of gender to that of sex constitutes a change of the human condition that is without precedent. But the fact that gender might be irrecuperable is no reason to hide its loss by imputing sex to the past, or to lie about the entirely new degradations that it has brought to the present.

I know of no industrial society where women are the economic equals of men. Of everything that economics measures, women get less. The literature dealing with this economic sexism has recently turned into a flood. It documents sexist exploitation, denounces it as an injustice, usually describes it as a new version of an age-old evil, and proposes explanatory theories with remedial strategies built in. Through the institutional sponsorship of the United Nations, the World Council of Churches, governments, and universities, the latest growth industry of career reformers thrives. First the proletariat, then the underdeveloped, and now women are the favored pets of "the concerned." You can no longer mention sex discrimination without creating the impression that you want to contribute to the political economy of sex: Either you want to promote a "non-sexist economy," or you are engaged in whitewashing the sexist economy we have. Although I shall build my argument on this evidence of discrimination, I do not want to do either. To me, the pursuit of a non-sexist "economy" is as absurd as a sexist one is abhorrent. Here I shall expose the intrinsically sexist nature of economics as such and clarify the sexist nature of the most basic postulates on which economics, "the science of values under the assumption of scarcity," is built.

Sexism and Economic Growth

I shall explain how all economic growth entails the destruction of *vernacular gender* (chapters 3–5) and thrives on the exploitation of *economic* sex (chapter 2). I want to examine the economic apartheid and subordination of women and yet avoid the socio-biological and structuralist traps that explain this discrimination as "naturally" and "culturally" inevitable, respectively. As a historian, I want to trace the origins of women's *economic* subservience; as an anthropologist, I want to grasp what the new gradation reveals about kinship where it occurs; as a philosopher, I want to clarify what this repetitive pattern tells us about the axioms of popular wisdom, namely, those on which the contemporary university and its social sciences rest.

It was not easy to spell out what I have to say. More than I realized when I began, the ordinary speech of the industrial age revealed itself as *both* genderless and sexist. I knew that gender was dual, but my thinking was constantly distorted by the genderless perspective that industrialized language necessarily enforces. I found myself caught up in a distracting web of *key words*. I now see that key words are a characteristic feature of modern language, but clearly distinct from technical terms. "Automobile" and "jet" are technical terms. And I have learned that such words can overwhelm the lexicon of a traditional language. When this occurs, I speak of technological creolization. A term like "transportation," however, is a key word. It does more than designate a device—it imputes a basic need.[2]

2 KEY WORDS

I have been led to the study of key words by Raymond Williams, *Key Words: A Vocabulary of Culture and Society* (New York: Oxford University Press, pbk., 1976). This book is unlike any other "on words" that I know. Each entry conveys the surprise and passion of an aging man telling us about the inconstancy of a word on which his own integrity has rested. As a result of his guidance I have (1) ventured into the exploration of new types of key words and (2) attempted to identify the conditions under which a spider's web of key words could establish its network in everyday language. In formulating the method I use in such explanations, I have been guided by Peter Berger, Brigitte Berger, and Hansfried Kellner, *The Homeless Mind: Modernization and Consciousness* (New York: Vintage Books, 1974). For an introduction to a characteristically German type of historical semantics, see Irmline Veit-Brause, "A Note on *Begriffsgeschichte*," *History and Theory* 20, no. 1 (1981): 61–67. For the study

An examination of modern languages shows that key words are strong, persuasive, in common usage. Some are etymologically old but have acquired a new meaning totally unlike their former intent. "Family," "man," "work" are familiar examples. Others are of more recent coinage but were originally conceived for specialized use alone. At a certain moment they slipped into everyday language and now denote a wide area of thought and experience. "Role," "sex," "energy," "production," "development," "consumer" are well-known examples. In every industrialized language, these key words take on the semblance of common sense. And each modern language has its own set that provides that society's unique perspective on the social and ideological reality of the contemporary world. The set of key words in all modern industrialized languages is homologous. The reality they interpret is everywhere fundamentally the same. The same highways leading to the same school and office buildings overshadowed by the same TV antennas transform dissimilar landscapes and societies into monotonous uniformity. In much the same way, texts dominated by key words translate easily from English into Japanese or Malay.

Universal technical terms that have become key words, such as "education," "proletariat," and "medicine," mean the same thing in all modern languages. Other traditional terms with very different word fields, when used as key words, correspond almost exactly to each other across different languages. Examples are "humanity" and "*Menschheit*." Therefore, the study of key words calls for some comparison between languages.[3]

---

of specific, modern webs of utterances, I have been strongly influenced by Michel Foucault, *Power/Knowledge: Selected Interviews and Other Writings, 1972–77* (New York: Pantheon, 1981) and his earlier *The Archaeology of Knowledge* (New York: Harper and Row, 1976; orig.—Paris: Gallimard, 1969).

For the comparative semantics of key words in the principal Western European languages, Johann Knobloch, et. al., eds. *Europäische Schlüsselwörter*, 3 vols. (Munich: Max Hüber, 1963–67).

3 WORD FIELDS

Word fields have been traced and mapped in monographs and in dictionaries. For an international critical bibliography with essay-length

Sexism and Economic Growth

To explain the appearance of a dominance of key words in a language, I learned to distinguish *vernacular speech,* into which we grow through daily intercourse with people who speak their own minds, from *taught mother tongue,* which we acquire through professionals employed to speak for and to us. Key words

---

commentaries on word-field studies, see H. Gipper and H. Schwarz, *Bibliographisches Handbuch zur Sprachinhaltsforschung; Schrifttum zur Sprachinhaltsforschung in alphabetischer Folge nach Verfassern, mit Besprechungen und ·Inhaltshinweisen* (Cologne: Arbeitsgemeinschaft für Forschung des Landes Nordrhein-Westfalen, 1961). The book is complete only to the letter L, but two thematic indices to this first half of the book have already appeared. The twentieth-century semblance of common sense, which key words reflect, transcends individual languages; research into this popular wisdom frequently requires comparisons. For the English language, the prime instrument for research is A *Supplement to the Oxford English Dictionary,* ed. R.W. Burchfield, 3 vols. (Oxford: Clarendon Press, 1972). "The vocabulary treated is that which came into use during the publication of the successive sections of the main dictionary (the *OED*)—that is, between 1884, when the first fascicle of the letter A was published, and 1928, when the final section of the dictionary appeared, together with accessions to the English language in Britain and abroad from 1928 to the present day." Also, William Little, H.W. Fowler, and Jessie Coulson, comp., *The Shorter Oxford English Dictionary on Historical Principles,* 2 vols., rev. and ed. C.T. Onions; third edition completely reset with etymologies revised by G.W.S. Friedrichsen and with revised addenda (Oxford: Clarendon Press, 1973). This presents in miniature all the features of the main work, including older colloquial English, obsolete, archaic, and dialectal words and uses. Always useful: H.L. Mencken, *The American Language: An Inquiry into the Development of English in the United States*—the fourth edition and the two abridged supplements with annotations and new material by Raven I. McDavid, Jr., with the assistance of David W. Maurer (New York: Knopf, 1980). A one-volume abridged edition in paperback also exists. For French, very handy: Paul Robert, *Dictionnaire alphabétique et analogique de la langue française* (Paris: Nouveau Littré, 1967) (on the cover: *Petit Robert*). This is an excellent and up-to-date abridgement of the six-volume major work. An attempt is now being undertaken in France to equal the *OED* and its supplements with Paul Imbs, ed., *Trésor de la langue française; Dictionnaire de la langue du XIXe et du XXe siècle* (1789–1960) (Paris: CNRS, 1971–). However, the scope of this comprehensive, historical dictionary was reduced drastically beginning with volume three. For Spanish, I give preference to J. Corominas, *Diccionario crítico etimológico de la lengua castellana* (Madrid: Gredoš, 1954–57). Enlarged "*adiciones, restificaciones*

are a characteristic of taught mother tongue. They are even more effective than the mere standardization of the vocabulary and grammatical rules in their repression of the vernacular because, having the appearance of a *common* sense, they put a pseudo-vernacular gloss on engineered reality. Key words, then, are also more important for the formation of an industrialized language than creolization by technical terms because each one denotes a perspective common to the entire set. I have found that the paramount characteristic of key words in all languages is their exclusion of gender. Therefore, an understanding of gender, and its distinction from sex (a key word), depends on the avoidance or wary use of all terms that might be key words.

Linguistically, then, I found myself in a double ghetto when I started to write this essay: I was unable to use words in the traditional resonance of gender, and unwilling to repeat them with their current sexist ring. I first noticed the difficulty when I tried to use earlier versions of this text in my lectures during 1980–82. Never before had so many colleagues and friends attempted to

---

e indices" will be found in the fourth volume of the reprint (Bern: Francke, 1979). Most entries contain a bibliography that refers to critical studies on the term. In German, Jacob & Wilhelm Grimm's *Deutsches Wörterbuch* (orig. 1854–1960, 16 vols.) is now being revised but is accessible to few people. Instead try Hermann Paul, *Deutsches Wörterbuch.* 5th ed. Völlig neu bearb. und erw. Aufl. v. N. Werner Betz (Tübingen: Niemeyer, 1966). Due to peculiar German interest in the history of ideas and the history of concepts, two major German reference tools have no equal in other languages, and can often be used for the study of key words in other European languages. First, there is Joachim Ritter, ed., *Historisches Wörterbuch der Philosophie*, rev. ed. (Basel: Schwabe; Darmstadt: Wissenschaftliche Buchgesellschaft, 1971–). Six of the planned ten volumes have appeared so far. Secondly, Otto Brunner, Werner Conze, and Reinhart Koselleck, eds., *Geschichtliche Grundbegriffe; historisches Lexikon zur politisch-sozialen Sprache in Deutschland* (Stuttgart: E. Klett, 1972–). This will comprise, when finished, 130 monographic articles on socio-political terms and concepts. For Italian, Salvatore Battaglia, *Grande dizionario della lingua italiana*, 8 vols., ed. Giorgio Bárberi Squarotti (Turin: Unione Tipografico, 1961–). Planned on historical principles, its indices give easy access to numerous, also modern, citations. To establish the contrast between vernacular synonyms and uniquack key words, I use Carl Darling Buck, *A Dictionary of Selected Synonyms in the Principal Indo-European Languages: A Contribution to the History of Ideas* (Chicago: University of Chicago Press, 1949).

dissuade me from a task on which I had embarked. Most felt that I should turn my attention to something less trivial, less ambiguous, or less scabrous; others insisted that, in the present crisis of feminism, talk about women was not for men. Listening carefully, I came to see that most of my interlocutors felt uneasy because my reasoning interfered with their dreams: with the feminist dream of a genderless economy without compulsory sex roles; with the leftist dream of a political economy whose subjects would be equally human;[4] with the futurist dream of a modern society where people are plastic, their choices of being a dentist, a male, a Protestant, or a gene-manipulator deserving the same respect. The conclusion about economics *tout court*, which my perspective on sex discrimination revealed, upset each dream with equal force, since the desires that these dreams express are all made of the same stuff: genderless economics (see chapter 7).

An industrial society cannot exist unless it imposes certain unisex assumptions: the assumptions that both sexes are made for the same work, perceive the same reality, and have, with some minor cosmetic variations, the same needs.[5] And the assumption

4 THE HUMAN

Before the eighteenth century, "humane" was the normal spelling for the main-range meanings characteristic of the human species: its members were humane, but all *humans* were either men or women or children. Only during the late eighteenth century did the word acquire the meaning it has today—kind, gentle, courteous, sympathetic. *Humanity* has had a different but related development. Since the fourteenth century, the term has meant something similar to, but not identical with, the Italian *umanitá* and the French *humanité*, generally synonymous with courtesy, politeness, and a strong sense of civility. From the sixteenth century onward, it extends to kindness and generosity. The use of "humanity" to indicate, neutrally, a set of human characteristics or attributes is not common, in its abstract sense, before the eighteenth century, while today this is its first meaning. "Human" now has the same abstract sense. In addition, it indicates *condoned fallibility*, human error: "He has a human side to him." Consult Williams, (*op. cit.*, p. 121ff, FN 2). For a bibliography on the concept and term, see Michael Landmann, *Philosophical Anthropology* (Philadelphia: Westminster Press, 1974).

5 GENDERLESS INDIVIDUALISM

Historians, even those who focus on the history of economic ideas, have not yet noted that the loss of gender creates the subject of formal economics. Marcel Mauss was the first to recognize that "only recently have

of scarcity, which is fundamental to economics, is itself logically based on this unisex postulate. There could be no competition for "work" between men and women, unless "work" had been redefined as an activity that befits humans irrespective of their sex. The subject on which economic theory is based is just such a genderless *human*. Then, with scarcity accepted, the unisex postu-

---

our Western societies made man into an *economic animal"* (1909). Westernized man is *Homo oeconomicus*. We call a society "Western" when its institutions are reshaped for the *disembedded* production of commodities that meet this being's basic needs. On this, see Karl Polanyi, **The Great Transformation* (New York: Octagon Books, 1975). On his influence: S.C. Humphreys, "History, Economics and Anthropology: The Work of Karl Polanyi," *History and Theory* 9, no. 2 (1968) 165–212. The novel definition of man as the subject and client of a "disembedded" economy has a history. As an introduction to this history, I highly recommend Louis Dumont, **From Mandeville to Marx: Genesis and Triumph of Economic Ideology* (Chicago: University of Chicago Press, 1977). The perception of ego as a *human*, and the demand that social institutions fit the ego's egalitarian human needs, represent a break with all pre-modern forms of consciousness. But to define the precise character of this radical discontinuity in consciousness remains very much a controversial issue. For one orientation on the dispute, see Marshall Sahlins, *Culture and Practical Reason* (Chicago: University of Chicago Press, 1976). Sahlins identifies the difference between then and now as a "distinctive mode of symbolic production" that is peculiar to Western civilization (p. 220). I do not quarrel with Sahlins on this point. However, in this context I argue that there is a profound discontinuity between all past forms of existence and Western individualism; and this change constitutes a fundamental rupture. It consists primarily in the *loss of gender*. And this loss of social gender has not yet been treated adequately in the history of individualism. A historiography of economic individualism might best begin with Elie Halevy, **The Growth of Philosophical Radicalism* (Clifton, NJ: Kelly reprint, 1972), based on an abridged translation by M. Morris in 1952. He charts and explains in detail the highly discrepant effects Bentham had on his various disciples. He calls Bentham and his disciples "radical" because they consciously broke all ties with previous philosophical traditions. On the transformation of personality structure, at the deepest levels, that created the English working class between the years 1790 and 1830, see E. P. Thompson, *The Making of the English Working Class* (New York: Random House, 1966). Utilitarianism could produce faith in bureaucratic paternalism based on legislative intervention, or belief in anarchical individualism and *laissez faire*. Halevy describes how both positions were held by Bentham's pupils. See also: Leszek Kolakowski, *Main Currents in Marxism: Its Rise, Growth and Dissolution*, 3 vols. (London: Oxford University

late spreads. Every modern institution, from school to family and from union to courtroom, incorporates this assumption of scarcity, thereby dispersing its constitutive unisex postulate throughout the society. For example, men and women have always grown up; now they need "education" to do so. In traditional societies, they matured without the conditions for growth being perceived as scarce. Now, educational institutions teach them that desirable learning and competence are scarce goods for which men and women must compete. Thus, education turns into the name for learning to live under an assumption of scarcity. But education, considered as an example of a *typical* modern need, entails more: It assumes the scarcity of a genderless value; it teaches that he or she who experiences its process is primarily a human being in need of genderless education. Economic institutions, then, are based on the assumption of scarcity in genderless values, equally desirable or necessary for competing neuters belonging to two

Press, 1978). In the mirror of twentieth-century Marxism, the social history of this century can be read as a conflict between groups espousing these opposite policies deduced from utilitarian principles. Dumont (see above, this footnote) explores the fundamental commonality of utilitarian thought. He offers a careful and solid textual analysis of Mandeville, Locke, Smith, and Marx. Each of these thinkers conceptualizes "human" as "individual," determined by basic needs under the assumption of universal scarcity. What "individual" means is further clarified by C.B. MacPherson, *The Political Theory of Possessive Individualism: Hobbes to Locke* (London: Oxford University Press, pbk., 1962) and, by the same author, *The Real World of Democracy* (London: Oxford University Press, 1966) and *Democratic Theory: Essays on Retrieval* (London: Oxford University Press, 1972). He carefully substantiates his intuition that the fundamental common trait of the individual, which underlies all modern democratic thought, is its *possessive* quality. He shows that all humanisms of the nineteenth and twentieth centuries rest on the ultimate value of the free, self-developing, possessive individual, insofar as freedom is seen as a possession, namely a freedom from any but economic relations with others. In this present essay, I argue that a second characteristic is equally constitutive of the subject of modern social theory and practice: The *possessive* individual is *genderless*, anthropologically construed as a merely sexed neuter. Logically, as I shall argue, only the individual who is both possessive and genderless can fit the assumption of scarcity on which any political economy must rest. The institutional "identity" of *Homo oeconomicus* excludes gender. *He* is a *neutrum oeconomicum*. Therefore, the loss of social gender is an integral part of the history of scarcity and of the institutions that structure it.

biological sexes.[6] What Karl Polanyi has called the "disembedding" of a formal market economy, I am describing, anthropologically, as the transmogrification of gender to sex.

Relentlessly, economic institutions transform the two culturally embedded genders into something new, into economic

6 INVIDIOUS INDIVIDUALISM

The contemporary, genderless, possessive individual, the subject of the economy, lives by decisions based on considerations of marginal utility. Every economic decision is embedded in a sense of scarcity, and thus tends toward a kind of envy unknown to the past. Modern *productive* institutions at the same time foster and mask invidious individualism, something the *subsistence-oriented* institutions of all past ages were designed to reduce and to expose. This is the argument of Paul Dumouchel and Jean-Pierre Dupuy, *L'enfer des choses: René Girard et la logique de l'économie* (Paris: Seuil, 1979). The authors attempt to clarify the typological contrast between modern institutions, which generate and then disguise envy, and those that had the inverse function and were replaced. In independent essays, the two authors apply to economics the results reached through literary analysis by René Girard, *Deceit, Desire and the Novel: Self and Other in Literary Structure*, trans. Yvonne Freccero (Baltimore: Johns Hopkins Press, pbk., 1976). Also see R. Girard, *Violence and the Sacred* (Baltimore: Johns Hopkins University Press, 1977). Girard finds in the nineteenth-century novel a source of evidence for a historic transformation of desire: the evolution of "needs" based on invidious comparison with the other's aspirations. Rather than analyzing Dostoyevsky's figures through Freudian categories, he demystifies Freud by looking at him though the eyes of the brothers Karamazov. In this perspective, what is considered economic progress appears as the institutional spread of triangular, or "mimetic," desire. The history of economic individualism coincides with the modernization of envy. In this essay, I discuss the appearance of a new kind of envy, characteristic of the relations between the sexes, one that arises only as gender fades from a society. I do not find an explicit history-of-envy treatment of this theme in the available literature. Fundamental for the anthropology of envy remains George M. Foster, "Peasant Society and the Image of Limited Good," *American Anthropologist* 67, no. 2 (April 1965): 293–315 and, by the same author, *"The Anatomy of Envy: A Study in Symbolic Behavior," Current Anthropology* 13, no. 2 (April 1972): 165–202. "Sensing the ever-present threat of envy to himself and to his society, man fears: He fears the consequences of his own envy, and he fears the consequences of the envy of others. As a result, in every society people use symbolic and non-symbolic cultural forms whose function is to neutralize or reduce or otherwise control the dangers they see stemming from envy, and especially their

neuters distinguished by nothing more than their disembedded sex. A characteristic but quite secondary bulge in the blue jeans is now all that differentiates and bestows privilege on one kind of human being over the other. *Economic* discrimination against women cannot exist without the abolition of gender and the social construction of sex.[7] This I shall attempt to establish with my

---

fear of envy." For the perception of envy in classical antiquity, see Svend Ranulf, *The Jealousy of the Gods and Criminal Law in Athens: A Contribution to the Sociology of Moral Indignation*, 2 vols. (London: Williams & Norgate; Copenhagen: Levin & Munksgaard, 1933–34). On *hybris* calling for nemesis: David Grene, *Greek Political Theory: The Image of Man in Thucydides and Plato* (Chicago: University of Chicago Press, Phoenix Books, 1965)—the original title was *Man in His Pride*—and E.R. Dodds, *The Greeks and the Irrational* (Berkeley: University of California Press, 1968), esp. chapter 2. For the late classical attitude toward envy, a study on its opposite is helpful: R.A. Gauthier, *Magnanimité: L'idéal de la grandeur dans la philosophie païenne et dans la théologie chrétienne* (Paris: Vrin, 1951). For the Christian treatment of envy as a vice, see Edouard Ranwez, "Envie," *Dictionnaire de Spiritualité* (1932–); also, Lester K. Little, "Pride Goes Before Avarice: Social Change and the Vices in Latin Christendom," *The American Historical Review* 76 (February 1971): 16–49. On the iconography of envy during the Middle Ages, see Mireille Vincent-Cassy, *"L'envie au Moyen Age," *Annales, ESC* 35, no. 2 (March–April 1980): 253–71 and, by the same author, "Quelques réflexions sur l'envie et la jalousie en France au XIVe siècle," in Michel Mollat, *Etudes sur l'histoire de la pauvreté* (Moyen Age–XVIe siècle), 8, Série Etudes (Paris: Publications de la Sorbonne, 1974): 487–503. A history of envy would be something quite different from the attempt of a modern psychologist or sociologist to try to impute what he considers to be "envy" to people in other ages. Characteristic of such historical treatments are Melanie Klein, *Envy and Gratitude* (New York: Delacorte Press, 1975), esp. pp. 176–235, who starts with the Freudian assumption that women have always coveted what in classical English is called the "tool"; and Helmut Schoeck, *Envy, A Theory of Social Behavior* (New York: Harcourt, Brace and World, 1970), who totally misses the point that the emotion and the perception of envy have a history. Malevolent disparagement between men and women is not a new social phenomenon; the institutionalization of lifelong invidious comparison between genderless individuals is historically unprecedented.

7 SEX AND SEXISM

The word "sex" is derived from the Latin *sexus* and is related to *seco*, *sec-, a root for division: seg-ment. Grammatically, the word must always be

argument. And if this is true—namely, that economic growth is intrinsically and irremediably gender-destructive, that is, sexist—the sexism can be reduced only at the "cost" of economic shrinkage. Further, the decline of sexism requires as a necessary, albeit insufficient, condition the contraction of the cash nexus and the

---

accompanied by either *virile* (male) or *muliebre* (female). During the Enlightenment, while "the human" took form as an ideal, the French use of the term was restricted to the segregation of women. *"Le sexe"* merits ten lines in Diderot's *Encyclopédie*: "Le sexe absolument parlant, ou plutôt *le beau sexe*, est l'épithète qu'on donne aux femmes . . . les plus chères délices du citoyen paisible . . . [dont] l'heureuse fécondité perpétue les amours et les grâces. . . ." Only in the last quarter of the nineteenth century did the term come to mean something common to both men and women, although its weight, shape, and significance were posited as different in the two. For both, however, it meant a kind of plumbing system channeling a genderless force that, by the end of the century, Freud called "libido." The new, genderless meaning of the modern "sex" appears clearly in such terms as "sexuality." When functioning as a key word, sex is paradoxically genderless. And the formation of genderless sexuality is one of the necessary prerequisites for the appearance of *Homo oeconomicus*. For this reason I oppose *economic sex* to *vernacular gender*. By the former, I designate a complementary duality; by the second, the polarization of a common characteristic. Both gender and sex are social realities with only a tenuous connection to anatomy. Individualized economic sex is all that is left of social gender in the self-conscious pseudo-gender of the contemporary *well-sexed human*. Gender just cannot thrive in an environment shaped by economics. However, the background condition for this transformation, the despoliation of a social environment suitable for vernacular gender, is a subject so far ignored by ecologists. Obviously, I am using *gender* and *sex* as ideal types in the sense of Max Weber, *The Methodology of the Social Sciences*, trans. and ed. E.A. Shils (Glencoe, IL: Free Press, 1949): 93ff. An ideal type is a conceptual construct (*ein Gedankenbild*), which is neither historical reality nor even "true" reality. It is even less fit to serve as a schema under which a real situation or action is to be subsumed as one item. An ideal type has the significance of a purely ideal, *limiting* concept with which the real situation or action is *compared* and surveyed for the explication of certain of its significant components. For me, *gender* and *sex* are ideal, limiting concepts to designate a polarity: the industrial transformation of society from a "gendering" into a "sexing" system. For both, for gender and for sex, anatomy is but the raw material. Both gender and sex transform the genital organs into a social reality. Gender transforms the penis into innumerable types of phalluses; sex only *produces* the one, international, threatening,

Sexism and Economic Growth

expansion of non-market-related, non-economic forms of subsistence.

Up to now, two major motifs have emerged that impel us to adopt negative growth policies: environmental degradation[8] and paradoxical counterproductivity.[9] Now a third urges us: Negative

---

enviable "penis." (On the analogous homogenization of womb and vagina, see FNs 87, 90.) Gayle Rubin (Cf. FNs 22, 76) underscores the fact that among *human* groups the existence of gender systems is universal, although the configuration of these systems varies widely. However, regardless of its unique content, each society exhibits an ideology that presents gender categories as unalterable. I agree, but further argue that a *sexed* society exhibits an ideology that presents gender as irrevocably passé. (On patriarchy vs. sexism, see FN 21.) On the subtle range of variation of gender symbols, see FNs 116, 117, as well as L. Kriss-Rettenbeck, *"Feige": Wort, Gebärde, Amulett* (Munich, 1955) and M.L. Wagner, "Phallus, Horn und Fisch. Lebendige und verschüttete Vorstellungen und Symbole, vornehmlich im Bereich des Mittelmeerbeckens," *Domum Natalicium* (Zurich: Carol Jaberg, 1973): 77–130. Also see FN 118.

8 ENVIRONMENTAL DEGRADATION

Here I refer to the growing recognition of limits that change the fundamental assumptions of political economy. Though ecology (as science and as belief system) has only a short history, it is now moving toward maturity. The mark of a maturing discipline is its growing reference to its own history. The term *Oekologie* was first coined 1866 by E. Haecker, relating animal morphology to Charles Darwin's theory of evolution. Robert P. McIntosh, *"The Background and Some Current Problems of Theoretical Ecology," *Synthèse* 43 (1980): 195–255, provides a critical and analytic historiography of ecology in the bio-sciences. Ecology as a political science is of much more recent origin. For an introduction to present issues, see William Ophuls, *Ecology and the Politics of Scarcity: Prologue to a Political Theory of Steady State* (New York: W.H. Freeman, 1977). In my opinion, political ecology cannot mature unless it incorporates two distinctions, now neglected: first, the juristic distinction between *the commons* and *productive resources* (see FN 10) and, second, the distinction between complementary domains and genderless space (see text pp. 105 ff.). See also FNs 78, 79, 84–87.

9 COUNTERPRODUCTIVITY

Counterproductivity is a social indicator that measures a group- or class-specific frustration resulting from the obligatory consumption of a good or service. Time loss through the acceleration of traffic patterns, medicine that makes one sick rather than well, stultification by educational curricula

· 1 5 ·

growth is necessary to reduce sexism. This proposition is hard to accept for the well-meaning critics who have tried during the past year to divert me from my present line of argument; they feared either that I would make a fool of myself or that their dreams of growth with equality would appear to be fantasies. I believe, however, that this is the time to turn social strategies topsy-turvy, to recognize that peace between men and women, whatever form it might take, depends on economic contraction and not on economic expansion. Up to now, no goodwill and no struggle, no legislation and no technique, have reduced the sexist exploitation characteristic of industrial society. As I shall show, the interpretation of this economic degradation by sex as just more machismo under market conditions will not wash. Up to now, wherever equal rights were legally enacted and enforced, wherever partner-

---

or news, dependence induced through political or social guidance—all are examples. The phenomenon can be viewed as measuring the *intensity* with which a modern institution, by *technical necessity*, denies a majority of its clients the purported benefit for which one of its characteristics—for example, speed in transportation—was originally engineered and publicly financed. Counterproductivity is not congestion, a frustration that results simply from the fact that commodities of the same kind get into each other's way, be these cars, curricula, or therapies. In my opinion, counterproductivity is the result of a *radical monopoly of commodities over vernacular values*, which I still called use values in Ivan Illich, *Tools for Conviviality* (New York: Harper and Row; London: Marion Boyars, 1971), esp. chapter 3, part 2, and Ivan Illich, "Energy and Equity" in *Toward a History of Needs* (New York: Pantheon, 1977): 110–43. This radical monopoly stems ultimately from the transformation of the commons—for instance, those regulated by traditional laws on the *right of way* for pedestrians—into public utilities necessary for the production or circulation of commodities. Ivan Illich, *Medical Nemesis* (London: Marion Boyars, 1975; New York: Pantheon, 1976) was written to illustrate how counterproductivity works specifically on the levels of technique, social structure, and cultural symbols. Jean-Pierre Dupuy, *Valeur sociale et encombrement du temps: Monographie du séminaire d'économétrie* (Paris: CNRS, 1975), and ean-Pierre Dupuy and Jean Robert, *La trahison de l'opulence* (Paris: PUF, 1976) clarify that counterproductivity is not a measure of individual impediments that can be overcome by political or technical means but is ultimately a social indicator that reflects technological characteristics. A brilliant and vivid outline for public discussion on the issue is Wolfgang Sachs, "Are Energy-Intensive Life Images Fading? The Cultural Meaning of the Automobile in Transition" (Berlin: [ms.] Technische Universität, 10/1981). See also FNs 60, 112.

ship between the sexes became stylish, these innovations gave a sense of accomplishment to the elites who proposed and obtained them, but left the majority of women untouched, if not worse off than before.

The ideal of unisex economic equality is now dying, much like the ideal of growth leading to a convergence of GNP north and south of the equator is. However, it is now possible to invert the issue. Instead of clinging to the dream of anti-discriminatory growth, it appears more sensible to pursue economic shrinkage as the policy along which a non-sexist or, at least, a less sexist society can come into being. Upon reflection, I now see that an industrial economy without a sexist hierarchy is as farfetched as that of a pre-industrial society without gender; that is, without a clear division between what men and what women do, say, and see. Both are pipe dreams, regardless of the sex of the dreamer. But the reduction of the cash nexus, that is, of both commodity production *and* commodity dependence, is *not* in the realm of fantasy. Such a cutback, however, means the repudiation of everyday expectations and habits now thought "natural to man." Many people, including some who know that rollback is the necessary alternative to horror, view the choice as impossible. But a rapidly growing number of experienced people, together with an increasing number of experts (some convinced and others opportunistic), agree that cutting back is the wise choice. Subsistence that is based on a progressive unplugging from the cash nexus now appears to be a condition for survival. Without negative growth, it is impossible to maintain an ecological balance, achieve justice among regions, or foster people's peace. And the policy must, of course, be implemented in rich countries at a much higher rate than in poor ones. Perhaps the maximum anyone can reasonably hope for is equal access to the world's scarce resources at the level currently typical for the poorest nations. The translation of such a proposition into specific action would require a multi-faceted alliance of many diverse groups and interests that pursues the recovery of the commons, what I call "radical political ecology."[10] To bring those aggrieved by the loss of gender

10 THE RECOVERY OF THE COMMONS

"Commons" is an old English word. *Almende* and *Gemeinheit* are corresponding German terms [see Ivan Illich, *Das Recht auf Gemeinheit*

into this alliance, I shall here establish the linkage between shift from production to subsistence and the reduction of sexism.

To demonstrate that this kind of relationship between sexism and economics does indeed exist, I must construct a theory. This theory is a prerequisite for a history of scarcity.[11] Throughout

---

(Hamburg: Rowohlt, 1981), introduction]. The Italian term is *gli usi civici*. "Commons" referred to that part of the environment that lay beyond a person's own threshold and outside his own possession, but to which, however, that person had a recognized claim of usage—not to produce commodities but to provide for the subsistence of kin. Neither wilderness nor home is commons, but that part of the environment for which customary law exacts specific forms of community respect. I will discuss the degradation of the commons through its transformation into a productive resource in *Vernacular Values* (*op. cit.* FN 1). Those who struggle to preserve the biosphere, and those who oppose a style of life characterized by a monopoly of commodities over activities, by reclaiming in bits and pieces the ability to exist outside the market's regime of scarcity, have recently begun to coalesce in a new alliance. The one value shared by all currents within this alliance is the attempt to recover and enlarge, in some way, *the commons*. This emerging and converging social reality has been called the "archipelago of conviviality" by André Gorz. The key instrument for mapping this new world is Valentina Borremans, *Reference Guide to Convivial Tools*, Special Report no. 13 (New York: *Library Journal*, 1980), a critical guide to over a thousand bibliographies, catalogues, journals, etc. Periodical information and bibliographies on the struggle for a new commons can be found in such journals as: *TRANET*: Trans-National Network for Appropriate Alternative Technology, P.O. Box 567, Rangeley, ME 04980; *CoEvolution Quarterly*, Steward Brand, ed., P.O. Box 428, Sausalito, CA 94965.

For a more limited but lively survey, see George McRobie, **Small Is Possible* (London: Intermediate Technology Publications, 1981) and, more political, Harry Boyte, **The Backyard Revolution* (Philadelphia: Temple University Press, 1980). A major intellectual obstacle to the common formulation of the new claim on the commons is the consistent tendency among philosophers, jurists, and social critics to confuse *the commons* with industrial-age *public utilities*. I argue that the commons, which were protected by legal precedents prior to industrialization, were in fact *gendered domains* (cf. FN 79).

11 SCARCITY

In this essay, I use the term in a narrow sense only, the one used by economists since L. Walras first inaugurated that precise meaning in 1874.

the essay, the theoretical argument is frequently highlighted with examples, rather than massively encumbered with data. The former are inserted in order to illustrate the theory and stimulate research, and the latter—when they exist—are integrated into the thematic footnotes. Because of the newness of this theoretical outlook and the paucity of empirical studies from this perspective, I occasionally found it necessary to use new language. Whenever possible, however, I used old words in new ways to say precisely what both the theory and the evidence demanded.

In this sense, scarcity defines the field in which the laws of economics relate (1) *subjects* (possessive, invidious, genderless individuals—personal or corporate), (2) *institutions* (which symbolically foster mimesis), and (3) *commodities*, within (4) an environment in which the commons have been transformed into *resources*, private or public. Thus used, scarcity should not be confused with (i) *rare* birds of interest to some ornithologist, (ii) a *meager* or niggardly diet on which camel drivers have lived for centuries in the desert, (iii) a *deficient* diet, as diagnosed by a social worker who visits a family, (iv) the *last reserves* of wheat in a typical eleventh-century French village—in which case custom or violence would assure that all get some, however small the amount. A useful source of references and bibliographies, although not yet a history of scarcity, is Bálint Balla, *Soziologie der Knappheit. Zum Verständnis individueller und gesellschaftlicher Mängelzustände* (Stuttgart: Enke, 1978). Niklas Luhman, "Knappheit, Geld und die bürgerliche Gesellschaft," *Jahrbuch für Sozialwissenschaft* 23, (1972): 186–210 has attempted to identify five characteristics of "social contingency" in regard to contemporary (and unquestioned) reliance on the regime of scarcity. Historically, the regime of scarcity was introduced through the proliferation of money as a scarce means of exchange; see Karl Polanyi, *Primitive, Archaic and Modern Economics: Essays of Karl Polanyi*, ed. G. Dalton (Boston: Beacon Press, 1971): 175–203, who distinguishes among the uses of money to conserve values, to measure value, and as a means of exchange. For a survey of psychoanalytical theories trying to explain the origins of scarcity, see Ernest Borneman, *Psychonalyse des Geldes* (Frankfurt: Suhrkamp, 1975), comprised of contributions by two dozen authors. Unless the distinction between scarce productive resources and shared, porous commons is philosophically and legally recognized, the coming *steady state society* will be an oligarchic, undemocratic, and authoritarian expertocracy governed by ecologists. This is cogently argued by William Ophuls, *Ecology and the Politics of Scarcity* (San Francisco: W.H. Freeman, 1979). The fading of gender and the growing intensity and variety of scarcities are two sides of the same process of *Westernization* (see a.a. FN 105). For this reason, I consider my current work on gender a preparatory study on which to build a history of scarcity.

My theory allows me to oppose two modes of existence, which I call the *reign of vernacular gender* and the *regime of economic sex*. The terms themselves indicate that both forms of being are dual *and* that the two dualities are *very* different in kind.[12] By social gender I mean the eminently local and time-bound duality that sets off men and women under circumstances and conditions that prevent them from saying, doing, desiring, or perceiving "the same thing." By economic, or social, sex I mean the duality that stretches toward the illusory goal of economic, political, legal, or social equality between women and men. Under this second construction of reality, as I shall show, equality is mostly fanciful. The essay, then, is cast in the form of an

12 DUALITY

It is conventional to use some kind of duality in sociological analysis. The duality that I propose is not related to any of those I know. In the duality I propose, the asymmetric complementarity of gender is opposed to the polarization of homogeneous characteristics that constitutes social sex. If I were addressing mathematicians, I would be tempted to speak about homomorphic pairs of domains, taken from heterogeneous spaces. For an orientation to the complexities of the issue, consult Lynda M. Glennon, *Women and Dualism: A Sociology of Knowledge Analysis* (New York: Longman, pbk., 1979). By using content analysis of feminist literature, the author shows how feminists have recently questioned the logic of duality, thereby challenging the "laws" of sociological conventions that relate a large number of analytic dualities to gender. She focuses primarily on dichotomized typologies since Ferdinand Töennies, barely mentioning earlier types. For her it was Töennies, *Gemeinschaft und Gesellschaft* (1887), who watered the soil from which other modern dualities grew: Maine's status society and contract society; Spencer's militant and industrial forms; Ratzenhofer's conquest state and culture state; Wundt's natural and cultural polarity; Durkheim's mechanical and organic solidarity; Cooley's primary and secondary (implicit) groups; MacIver's communal and associational relation; Zimmerman's localistic and cosmopolitan communities; Odum's folk state pair; Redfield's folk urban continuum; Soroking's familistic and contractual relations; Bercker's sacred and secular societies . . . just as he did for other dualities less tied to particular names, such as primitive-civilized; literate–non-literate; rural-urban; developed-underdeveloped; or prevalence of the public and the private, matriarchal/patriarchal (see also FN 54). In this essay I oppose gender and sex. I try to introduce the opposition of two dualities into social analysis: Gender stands for one, sex for the other. Besides indicating duality and a more or less explicit reference to genital difference, the two *social pairs* have little in common.

epilogue on the industrial age and its chimeras. Through writing it, I came to understand in a new way—beyond what I had seen in *Tools for Conviviality* (1971)—what this age has irremediably destroyed. Only the transmogrification of the commons into resources can be compared to that of gender into sex. I describe this from the perspective of the past. About the future, I know and say nothing.

II. Economic Sex

Proof of economic discrimination against women does not have to be established here. The evidence is already overwhelming. Fifteen years of feminist research has removed all doubts. However, two major tasks remain. First, we must learn to distinguish three separate arenas in all modern economies. In each of these arenas women are economically discriminated against, albeit in different ways. The three forms of discrimination were heretofore confused. Second, we must grow to understand the difference between this threefold *economic* discrimination against women and the patriarchal subordination of women in societies not yet penetrated by the cash nexus. Thus, sexist discrimination will serve as a speculum that mirrors what is called "economy" in advanced industrial societies. Any economy based on formal exchanges between the producer and the consumer of goods and/or services is first divided into a statistically reported and an unreported sector—the arenas of *reported* and *unreported discrimination* against women on the job. And then there always exists another economy, the shadow of the former, which is the third arena of *discrimination* against women: that found in the nether sector of *shadow work*.

The Reported Economy

Over the years, discrimination against women in paid, taxed, and officially reported jobs has not changed in severity but has

Economic Sex

grown in volume.[18] Presently, 51 percent of U.S. women are in the labor force; in 1880, only 5 percent were employed outside the home. Today, women comprise 42 percent of the U.S. labor force; in 1880, only 15 percent. Today, half of all married women have their own income from a job, while only 5 percent had

1 3   WORK AND SEX

Both "work" and "job" are key words today; see J. Knobloch, ed. (op. cit. FN 2) 2: 258–354 and O. Brunner (op. cit. FN 3) 1: 154–243. The vocabulary surrounding the idea of work is mostly technical and new: Arthur E. Bestor, Jr., "The Evolution of the Socialist Vocabulary," Journal of the History of Ideas 9, no. 3 (June 1948): 259–302. Most non-European languages have experienced great difficulties in translating the term "work"; for a bibliography, see Ivan Illich, "El derecho al desempleo creador," Tecno-Politica, Doc. 78/11, APD 479, Cuernavaca, Mexico. In the Middle Ages the relationship of work to income was tenuous: Helmut Stahleder, Arbeit in der mittelalterlichen Gesellschaft (Munich: Neue Schriftenreihe des Stadtarchivs München, 1972). Attitudes toward this relationship changed slowly with mechanization: Lynn White, Jr., "Medieval Engineering and the Sociology of Knowledge," Pacific Historical Review 44 (1975): 1–21. Only Martin Luther gave a contemporary meaning to "work": Hildburg Geist, "Arbeit: die Entscheidung eines Wortwertes durch Luther," Luther Jahrbuch (1931): 83–113. He discovered that work was somehow laudable in itself. "He was the true inventor of the modern doctrine that there is something inherently dignified and praiseworthy about labor, that the man who bears the burden in the heat of the day is somehow more pleasing to God than the man who takes his ease in the shade" (H.L. Mencken, op. cit. FN 3). The history of sex discrimination at work coincides with the slow establishment of wage labor as the prototype of work that should be dignified, gratifying, meaningful, and accessible to all. Well into the eighteenth century, even the rather small percentage of legitimate wage earners derived most of their own subsistence from participation in the household of their employers: Bronislaw Geremek, Le salariat dans l'artisanat parisien aux XIII–XVe siècles (Paris: Mouton, 1968). The necessity to live primarily off wages was a sign not of simple poverty but of misery. This is one of the main themes in Michel Mollat (op. cit. FN 6). A full set of legal rights was derived from poverty during the Middle Ages, and these were unrelated to work: G. Couvreur, Les pauvres ont-ils des droits? Recherches sur le vol en cas d'extrême nécessité depuis la Concordia de Gratien (1140) jusqu'à Guillaume d'Auxerre, mort en 1231 (Rome/Paris: Univ. Gregoriana, 1961). Also: B. Tierney, Medieval Poor Law: A Sketch of Canonical Theory and Its Applications in England (Berkeley: University of California Press, 1959). On the attitudes toward wage labor in Medici Florence, read Judith C.

outside, paying jobs a century ago. Today, the law keeps all curricula and careers open for women, but in 1880 many of both were closed to them. Today, women averagely spend twenty-eight years in employment; in 1880, the average was five. These all seem like significant steps toward economic equality, until you apply the one measuring stick that counts. The median yearly earnings of the average full-time employed woman still hovers around a magical ratio (3:5) of a man's average earnings: 59 percent, give or take 3 percent—the same percentage as one hundred years ago.[14] Neither educational opportunities nor legislative provi-

---

Brown and Jordan Goodman, "Women and Industry in Florence," *Journal of Economic History* 40, no. 1 (March 1980): 73–80. This study is based on two surveys of Florentine shops in 1561 and 1642, respectively. As the artisan sector grew from the late sixteenth century on, men were bid away from textile production into luxury trades. Women entered almost exclusively into the wool, silk, and clothing industries, which shifted, in response to changing demand, from the making of luxury clothes to more simple ones the production of which could be easily routinized. Thus, a rough sexual division of labor took place, separating the sexes between market- and non-market-related activities. Men supplied the artisan skills, and women the unskilled labor required for simple spinning and weaving and sewing. Consistently since then, with the expansion and generalization of wage labor, the economic discrimination of women at work has increased. More women find in lower-income wage labor the daily proof of their lower economic value. In the USA, for instance, the opportunities for women to enter various fields were much greater in colonial times than by the mid-nineteenth century: Elisabeth Anthony Dexter, *Career Women of America, 1776–1840* (Clifton, NJ: Augustus Kelley, 1972). For comparisons on wages and hours worked, Edith Abbott, *Women in Industry: A Study in American Economic History* (New York: Appleton, 1916) is still an unsurpassed summary. For more recent tables and statistics and bibliography, see Valerie Kincade Oppenheimer, *The Female Labor Force in the United States: Demographic and Economic Factors Governing Its Growth and Changing Composition*, Population Monograph no. 5 (Berkeley: University of California, Institute of International Studies, 1970) and Alice Kessler-Harris, "Women's Wage Work as Myth and History," *Labor History* 19 (1978): 287–307.

14 THE WIDENING WAGE GAP

In the USA, the wage gap between men and women continues to grow hand in hand with the enactment of anti-discrimination laws and organized feminist pressure. With the current stagflation, it might now reach an all-

sions nor revolutionary rhetoric—political, technological, or sexual—have changed the magnitude by which women, in their earnings, stand below men.[15] What at first sight looks like so many steps toward equity is, in the perspective of the average woman, only a series of events by which more women have been

---

time measured record: 55 percent. The wage gap is larger in the States now than it was twenty years ago, even though the country has had a federal pay law since 1963. The $2,827 median wage or salary income of women employed full-time year-round in 1956 was 63 percent of the $4,466 median income of men. Although women's median income rose to $6,488 in 1973, men's median income rose even faster to $11,468. Thus, the full-time, year-round wage and salary income of women fell to 57 percent of men's income during the Kennedy years and the Vietnam War. Comparable standardized wage gaps for some other countries: Austria, 64.4 percent (1975); Canada, 59 percent (1971); France, 66.6 percent (1972); Sweden, 86 percent (1974). I have taken this information from Ronnie Steinberg Ratner, *Equal Employment Policy for Women: Strategies for Implementation in the USA, Canada, and Western Europe* (Philadelphia: Temple University Press, 1978): 20–23. This is a collection of original essays surveying a variety of institutional means by which women's equal employment opportunities have become "effective" during the postwar years: This so-called multiple effectiveness of equal employment rules has not affected average lifelong income differentials (see FN 15). Among industrialized nations, Japan has been an exception: In 1960, women's wages were 43 percent of men's; in 1974, 54 percent. Simultaneously, however, the *social* discrimination of women became more acute. On the background of this evolution, see Kazuko Tsurumi, *Women in Japan: A Paradox of Modernization* (Tokyo: Sophia University, Institute of International Relations, 1977). For a recent bibliography, see *Women at Work: An ILO News Bulletin*, no. 2, (Geneva: International Labor Organization Office for Women Workers' Questions, 1979). For easy reference to statistics on women's incomes, monetary and non-monetary (such as health services) by educational level, see Jeanne Mager Stellman, *Women's Work, Women's Health: Myths and Realities* (New York: Pantheon, 1977). For literature on the same theme: Mei Liang Bickner, *Women at Work: An Annotated Bibliography*, 2 vols. (Los Angeles: Manpower Research Center, Institute of Industrial Relations, University of California, 1974 and 1977). A special form of women's work is *paid housework*, which is more sex-specific than any other modern occupation and is characterized by a wage differential between men and women more extreme than for other forms of work. For the first major history of this economic activity, which was also born during the nineteenth century, and a guide to further literature, see David Katzman, *Seven*

GENDER

quietly incorporated into the population that is economically
discriminated against on grounds of sex. The current median lifetime income of a female college graduate, even if she has an
advanced degree, is still only comparable to that of male high
school dropouts.

Days a Week: Women and Domestic Service in Industrializing America
(New York: Oxford University Press, 1978). For comparison, see I.
Davidoff and R. Hawthorn, *A Day in the Life of a Victorian Domestic
Servant* (London: Allen & Unwin, 1976) and Pierre Guiral and Guy
Thuiller, *La vie quotidienne des domestiques en France au XIXe siècle*
(Paris: Hachette, 1976). The total number of women exploited in domestic service worldwide is much larger today than in the nineteenth century,
but located in the Third World. See, for instance, Elisabeth Jelin, "Migra-
tion and Labor Force Participation of Latin American Women: The Domestic Servant in the Cities," *Signs* 3, no. 1 (1977): 129–41. Women
more than men migrate to cities. The market for them is literally unlimited. Female household servants in large parts of Latin America can be
found in households so low on the social ladder that, for comparison, it
would be necessary to look at conditions in nineteenth-century Europe.

15 STATISTICS ON DISCRIMINATION

To cull from the US census as much as such data can say, consult Robert
Tsuchigane and Norton Dodge, *Economic Discrimination Against Women
at Work* (Lexington, MA: D.C. Heath, Lexington Books, 1974). This is a
dry, technical, statistical analysis of income discrimination against women
in the United States. The authors recognize the complexity of translating
quantitative data into a normative concept: *total discrimination*. As a measure of the difference between total male and total female earnings in the
economy, Tsuchigane considers total discrimination to be the sum of three
types of discrimination: *income* discrimination, *occupational* discrimination, and *participation* discrimination. ". . . Simply stated, to the degree
women earn less than men doing the same work, income discrimination
exists. If the proportion of women in low-paying jobs is larger than in high-
paying jobs, occupational discrimination exists. To the extent that the
labor-force-participation rate of women is lower than that of men, participation discrimination exists" (*Ibid.*, p. 6). Comparing the census data,
especially for 1960 and 1970, the authors find a small decrease in total
discrimination, which gives me no comfort; the decrease is attributed to a
small decrease in occupational discrimination (a few more women got
much better-paying jobs) combined with a substantial decrease in participation discrimination (a larger percentage of women went to work every
day of the year in 1970), and in the author's method these two changes
weigh heavily enough in decreasing "total discrimination" to offset "a con-

· 2 6 ·

When I was first faced with this evidence I could not believe it. I reacted as I had years earlier when confronted with other evidence—when I was studying the effectiveness of the medical establishment. I had been unable to believe that since 1880 the probable lifetime remaining to a middle-aged male in the U.S. had not appreciably changed. I also could not believe that a twenty-five-fold increase in constant dollars for medical care, of which a disproportionate amount now went for the treatment and prevention of diseases affecting people in the fourth quarter of their lifespan, had resulted in no important increase in adult life expectancy. It took months for the significance of this information to sink in. It is true that the survival rate of infants has increased enormously; more people live to be forty-five. Bodies mangled in accidents can be reconstructed with plastic and aluminum; many infectious diseases have almost been wiped out. But the probable remaining lifespan of an adult man has not been significantly altered. And the increase or decrease that has occurred around the timeless threshold of death has little to do with medical efforts. Knowledge about the impotence of money, surgery, chemistry, and goodwill in the struggle against death is constantly

siderable and surprising increase in income discrimination during that same period" (*Ibid.*, p. 16). In plain English this means that, while more women were drafted into the labor force as the economy expanded and while, under feminist pressure, the differential between the majority of women and the well-paid minority became almost as large as it is among men, for equal work in most jobs today women get an even smaller fraction of the salary paid to men. Moshe Semyonov, "The Social Context of Women's Labor-Force Participation: A Comparative Analysis," *American Journal of Sociology* 86, no. 3 (1980): 534–50, confirms this trend, internationally, by utilizing an ample bibliography and data from sixty-one societies. The integration of more women into the labor force has consistently resulted in increasing occupational discrimination. The odds that employed women can achieve high status and well-paid occupations decrease everywhere with the proportion of women in the labor force. In the USSR a hard look at specialized sources and obscure publications shows the same pattern: Alastair McAuley, *Women's Work and Wages in the Soviet Union* (London: Allen & Unwin, 1979). The double burden (housework *cum* employment) seems to be heavier. The positive points that are noticeable in the USSR are irrelevant to incomes: A higher percentage of women are teachers and professors (who in the USSR are low paid), and almost one-third of MPs (powerless and exceptionally silent) are women.

repressed in our societies. It belongs to those facts that must seemingly be denied by ritual and myth.[16]

Although totally different, economic discrimination against women as a group constitutes a reality that is equally unpalatable to most non-cynical contemporaries. As polio and diphtheria have

16 EGALITARIAN RITUALS

Modern institutions are counterproductive (see FN 9). The good intentions of certain individuals, be they medical doctors, feminist organizers, or high-school teachers, at best gild the edges of this counterproductivity. For example, the contemporary medical establishment is inevitably a major threat to health. John Bradshaw, *Doctors on Trial* (London: Wildwood House, 1979) has restated my argument in much more readable language. And medicine is only one example of many. Generally, service institutions are rituals that veil for both providers and clients the ever-widening gap between the myth they pursue and the material reality to which they give social structure: Ivan Illich, "The Ritualization of Progress" (chapter 2), *Deschooling Society* (London: Calder and Boyars, 1971). Today's organized pursuit of economic equality for women, the "feminist enterprise," fits the same pattern. To appreciate the size of this informal enterprise during the 1960–75 period, consult Marija Matich Hughes, *The Sexual Barrier: Legal, Medical, Economic, and Social Aspects of Sex Discrimination* (Washington, D.C.: Hughes Press, 1977). So far, affirmative action in favor of women's economic equality has been futile as an attempt to reduce the wage gap for the majority. The effort has led to the creation of jobs for women employed to defend women's rights, and has considerably improved the status, opportunities, and incomes in the upper, mostly professional ranges of society. For instance, the increasing involvement of women, internationally, in medicine is well documented in Sandra L. Chaff, *Women in Medicine: A Bibliography of the Literature on Women Physicians* (Metuchen, NJ: Scarecrow Press, 1977). Technical assistance to women has had the same counterproductive effect—the relative deprivation of the majority of women—as international technical assistance has had on the economic development of poor nations. In order to achieve the necessary kind of self-criticism, of which medicine—like most unions, the military, and communist parties—has proven incapable, feminism would have to question seriously the assumption that its fundamental goals can be effectively and not just ritually pursued under a regime of scarcity. The medical and educational systems are frequently used to illustrate a development common to all industrial-age institutions *as they expand*: They are forced to produce exponentially symbols that conceal their own counterpurposive effects. On the paradoxical socio-political support for inevitably counterproductive causes, see the theoretical research by Jean-Pierre Dupuy, *Epistémologie économique et analyse de systèmes*

almost disapppeared, so has the exclusion of girls from grammar and high schools. Just as we have seat belts to protect us against crashes, so we have TV monitors to protect against rape. Just as we have affirmative action for the health of the poor, so we have special scholarships to get women to the top.

It is hard to face the fact that no program whatsoever has changed either average adult life expectancy or the wage differential between the sexes.[17]

(Paris: Cerebe, 1979). The exponential growth necessary to mask counterproductivity is not limited to education or medicine or transportation. For a full century, the economic equality of women citizens has been constantly on the agenda of hundreds of associations: Albert Krichmar, *The Women's Rights Movement in the United States, 1848–1970: A Bibliography and Sourcebook* (Metuchen, NJ: Scarecrow Press, 1972). Tens of thousands of women made a career of the struggle toward this goal and constantly reported progress. Many more gave time, effort, and enthusiasm to the cause. All the three major modern law systems, the Roman, English, and even the Islamic, made commitments to the enactment of *economic* equality: Kathleen Newland, *The Sisterhood of Man: The Impact of Women's Changing Roles on Social and Economic Life Around the World* (New York: Norton, 1979). The legal battle against economic discrimination survives with continual reports of "victories": *Women's Rights Law Reporter* (Newark, NJ: Rutgers Law School, quarterly). All this remains without measurable effect on the one point that counts and which is increasingly obscured by the flood of rhetoric and tokens: the gap between women's and men's cumulative real-money income, which demonstrates the inferior economic value of women.

17 WOMEN AND LAW

All known unwritten, customary law is gender-specific (see FNs 81–84). European written law is decidedly patriarchal (see FN 21) and the law of the modern nation-state is unfailingly sexist. Exploration of the impact that the transition from patriarchy to sexism has had on the legal standing of women has not received sufficient attention. For several interesting attempts to touch on this issue, see Diana Leonard Barker and Sheila Allen, eds. *Sexual Division and Society: Process and Change* (London: Tavestock Publications, 1976), especially Yves Dézalay, *"French Judicial Ideology in Working-Class Divorce"*: "Modern judicial statements, in their ambiguity, mix the professional control of men and the conjugal control of women, defining the reciprocal obligations of the two parties as equal. A lot of men in fact consider that it is because of their wives that they are forced to 'kill' themselves working, and this, in their eyes, makes up for whatever sacrifice their wives are obliged to make in marriage." Historical

The unchanged wage differential between the sexes is just one aspect of the economic discrimination practiced against women on the job, just as the unchanged male adult life expectancy is only one aspect of modern medicine's failure to improve "health." It can also be argued that the enormous exertions of the modern health establishment *have* added significantly to adult life expectancy. Without these efforts, some argue, life expectancy in a world of smog and stress would be even further below that of adults in many poor countries. In the same way, it can be argued that the concerted struggles of legislators, unions, feminists, and idealists have prevented the wage differential from increasing in a progressively commodity-intensive and therefore sexist society. It can be argued that such a pessimistic view of industrial society is entirely appropriate. There is good evidence that the decline of life expectancy at all ages that has been observed over the last twenty years in the USSR[18] is only the forerunner of a similar trend to be expected in most industrialized countries, and that the cancellation, due to the present job crisis, of many so-called advances toward equal opportunity is actually a movement that will not be reversed.[19] However, whether you take the optimist's or

---

research is needed to distinguish among (1) gendered law (which enhances ambiguous and balanced complementarity between genders), (2) patriarchal law (which disparages the female gender), and (3) sexist law (which disestablishes gender in favor of fanciful sexual equality).

18 WOMEN IN SOCIALIST COUNTRIES

The relative degradation of women's economic value seems fundamentally unaffected by the political ideology that has been established in an industrialized country. Two recent studies are noteworthy: M.P. Sacks, "Unchanging Times: A Comparison of the Everyday Life of Soviet Working Men and Women Between 1923 and 1966," in D. Atkinson, A. Dallin, and G.W. Lapidus, eds., *Women in Russia* (Sussex: Harvester Press, 1978) and A. Heitlinger, *Women and State Socialism: Sex Inequality in the Soviet Union and Czechoslovakia* (London: Macmillan & Co., 1979). Plan and market are different mechanisms, albeit equally precise in their relative devaluation of women. See also A. McAuley (*op. cit.* FN 15).

19 WOMEN AND RECESSION

The worldwide deterioration of economic activity in the seventies and subsequent weak recoveries coincided with the end of a period during which the participation of women in wage labor had sharply increased.

Economic Sex

the pessimist's stance, one thing seems empirically clear: The proportion of earnings withheld because of sex from half the total population seems a factor as fixed as the remaining lifespan of adult males; or, as others argue, as fixed as the incidence of cancer as a herd phenomenon in the human race.

During the sixties, women's research dealt mostly with two themes: physical violence against women by rapists, husbands, or physicians; and working conditions for wage labor. The patterns discovered by both kinds of research are extremely uniform, and depressing. In every country, discrimination and violence spread at the same rate as economic development: the more money earned, the more women earn less—and experience rape.[20] Sel-

---

The rising number of women entering the work force has been, however, accompanied by rising female unemployment reported in all countries of North America and Western Europe except England (where the official figures on jobless women are believed to be under-estimated by as much as 50 percent). This was the situation when the current overall reduction of the work force became noticeable. It found women more concentrated than men in a few industries and a narrow range of occupations, mostly services. At first women were to some extent shielded from the recession, which initially affected the production industries and manual occupations in which women were comparatively rare. But, as the slowdown becomes widespread, women become more vulnerable to job loss and find it harder to find a new job, especially those jobs that were traditionally men's work and for which men now more fiercely compete. See Diane Werneke, "The Economic Slowdown and Women's Employment Opportunities," *International Labor Review* 117, no. 1 (January–February 1978): 37–52. For easily consulted international comparisons on employment and relative earnings, see Marjorie Galenson, *Women and Work: An International Comparison* (Ithaca, NY: Cornell University, 1973). Women are now consistently under-represented in the estimate of unemployment because they give up faster than men all active search for jobs that, anyway, they have less chance of getting. See *The Economic Role of Women in the ECE Region* (New York: UN Publications, 1980).

20 SEXIST RAPE

The social history of rape still remains to be written, in part because *modern, sexist rape under assumptions of general conditions of scarcity* still has not been clearly distinguished from age-old forms of physical, genital violence against women. In the perspective of FN 11, what American women now fear most is rape as the supreme physical expression of modern sexism—and sexism as an experience that always tastes of this

dom has such an injustice been ingnored for so long and then, within ten years, been so smugly acknowledged. Research on work during this first wave of women's studies at American universities dealt primarily with wage labor: low pay, limited opportunities, degrading roles, misrepresentation on union boards, and

---

modern rape. I argue that this modern rape is implicitly fostered by the obliteration of gender. I can detect no trace of this distinction in Susan Brownmiller, *Against Our Will* (New York: Bantam, 1976). The distinction is implicitly recognized by Pamela Foa and Susan Roe Petersen in their contribution to Mary Vetterlin-Braggin et al., *Feminism and Philosophy* (Totowa, NJ: Littlefield, 1971), who state that rape, as a social institution, reflects society's attitudes toward heterosexual intercourse (on this, more in FN 110). The need for a history of rape is argued by E. Shorter, "On Writing the History of Rape," *Signs* 3, no. 2 (1977): 471–82, an article that led to some controversy in the same journal. The difficulty of substantiating statistically the claim I make in the text above will appear in Allan G. Johnson, "On the Prevalence of Rape in the United States," *Signs* 6, no. 1 (1980): 136–46. The author strongly disproves Shorter's statement that "the average woman's chances of actually being raped, i.e., to feel raped, to experience rape, in her lifetime are still minimal" in the U.S. Johnson produces data that show that an urban female at age twelve currently runs the risk of being raped at least once in her lifetime by someone other than her husband or father by a probability of somewhere between 1:3 and 1:2. That it is difficult to make believable statements about rape underlines the difficulty of writing its history based on statistics. Precisely this fact should encourage reflection about the changing social reality surrounding fear of rape. Today, rape is feared more than in the past. The new sexist insult combined with injury creates something different. As with rape under the assumption of scarcity, so also prostitution under the assumption of scarcity: To age-old injuries is added a new sexist insult. To get a sense of this evolution from craft to profession, compare the two articles by Jacques Rossiaud, "Prostitution, jeunesse et société dans les villes du sud-est au XVème siècle," *Annales, ESC,* 31, no. 2 (March–April 1976): 289–325 and, by the same author, "Fraternités de jeunesse et niveaux de culture dans les villes du sud-est à la fin du moyen âge," *Cahiers d'histoire* 21 (1967): 67–102. (See the translation into English by Elborg Forster: "Prostitution, Youth, and Society in the Towns of Southeastern France in the Fifteenth Century" in Robert Forster and Orest Ranum, eds., *Deviants and the Abandoned in French Society* (Baltimore and London: Johns Hopkins University Press, 1978): 1–46. With the incorporation of the typical housewife into the economy through her transformation from a subsistence- to a shadow-worker, the social reality of the prostitute has also radically changed. The prostitute belonged

precarious job security. Worldwide, most women work in non-unionized urban jobs, and in only a few categories; when they do belong to a union, they are seldom taken into account in contracts. Even when the union is made up primarily of women, men are the key representatives for it during contract negotiations. However you look at it, new research on the fact that economic progress increases economic discrimination is pointless. Such research could only result in sterile redundance, more academic degrees for would-be careerists, and more smugness by those who would use it to bolster their hand-me-down explanatory theories.[21]

---

to the minority of women engaged in disembedded market activities—her services were economically distinct from those rendered by the mistress or maid embedded in the household's subsistence. As women during the nineteenth century entered the formal economy, mainly as shadow workers, the decent woman and the whore found themselves in unprecedented economic, and therefore violent, competition, which led to a new, brutal, institutional exclusion and management of prostitution. As an introduction to the extensive literature on this process, see Alain Corbin, *Les filles de noce: Misère sexuelle et prostitution, 19e et 20e siècles* (Paris: Aubier Montaigne, 1978).

2 1   P A T R I A R C H Y   A N D   S E X I S M

The most common explanation for economic sexism is patriarchy, and for many authors the two terms are used interchangeably. I carefully distinguish between them (see also FN 7). I take patriarchy to mean a pattern of male dominance in a society under the aegis (which in Greek means *shield*) of gender. More specifically, in the context of European history patriarchy is a power imbalance under conditions of asymmetric gender complementarity that acquired its own special style in early Mediterranean society. Julian Pitt-Rivers, *The Fate of Shechem, or the Politics of Sex: Essays in the Anthropology of the Mediterranean* (New York and London: Cambridge University Press, 1977) (see esp. chapter 7) argues that the politics of sex (which in Western societies seems "natural") was muddled with pre-Homeric state formation. Elementary systems of marriage, in which women were exchanged for women, were replaced here by a new system in which women are exchanged for political status. Jane Schneider, *"Of Vigilance and Virgins: Honor, Shame, and Access to Resources in Mediterranean Societies," *Ethnology* 10 (1971): 1–24, identifies a particular set of ecological forces that fragmented pastoral societies into tiny economic units precluding the size and internal stratification typical of Asian societies, and limiting the capacity to organize violence.

Most of the early postwar feminist research was movement-borne and action-oriented. Some of its proponents followed liberal rhetoric calling for equal opportunity–*cum*–affirmative action; others busied themselves with holy writ, chewing on Marx, Freud, and Reich to get another establishment's approval. Repro-

---

She claims that under these circumstances women could become contested as a resource, much like water and pastureland. More importantly, the constant threat of mortal conflict between fathers and sons would be mediated by their common abiding interest in the "honor" of their women, which they controlled. Sherry B. Ortner, *"The Virgin and the State," *Michigan Discussions in Anthropology* 2 (Fall 1976): 1–16, further elaborates: Under such circumstances a private male dominion over these women whose purity the men protect can come about. This *dominion of men over women's domain* cannot simply be identified with the domestic (as opposed to the public) sphere. According to Schneider, this private encroachment of male dominion upon the "purity" of women distinguishes gender dominance in circum-Mediterranean societies from similar patterns in other societies. The rise of Mediterranean states and later democracies has been constantly confused with the institutionalization of this split. I therefore do not exclude the possibility of identifying different styles of patriarchy. Patriarchy under conditions of "broken gender" (see FNs 77, 120, 121) is arguably a case in point. Patriarchy I take to mean a power imbalance under the assumption of gender (see FN 84). Sexism is clearly not the continuation of patriarchal power relations into modern societies. Rather, it is a hitherto unthinkable individual degradation of one-half of humanity on socio-biological grounds (FNs 58 and 60). The lower prestige assigned by patriarchal societies (of the Mediterranean or of any other type) must therefore be carefully distinguished from the personal degradation of each individual woman who, under the regime of sex, is forced to compete with men. For guidance to the literature on the reasons given for sexism in wage labor: Natalie J. Sokoloff, "Bibliography of Women and Work: The 1970s," *Resources for Feminist Research/Documentation sur la recherche féministe* 10 (Toronto, 1981): 57–61. She offers interesting categories to classify explanatory theories for disadvantaged positions in the labor market—although these are defined, overwhelmingly, with genderless concepts. The article includes only post-1970 publications about what sociologists tend to call work, which is mainly wage labor, and classifies the material into Basic Data, Feminist Critique of These, Status Attainment Theory, Dual Labor Market Theory, Sex Stratification Theory, Radical Sociology (Marxist), Male Models of Contemporary Monopoly Capital Theorists on the Labor Market, Application to Women of These, Early Marxist Feminism, and Female-oriented Radical Feminist Mentors Used by Later Marxist Feminism. Blindness to the distinction between social gender and social sex

duction was discovered.[22] Women's rights and workers' rights then seemed compatible with industrial development and progress. In spite of its weakness and dullness, this research remains fundamental for our understanding of how industrial society works. It revealed a surprising homogeneity of discrimination

---

leads most of these sociologists to analyze the conflict now, as in past ages, as one that sets two classes of individuals against each other: women and men. The same blindness leads a brilliant mythologist in the opposite direction: Mary Daly, *Gyn/Ecology: The Metaethics of Radical Feminism* (Boston: Beacon Press, 1978). More clearly than most, she recognizes what I call sexism as "the prevailing religion of the entire planet"—but, ahistorically, she does not oppose it to patriarchy.

2 2   ''R E P R O D U C T I O N''

The term "reproduction" fits "production" as Eve fits Adam. When he wrote his economic philosophical manuscripts, Karl Marx could do without either. Both reproduction and production are now so wildly used that they have ceased to designate anything in particular. Agnes Heller, *"Paradigm of Production: Paradigm of Work," *Dialectical Anthropology* 6 (1981): 71–79, says: "Those interpreters of Marx who apply the concept of production to all spheres of human interaction, not as a figure of speech but in the sense of homology (speaking of 'production of art' or 'production of ideas'), merge two different paradigms into one . . . without being aware of the switch." For a critical attempt to apply the concept of reproduction to the analysis of women's status and functions, see Gayle Rubin, *"The Traffic in Women: Note on the Political Economy of Sex," in Rayna Reiter, ed., *Toward an Anthropology of Women* (New York: Monthly Review Press, 1975): 157–210. I was greatly helped by reading this paper—despite my comment in FN 76. See also Felicity Edholm, Olivia Harris, and Kate Young, *"Conceptualizing Women," *Critique of Anthropology* 9/10, no. 10 (1977): 101–30. Unfortunately, however, a good part of so-called women's history in the USA has become a hothouse for myths that will not survive in the open air of the 1980s. Feminist studies have so far failed to uncover the sexist perspective in any and all economies that rely on the polarization of activities as either productive or reproductive. Women academics grab at the semblance of legitimacy that comes from putting on the hand-me-down Marxoid categories discarded by social historians. North American feminists construct a history of "modes of reproduction," and theories of "reproduction"—physical, social, economic, ideological—crop up like weeds in any discourse that would distinguish gender and sex. Representative of this trend, and far above average in quality, is Heidi I. Hartmann, "The Family as the Locus of Gender, Class, and Political Struggle: The Example of Housework," *Signs* 6, no. 3

against women at work in socialist and capitalist, rich and poor, Latin and Anglo, Catholic, Protestant, and Shinto societies; at equal levels of income, women in such different places as France and Japan got more or less the same kind of bad deal. The pattern of women's exclusion from privileged wages is more uniform than what is practiced against blacks, Koreans, Malasians, or Puerto Ricans and Turks. In addition, nowhere are women establishing a female regime; there is a Tanzania for Nyerere, and Israel for Begin, but no Amazonia in sight. The nation-state is invariably sexist.

The Unreported Economy

There are many kinds of economic activities on which governments and their economists cannot or do not report. In some cases, they cannot get the data; others they could not name or measure, even if they cared to record them. A plethora of names has been given to this accumulation of activities, which economists exclude from their usual statistics. Some call it the informal sector, others the D-sector, others the fourth sector, which they add to the primary "extraction," the secondary "manufacture," and the tertiary "service" sectors of the economy. Others speak about the household economy, the modern barter economy, the economy of "transfers in kind," or the non-monetary market. Still others speak about the area of self-service, self-help, and self-initiated activities. Marxists[23] have no difficulty

---

(Spring 1981): 366–94. I speak of reproduction when referring to photography, cell division, or gypsum copies of art works. I refrain altogether from the use of "social reproduction" except when I speak of the school system as a Xerox machine.

23 THE UNREPORTED ECONOMY

Seldom has a new entity been called by as many names. No agreement has been reached, so far, on how to call or how to circumscribe the set of activities that disturb, distort, or invalidate official economic reports. The following document the search for a terminology: Scott Burns, *The Household Economy: Its Shape, Origins and Future* (Boston: Beacon Press, 1975); Peter M. Gutmann, "The Subterranean Economy," *Financial*

labeling this kind of work; they call it "social reproduction," and then they themselves divide into sects, each of which claims to know best what that means. To complete the confusion, among feminists during the mid-seventies it became fashionable to call all these activities "women's work," and to describe men who do it, in a fem-sexist epithet, as *male housewives*.

The volume of this unofficial economy is not easy to measure. It is made up of a hodgepodge of gainful activities for which no legally recognized salary is paid and for which no social security accrues, as well as of activities remunerated in kind. Much of it consists of unofficial trading, in the barter of favors or in cold cash, all of which elude the tax collector and the statistician. In Yugoslavia you must bring the government doctor a chicken if you want his attention, and in Poland eggs for the clerk are appropriate to obtain a marriage license. In Russia more than three-

Analysts Journal (November–December 1977): 26–28; Yona Friedman, "Le 'secteur D' de l'économie," *Futuribles* 15 (May–June 1978): 331–38, Jean-Marie Delatour, "Une forme de dissidence passive: le travail noir," *Cadres CFDT* 289 (June, July, August 1979): 26–29; Rosine Klatzman, "Le travail noir," *Futuribles* 26 (September 1979): 26–29: Alessandra Nannei, "La resurrección de la economía subterránea," *Le Monde Diplomatique en Español* 2, no. 19 (July 1980): 4–5. The latter is a commentary on Giorgio Fua (1976), who ascribed the economic success of Italy to its huge underground economy. Nannei argues the various reasons the worker in the underground economy is relatively more exploited. See also Dieter Piel, *Das dunkle Gewerbe. Schwarzarbeiter und illegale Verleihfirmen prellen den Staat um Milliarden* (Hamburg: Die Zeit Dossier Nr. 38, 1981): 9–11 and "Schwarzarbeit: Unglaublich was da läuft," *Der Spiegel* 46 (1981): 62–81. This nameless congeries of disparate activities, I will paradoxically call, for lack of a better term, the "unreported" economy. I say "paradoxically" because on none will there be more reporting during the eighties. For a bibliography of economic studies, particularly in Third World countries, see Stuart Sinclair, *Bibliography on the "Informal" Sectors* (Montreal: McGill University, Center for Developing Area Studies, 1978). The term "informal sector" is increasingly used by professional economists as a useful shorthand notation to designate activities whose economic productivity they succeed in formalizing: from bazaars, sidewalk traders, and family stalls to bribery. I have argued elsewhere that the economic formalization of the informal sector, and its bureaucratic policing by professional agencies promoting self-care, will, during the last quarter of the twentieth century, take on a function analogous to colonialism in earlier decades.

fourths of all eggs, milk, cheese, and fresh vegetables purchased by individual households come from the black market; books circulate on the sly or through self-publishing. In the U.S., this market includes the marijuana grower from California who raises and markets a multi-billion-dollar cash crop, and the import agent of Afghan heroin, together with the policeman who is on his payroll. It also comprises the wetback who harvests the grapes, the lawyer for whom you cut the grass and who in exchange sees to it that your illegally constructed house passes county inspection, the mechanic who puts a new carburetor into the car of the accountant who, in turn, fills out the tax return for the gas station. All these clean-cut transactions, each a money-measured trade between contracting partners, are part of the unreported economy. Some of these activities actually use money as a medium of exchange; others barter; all are clearly economic transactions, and on none are statistics properly kept. Some of them are legal, others criminal. Some victimize the client more than professional services, others much less. For both parties, some are more monetarily advantageous than formal, bureaucratic proceedings, while others constitute outright exploitation. But all of them are explicit exchanges of services, products, or currency that fit a market model.

Some attempts have been made to measure the size of this underground economy, at least by comparing it to the gross national product. The British government assumes that it loses an amount equal to 7.5 percent of GNP (and not just of salaries!) through tax evasion.[24] This is probably only a small fraction of the market it cannot record. The Internal Revenue Service in

Since 1978 it has become notorious that fiscal agencies are increasingly concerned with the proportion of income accruing to citizens that either by definition is not "earned" income or almost inevitably goes unreported. I was referred to Richard Porter, *Some Notes on Estimating the Underground Economy* (August 10, 1979, Board of Governors of the Federal Reserve System) and M. Higgins, "Measuring the Hidden Economy," Second Report from OCPU (Bath: Center for Fiscal Studies, University of Bath, July 1980). An attempt to construct macro-economic measuring tools has been made by Edgar L. Feige, "A New Perspective on Macro-economic Phenomena, the Theory and Measurement of the Unobserved Sector of the United States Economy: Causes, Consequences, and Implications" (August 1980). In this sixty-three-page manuscript, he says:

Economic Sex

Washington, D.C., estimated that in 1976 activities generating
135 billion dollars in personal or corporate income were not reported to federal agencies. This is from a report on tax evasion,
not on legally ambiguous tax dodging via business expenses, fabricated loss, and the like, which might account for an equal
amount of revenue. Recent estimates suggest that in the U.S. this
forgotten economy is growing much faster than the formal economy, outdistancing even inflation.[25] If the monetary (but statistically unreported) and the non-monetary markets of the U.S. are
added together, their value certainly rivals the non-military economy on which economists base their overall indicators, predictions,
and prescriptions. And, while in the formal, taxed, and statistically
reported economy the labor force is to a large measure engaged in
the artificial creation of pseudowork, producing useless articles, unwanted services, futile social controls, and costly economic inter-
mediation, the real efficiency of the unreported economy is on the
average much higher. The thriving black-market economy is the
reason why countries like Italy have survived ten years during
each of which economists confidently predicted impending bank-
ruptcy, and why the people's democracies of Eastern Europe have
survived theoretically impossible levels of mismanagement.

Throughout, one thing is certain: Even if we carefully exclude from the unreported market all subsistence activities and all
typically female housework (both of which, in their own ways,
do not fit the market model), this formerly unobserved economy,
growing proportionately faster than the reported GNP, contains a
share of discrimination against women that has only occasionally
been dealt with as an issue. Yet, in this sector of the market economy, where new jobs are created as reported unemployment rises,
women might be getting an even worse deal than in the sector the
economist's data dragnets can filter and measure. Here, no anti-
discrimination or equal-opportunity laws apply. In contrast to
male moonlighters, drug dealers, and bribe takers, whose pursuits
are lucrative if sometimes unlawful, women are left with the
shoddy consolation of prostitution, puny extortions, and fencing.

"I wish to contend that the unobserved sector is so large as to rival the
observed sector and so variable in relation to observed income that it might
provide the key to understanding our contemporary state of economic
malaise."

Women who attempt moonlighting typically wash dishes next door or do typing at home—or, more recently, cover the night shift on the text composer.[26]

Most of the proponents of the Chicago-bred discipline that calls itself "new home economics"[27] and most recent policy

26 UNDER-REPORTING: ECONOMIC VERSUS POLITICAL

Estimates of the absolute and relative volume of the unreported economy as part of the GNP depend on the activities that are included in the calculations. One extreme is represented by Gary S. Becker, *A Treatise on the Family (Cambridge, MA: Harvard University Press, 1981) and, in France, H. Lepage, Autogestion et capitalisme (Paris: Masson, 1978). Ideally, these authors attempt to evaluate the various factors making up the now unreported economy in units derived from standard measurements current in the reported economy. "The imputed value of school work (done by pupils) rose steadily from less than 5 percent of GNP in 1929 to over 11 percent in 1973. . . . The estimated value of volunteer labor increased proportionately even more, from 0.6 percent of GNP in 1929 to 2 percent in 1973. But employee costs charged to business expenses showed a relative decline of almost one-half, from 2.5 percent of GNP in 1929 to 1.3 percent in 1973 . . . reflecting a tighter tax law." Similar statements come from John W. Kendrick, "Expanding Imputed Values in the National Income and Product Accounts," The Review of Income and Wealth 25, no. 4 (December 1979): 349–63. The extreme opposite of such accounting procedures is an approach that is political rather than technical, one taken since the early seventies by the English Power of Women Collective. The classical statement remains Mariarosa Dalla Costa, *Women and the Subversion of the Community and Selma James, *A Woman's Place, both pamphlets published together (Bristol: Falling Wall Press, 1972). Essentially, these authors propose to evaluate the reported economy not in its own terms but in terms of the time, toil, and nuisance that its organization imposes on people when unemployed, and who, for obvious reasons, are primarily women. For an elaboration of this position, see FN 49. The language used by Becker and by James is in stark contrast, so much so that at first sight the opposition of such authors seems ludicrous. It becomes meaningful only when they are taken as two equally failing attempts to measure, in terms of each other, two heterogeneous fields: toil measured in terms of commodity production and toil expended to satisfy basic needs by the use of commodities (see FN 30).

27 NEW HOME ECONOMICS

Scott Burns (op. cit. FN 23) provides an easy introduction to the "new home economics." For a bibliography see Richard Berk, "The New Home

Economic Sex

studies focusing on the unreported economy have at least one feature in common: They recognize that both black-market labor, which evades taxes, and unpaid housework (for which some demand payment out of tax funds) make a major contribution to the GNP. But new studies on the hidden economy also have led

---

Economics: An Agenda for Sociological Research," in Sarah Fenstermaker Berk, ed., *Women and Household Labor* (Beverly Hills: Sage Publications, 1980). This essay has a double advantage: It retraces the history of the new discipline and places the issue narrowly into the context of contemporary women's housework. A parallel approach that aims at the calculation of economic contributions made by activities within the household to the total GNP in underdeveloped countries has become fashionable. For the corresponding literature, which deals with the borderline between economic anthropology and "new home economics," see, for instance, Moni Nag, Benjamin White, and Creighton Peet, "An Anthropological Approach to the Study of the Economic Value of Children in Java and Nepal," *Current Anthropology* 19, no. 2 (1978): 293–306. In the context of gender studies, "new home economics" raises a fundamental point: It permits a sexual polarization *of the methods* used in assigning people's economic worth. If women's economic value is given any weight at all in the literature, much more often than men they are assigned *imputed* values. Harvey S. Rosen, "The Monetary Value of a Housewife: A Replacement Cost Approach," *The American Journal of Economics and Sociology* 33, no. 1 (January 1974): 65–73 can be used as a classical and very short introduction to the methods used here. The housewife produces either monetary income or household goods. The value of lost monetary income can be easily calculated as a foregone but measurable income stream. The value of household production must be imputed. This imputation, with its shortcomings, is—according to the author—better than assuming no value where no monetary transaction exists. "Most approaches used . . . divide the hours the housewife works into several categories of jobs and then apply the *going wage rate* and sum it up. . . . A second approach calculates replacement costs; it goes to the market and finds out how much it would cost to hire a substitute for the mother. . . . A third approach says that the housewife's value is equal to her *opportunity cost* in the labor market." I have proposed elsewhere a *fourth method,* playing the same game of imputation. I have suggested that one calculate the amount of capital that is invested in a certain type of "household plant," and then establish what salary is paid over a twenty-four-hour period in neighboring industries investing an equal amount of capital per workplace. All four methods make it possible to determine the "value" of a housewife in a derivative fashion. Her status as the second economic sex is measured, established, and confirmed in reference to wage labor and

GENDER

to a new confusion between hitherto unreported market activities and unpaid female housework. The inability to draw a clear distinction between unreported and unpaid work constitutes the theoretical weakness of the new economic school and makes the "new home economics" treacherous for women.[28] Women know

---

capital. Notice that housewives are being imputed monetary value for their shadow work during the very same decade, the seventies, in which wage labor has turned largely into busy work: pseudo-production of doubtful market value.

2 8   I L L E G I T I M A T E   U N E M P L O Y M E N T

In 1982, legitimate unemployment constitutes a relative privilege. Blacks, women, and dropouts have for a decade suffered from illegitimate unemployment, which is now catching up with the WASPM. Increasingly, people are squeezed out of illegitimate jobs. They lose their habitual income from untaxed or criminal activities; their earnings from unreported or unrecorded sources dry up; or they cease to pursue profitable activities that in the opinion of the courts, the unions, or the professions they should never have exercised in the first place. The correlation between legitimate and illegitimate unemployment cannot escape becoming a major policy issue. In a society that aims at full employment, most people who do unpaid work are not counted as "unemployed," while many people who do work in the unreported sector are carried on unemployment rolls and often get the corresponding benefits. Whether "the concept of unemployment was beyond the scope of any idea which early Victorian reformers had at their command, largely because they had no word for it (G.M. Young, *Victorian England*) or whether . . . (Victorians by their avoidance of the term) . . . proved their lack of understanding (of crowd feelings) as E.P. Thompson (*Making of the English Working Class*) would claim" is not easy to decide: R. Williams, *Key Words*, (*op. cit.*, pp. 273–75, FN 2). No matter the precise reason, the division of citizens into those who are *employed*, those who are *unemployed*, and those who are *neither* is characteristic only for the middle of the twentieth century. The social perception of a deviant category of "those without work" has a history—and a short one—that has been consistently overlooked. John A. Garraty, *Unemployment in History: Economic Thought and Public Policy* (New York: Harper and Row, 1978), in his introduction says, ". . . No one has ever before written a general history of unemployment. . . . I call this book *Unemployment in History* instead of *A History of Unemployment*. . . . It does not attempt to describe why there was unemployment, but how the condition of being without work has been perceived and dealt with in different societies from the beginning of recorded history." Garraty obviously assumes that "work" is at least coeval with history. Garraty's book

that they are excluded from the desirable jobs in the growing arena
of illegitimate work—even more so than from taxed wage labor—
while their housework is a form of *bondage*. Drawing a formal
distinction between "unreported" economic activities, from which
women are unequally excluded, and others, to which women are un-

---

is useful but weak, precisely because he overlooks that "work" as a classi-
fying category for human activities and "the worker" as a designation for a
special status are both of recent origin (see FN 13). After a century of
prominence, both categories are now fading. Micro-electronics are reducing the status of labor input in production. In addition, at present, attitudes
toward *unemployment as a form of deviance* cannot but change: As more
people derive more of their income from the unreported sector, many
policies that are enacted to favor *reported employment* will threaten their
unreported sources of livelihood. The correlation between the flow of these
unreportable sources and the volume of reportable jobs will become a
major policy issue. As an example, energy conservation and the transition
from conventional to renewable energy sources has a foreseeable impact
on levels and characteristics of employment, as well as on conventionally
measured unemployment. Arguably, this transition increases the number of
jobs available. More important than this, however, is this question: How
does the conversion affect the volume and the characteristics of unreportable sources of livelihood? "Soft" might also mean unorganizable labor. For
guidance to this issue: Skip Laitner, Center for Renewable Resources,
Suite 510, 1001 Connecticut Avenue NW, Washington, D.C. 20036. The
loss of unreported sources of livelihood (should we call it *illegitimate
unemployment?*) might soon frighten more people more deeply than reported unemployment. Statistics on the correlation between the two fundamental forms of unemployment are difficult to come by. A number of
authors, all writing in the *Review of Income and Wealth* have a straight-
forward approach to the distinction between economic and non-economic
activities. For them, a non-market service is economic if it could just as well
be purchased. Even with this restrictive criterion, they come to the following
generalization: The unobserved sector comes close to rivaling the entire
private sector in the USA, totaling over $1.2 trillion in 1976. In compari-
son with the observed sector, the unobserved sector has grown dramatically
over the last twenty years. The authors distinguish between monetary and
non-monetary components in the unobserved sector of the economy. They
"discover" that, when compared to the latter, the former is not stable, but
fluctuates. I take this to mean that the exclusion from the illegitimate labor
market (*illegitimate unemployment*) fluctuates like reported unemployment, albeit on a different cycle. One fundamental reason these authors do
not leave me satisfied is that they include part of what I shall presently
define as shadow work in their computation, and in this sense they over-

equally bonded, is crucial. Taking housework as a paradigm of an "ideal type" of economic activity, it has two characteristics that distinguish it from black-market labor: Its value is imputed and its performance cannot be disintermediated.[29] It is part of the modern nether economy that all contemporary money implies and that money therefore cannot measure.

---

estimate the unreported *market* economy. By implication, these authors falsify the nature and underestimate the volume of shadow work. For them, it is largely non-economic non-work: It constitutes satisfactory or desirable activities associated with consumption. For a different approach using similar conceptual tools for the French economy, specifically the household economy, see Pierre Kendé, "Vers une évaluation de la consommation réelle des ménages," *Consommation* 2 (1975): 7–44. NB: Sex-specific data on illegitimate unemployment do not seem to be available. The lack of any serious attempts to estimate and highlight discrimination in the unreported money economy constitutes a lacuna in women's studies.

29 DISINTERMEDIATION

"Disintermediation" is a technical term first used to describe a tendency in the behavior of investors: the displacement of funds from banks and savings institutions when groups of depositors decide to seek higher yields by investing on their own. Paul Hawken, *"Disintermediation: An Economics Buzzword That Neatly Explains a Lot of the Good That Is Going On," *Co-Evolution Quarterly* 29 (Spring 1981): 6–13 recommends the use of this term for the economic consequences of a broad spectrum of activities in which people increasingly bypass institutions to get more of what they really want for their money. They disintermediate (bypass, skirt, evade) the specialist, the union, the taxman, and with him the government. They disintermediate medical diagnosis and therapy and make arrangements to die from their own cancer at home. Above all, they circumvent the professionals who administer and coordinate those multiple services. The distinction I have made between the reported and the unreported economy corresponds in reality to a distinction between the highly intermediated and the highly disintermediated poles of the formal economy. The hard core of women's housework corresponds to neither of these two poles of the formal economy. The care of the sick child could be "intermediated" through a hospital. Cooking or childbearing, in practice, cannot. Rightly, these are paradigmatic for shadow work. As an ideal type, as a category of economic activity, shadow work is distinct from wage labor (be this reportable or not, paid in money or in kind), because shadow work for cultural reasons cannot be disintermediated.

Economic Sex

Shadow Work[30]

By the mid-seventies, the orientation of women's research on women's work and its economic analysis had changed. Studies began to struggle with insights that could not be properly expressed in the categories to which we had become accustomed in the fields of history, economics, ethnology, or anthropology. For their kind of research, the point was not women's smaller bite into the salary cake. Something quite different was of greater significance: how to explain that in every industrial society women are

30 SHADOW WORK

I created this term in conversation with Claudia von Werlhof (FN 49), although not to her full satisfaction. I coined the term to designate the consumer's unpaid toil that adds to a commodity an incremental value that is necessary to make this commodity useful to the consuming unit itself. I called the activity "work" to emphasize that the activity constitutes a burdensome loss of time; I called it "shadow" work to indicate that this toil is associated with (and preparatory to) the act of consumption. The sector of an industrial economy in which shadow work prevails I have called the *shadow*, or the *nether, economy*. I felt impelled to create these neologisms, shadow work and nether economy, to avoid a confusion between this consumption-associated unpaid toil and two other ideal types of activity: the first, like shadow work, part of every industrial economy; the second, embedded in culture and gender and, therefore, in the strict sense, non-economic. The three areas, all "unreported," had to be differentiated. I connected the genderless term "work" with the image "shadow," thinking of an iceberg. The peak alone is visible, and it can be seen from only one side (the other side being analogous to the *unobserved* sector of the economy). However, most of the iceberg remains below the water, its shape unobservable, although I can infer its size. The whole iceberg is the economy. It floats because of the major part, which lies below the water; because of the toil performed in the nether economy. The whole iceberg, above and below the waterline, has crystallized out of the water, out of gendered subsistence, and none of its three parts can be found, except marginally, in pre-industrial societies. The iceberg represents human existence under the assumption of scarcity. For criticism, see Claudia von Werlhof, "Schattenarbeit oder Hausarbeit? Zur Gegenwart und Zukunft der Arbeit: Eine feministische Kritik an Ivan Illich," in Th. Olk and H.-U. Olk, eds., *Soziale Dienste im Wandel 2— Professionelle Dienstleistung und Selbsthilfebewegung*, 1982 (Bielefeld: Fakultät für Soziologie, November 1981).

discriminated against in employment only to be forced, when off the job, to do a new kind of *economically* necessary work without any pay attached to it. It was obvious to all concerned that women regularly lose out when they apply for a job, when they seek advancement, when they try to hold on to a paying position. But outside of and along with wage labor, which had spread during the nineteenth century, a second kind of unprecedented economic activity had come into being. To a greater extent and in a different manner from men, women were drafted into the economy. They were—and are—deprived of equal access to wage labor only to be bound with even greater inequality to work that did not exist before wage labor came into being.[31]

3 1 HOUSEWORK

I was compelled to recognize the absence of a category into which I could fit, without forcing it, the "housework" of modern women, when I read the 1976 German original of Gisela Bock and Barbara Duden, *"Labor of Love—Love as Labor: On the Genesis of Housework in Capitalism," in Edith Hoshino Altbach, ed., *From Feminism to Liberation* (Cambridge, MA: Schenkman, 1980): 153–92. The two historians clarified for me the economic difference between the householding activities of women in traditional society and the unpaid activities of women keeping a home for a married wage earner. I recognized that in the case of the former I had to speak about a gender-specific assignment of culturally defined, concrete tasks, while in the case of the latter I was faced with the sexual polarization of the unpaid labor force—a sexual division of economic activities. To find an economic (and therefore genderless) term to designate the unpaid economic activities that were disproportionately imposed, during the nineteenth century, on women, I assigned housework to the category of shadow work. By doing so, I turn housework into the paradigm for shadow work and, further, I highlight the fact that sexual discrimination through bondage to shadow work constitutes an essential characteristic of the new activity. The nineteenth-century transition from the gendered assignment of concrete tasks to the sexual polarization of the labor force remains implicit in most recent historical studies on women as well as in studies on women in industrializing societies. The current state of research in English is represented in Sarah Fenstermaker Berk (*op. cit.* FN 27) and Nona Glazer-Malbin, "Housework," *Signs* 1, no. 4 (1976): 905–22. They examine the 1950–75 literature, which treats housework as a division of labor, adding the literature after 1970 concerned with the economic measurement of its value. See also Louise A. Tilly and Joan W. Scott, eds., *Women, Work, and Family* (New York: Holt, Reinhart, and Winston, 1978) and Sandra M. Burman, *Fit Work for Women* (London: Croom

Economic Sex

The best evidence of the existence of the new nether economy comes from historians of housework. Their writings made me understand that the difference between housework past and present cannot adequately be put into traditional language, nor satisfactorily expressed in the categories of class analysis or social-science jargon. What housework is now, women of old did not do. However, the modern woman finds it hard to believe that her ancestor did not have to work in a nether economy. Irrefutably, the new historians of housework describe the typical activity of the housewife[32] as something unlike anything women have done

---

Helm, 1979). On modernization and housework, see C.E. Clark, "Domestic Architecture as an Index to Social History: The Romantic Revival and the Cult of Domesticity in America, 1840–70," *Journal of Interdisciplinary History* 7 (1976) and Susan J. Kleinberg, "Technology and Women's Work: The Lives of Working-Class Women in Pittsburgh, 1870–1900," *Labor History* 17 (1976): 58–72. Also consult FNs 36, 37, 86.

While these footnotes were being typed, I received the uncorrected proofs of Susan Strasser, *Never Done: A History of American Housework* (New York: Pantheon, 1982). This is the first book dealing with American housework since it came into being as an historical reality; it tells what women in their homes *did*, *not* what they were *supposed to do*, not what sociological *functions* they performed, nor what their work *meant*. Every paragraph is crammed with precise information, always lively and sometimes superbly formulated.

3 2   THE HOUSEWIFE

The terminological bonding of "wife" to "house" in "housewife" is unique to English. Upon reflection, this conjugal relationship of the female and the apartment or house is jarring. Already in 1936, the Long Island Federation of Women's Clubs decreed that "housewives" should become "homemakers"; in 1942 a reformer in Kansas City launched a crusade to make it "household executive." In England, "housewife" was almost dead by 1939, when people tended to make fun of the German *Hausfrau*. But the word leaped back into the vocabulary and gave propagandists a chance to flatter women who could not be put into any other category. This is what H.L. Mencken (*op. cit.*, p. 246, FN 3) recounts. Today, this term, like "my better half," can hardly be used without giving a sarcastic twitch to the sentence in which it occurs. The word might now be fit for use as a technical term to designate the female shadow worker. Fun to read and superbly organized on the mystification of woman's work is chapter 7 of Ann Oakley, *Woman's Work: The Housewife, Past and Present* (New York: Vintage, 1974).

outside industrial society, as something that cannot be suitably accounted for as just one more facet of the unreported economy, and as something the dogmatic categories of "social reproduction" simply cannot meaningfully signify.

Looking more closely at the phenomena anthropologists and historians of housework study, I began to see that the contemporary labor market, both reported and unreported, constitutes only the tip of an iceberg. True to this metaphor, most of the toil that supports the visible tip is below the waterline, work done in the nether economy. As employment in the various kinds of wage labor increases, the submerged drudgery must expand even faster. And modern housework is a typical, but not exclusive, part of that nether world's reality—work that is not only unreported but also impenetrable by the economic searchlight. And, since no commonly accepted nomenclature has yet been devised to make the distinction between housework and unreported market activities explicit, I shall contrast the spectrum of remunerated work done in the reported and unreported economy with a nether economy of shadow work, which forms its complement.[33]

Unlike the production of goods and services, shadow work is performed by the consumer of commodities, specifically, the consuming household. I call shadow work any *labor* by which the consumer transforms a purchased commodity into a usable good. I designate as shadow work the time, toil, and effort that must be expended in order to add to any purchased commodity the

33 ECONOMIC ANTHROPOLOGY

Since 1957, when K. Polanyi, C. Arensberg, and Pearson, eds., *Trade and Market in the Early Empires* (now available in pbk., South Bend, IN: Regnery-Gateway, 1971) was published, much has been written on the question: Which of several alternative sets of analytic concepts are best suited to interpret behavior outside market systems? George Dalton, "Theoretical Issues in Economic Anthropology," *Current Anthropology* 10, no. 1 (February 1969): 63–102 is still an excellent introduction to this topic. It has become obvious, since then, that what economists call economic decisions within economic systems do not describe what anthropologists or historians describe as the behavior of primitives, peasants, or city dwellers of old. One fundamental reason economic concepts do not *fit* outside commodity-intensive society is the fact that these concepts assume conditions of formal scarcity (see FN 11) and exchanges between genderless subjects (see FNs 4 and 5).

value without which it is unfit for use. Therefore, shadow work names an activity in which people must engage to whatever degree they attempt to satisfy their needs by means of commodities. By introducing the term "shadow work," I distinguish the procedure for cooking eggs today from that followed in the past. When a modern housewife goes to the market, picks up the eggs, drives them home in her car, takes the elevator to the seventh floor, turns on the stove, takes butter from the refrigerator, and fries the eggs, she adds value to the commodity with each one of these steps. This is not what her grandmother did. The latter looked for eggs in the chicken coop, cut a piece from the lard she had rendered, lit some wood her kids had gathered on the commons, and added the salt she had bought. Although this example might sound romantic, it should make the economic difference clear. Both women prepare fried eggs, but only one uses a marketed commodity and highly capitalized production goods: car, elevator, electric appliances. The grandmother carries out woman's gender-specific tasks in creating subsistence; the new housewife must put up with the household burden of shadow work.[34]

Changes in housework reach far below the surface. Rising standards of living have made it more capital-intensive by providing numerous machines and gadgets. The investment in the household equipment of a median Canadian family—and the same would be true in every other modern home—is now higher than the median plant investment per factory job in two-thirds of

34 MYSTIFICATION OF SHADOW WORK

To recognize the existence of shadow work (which is neither a subsistence-oriented activity nor, experientially, a *quid pro quo*) has been consistently tabooed. To avoid the analysis of shadow work, four separate masks are used to disguise the nether economy: (1) In anthropology, housework is usually treated as a survival of subsistence activities; (2) economists (see FN 26) amalgamate it with the informal sector, considering it either a labor of love, repaid by the pleasure it gives, or as an activity within the unreported sector, compensated by some non-monetary reward; (3) Marxists use the catchall concept of reproduction to dispose of shadow work (see FN 22); and (4) there are those who add feminist shades to Marxist spectacles and fight tooth and nail to identify shadow work with woman's work. By doing so, they blur the fact that this is a category of human activity (a) exclusively characteristic of modern times and (b) structurally distinct from, and more fundamental than, wage labor.

all nations. As a result, housework has become more sedentary, and the incidence of varicose veins has decreased. For a minority of women, this has meant an interesting, well-paid part-time job and free time "to write their books or go fishing." But the "new" kind of housework most present-day women perform has also become more lonely, more dull, more impersonal, more time-polluting. Valium consumption and addiction to TV soap operas have often been regarded as indicators of this new, muffled stress.[35] But, much more fundamentally, housework has become the paradigm for the new unpaid economic activity that in a computer-policed and microprocessor-equipped society is economically more fundamental than productive labor, whether this production is recorded by economists or not.

Shadow work could not have come into existence before the household was turned into an apartment set up for the economic function of upgrading value-deficient commodities. Shadow work could not become unmistakably women's work before men's work had moved out of the house to factory or office. Henceforth, the household had to be run on what the paycheck bought—one paycheck for the engineer and almost inevitably several to feed the hod carrier's family, whose wife took in piecework, while his daughter hired out as a domestic. The unpaid upgrading of what wage labor produced now became women's work. Women were then defined in terms of the new use to which they were being put. Both kinds of work, wage labor and its shadow, proliferated with industrialization. The two new functions, that of the breadwinner and that of the dependent, began to divide society at large: He was identified with overalls and the factory, she with an apron

3 5 THE VALIUM ECONOMY

Medical sociology suggests several characteristics of sex-specific "health consumption." Women of working age get more costly services from and spend more time on medical care. Medicine is used on women more unashamedly as a technique for their control. While men use medicine effectively to get a vacation from wage labor, women try and frequently fail to use it for the purpose of eschewing shadow work. See Constance Nathanson, "Illness and the Feminine Role: A Theoretical Survey" in *Social Science and Medicine* 9 (1975): 57–62; and M. Barrett and H. Roberts, "Doctors and Their Patients: The Social Control of Women in General Practice" in C. and B. Smart, eds., *Women, Sexuality and Social Control* (London: Routledge & Paul Kegan, 1978); also FNs 80, 87.

and the kitchen. For the wage labor she was able to find as a side-line, she received sympathy and low pay.

While, during the nineteenth century, technological change revolutionized work outside the household, at first it had little impact on housework routine, except for tightening the enclosure into which each housewife was locked. Tap water put an end to her carrying the jugs to and fro, but also to her meeting friends at the well. While women's work was economically without precedent, technically it seemed to go on as always. Indoor plumbing and the new fuels, gas and electricity, which were to become nearly universal in U.S. urban areas by 1920 and in small towns by 1930, were for the great majority of people no more than technological possibilities at the turn of the century. Only as recently as the second quarter of this century did technology really change the material reality of housework; simultaneously, radio and TV began to act as substitutes for community conversation. Industry then started to produce machinery for *shadow work*. As industrial work became less labor-intensive, housework, without diminishing, became by several orders of magnitude more capital-intensive.[36]

3 6 HOUSEHOLD MACHINERY

Ruth Schwartz Cowan, "A Case Study of Technological and Social Change: The Washing Machine and the Working Wife" in Mary S. Hartman and Lois Banner, eds., *Clio's Consciousness Raised* (New York: Harper Colophon, 1974): 245–53 discusses how two generations of American women used their electrical appliances to create "more satisfying" homes, and it was only in the third generation that women began to suspect the satisfaction was a ruse. The initial effect to the diffusion of household technology among middle-class women was to raise their standards of household care and to transfer several functions that had previously been performed outside the home or by paid employees to the purview of the housewife. Concurrently, time priorities changed for the housewives; whatever time they saved —let us say in cooking—they were expected to transfer to other tasks, primarily childcare. The hypothesis, if proven, would be dismaying . . . because our thoughts about domestic and foreign planning have been predicated on the assumption that, if you want to curb poverty in India, you should introduce modern agriculture and birth control. But the relationship between the sexes is not likely to be improved simply by the introduction of male contraceptives and bigger and better vacuum cleaners. I have come to analogous conclusions about the effect of mechanization of everyday transport in *Energy and Equity* (orig. publ. London: Boyars, 1973). The conclu-

Economic progress is usually measured by the number of work places, meaning jobs, that are created. But it can with equal right be called that process by which more goods are offered on the market, each new commodity requiring a greater "input" of shadow work.[37] Development conventionally means that production has become more capital-intensive; it can just as well be described as the course through which more and more capital-intensive shadow work is made necessary for the achievement of a minimum level of well-being.[38] It is highly improbable that the

---

sions Schwartz Cowan reaches for female housework fit shadow work in general. Mechanical equipment associated with the household (the car no less than the washing machine) primarily constitutes a capital investment that transforms the home into a plant suited for the performance of capital-intensive shadow work. The proliferation of this equipment increases the time-volume of the shadow work performed, and, by rendering housework more genderless, it lays more solid material foundations for sexism in the home.

37-42   UNPAID WORK

37 For research on the impact that women's household labor has on economic status, labor, marriage roles, family discord, violence, treatment of women at work, see particularly (good bibliography) Susan M. Strasser, "An Enlarged Human Existence? Technology and Household Work in Nineteenth-Century America" in Sarah Fenstermaker Berk (op. cit., pp. 25–51, FN 27). On unpaid time use, see Kathryn E. Walker and Margaret E. Woods, Time Use: A Measure of Household Production of Family Goods and Services (Washington D.C.: Center for the Family of the American Home Economics Association, 1976). The time required to accomplish varying quantities of household work has been the central focus of this research, which wants to measure household-work output in terms of time use. The study is limited to one urban-suburban community in upstate New York, and to two-parent households with or without children. It provides no useful measurements of shadow work but rather shows the difficulty in obtaining them. For estimates of time budgets of housewives in France, see B. Riandey, "L'emploi du temps des mères de famille en France," in A. Michel, Les femmes dans la société marchande (Paris: PUF, 1978).

38 Jacques Attali, Les trois mondes: Pour une théorie de l'après-crise (Paris: Fayard, 1981) has considerably elaborated his past reflections on this masturbatory aspect of late-industrial economies. His many strong insights argue for the distinction, which I make here, between the nether economy and the unreported sector of production (no matter if this pro-

volume of productive wage labor will ever again increase any-
where in the world, or that make-work, now called "service," will
be paid for as extravagantly as has occurred up to now. Rather, I
expect that automated production will decrease the overall
volume of wage labor and lead to the marketing of commodities
requiring more, not less, unpaid toil by the buyer/user. This
shadow side of economic growth—a foreseeable increase in
shadow work as wage labor decreases—will further accentuate a
new kind of sexual discrimination, a discrimination *within* shadow
work.

Shadow work is not women's exclusive domain. It is as clearly
genderless as wage labor. Unpaid work to upgrade industrial production is done by males, too. The husband who crams for an
exam on a subject he hates, solely to get a promotion; the man
who commutes every day to the office—these men are engaged in
shadow work. True, the typical "consumer" is "the household,"
and this is run by a woman—the expression being but a euphe-
mism for her toil. But if women alone carried the burden of
shadow work, it would be silly to say that, within the realm of shadow work, discrimination works against women. Yet this is precisely
what happens. In shadow work much more intensely than in wage
labor, women are discriminated against. They are tied to more of
it, they must spend more time on it, they have less opportunity
to avoid it, its volume does not diminish when they take outside
employment, and they are penalized more cruelly when they refuse to do it. What women are cheated out of through discrimination in reported and unreported jobs is only a small fraction of the
shadow price due them for their unpaid shadow work in the
home.

Education provides a good example. In former times, growing
up was not an "economic" process; what a boy or girl learned
living at home was not scarce. Everyone learned to speak his vernacular tongue and the basic skills necessary for vernacular life.
Growing up could not possibly have been described, with rare

ductive labor is rewarded with money or by other considerations). However, the author does not himself insist on this distinction. For a comparison between my position and that of Attali, see Louis Puiseux, "Les
visionnaires de l'après-crise," *Politique Hebdo* (April 12, 1981): 8ff.

exceptions, as a process of capitalization of the labor force. Today, this is all changed. Parents have become teaching assistants within the educational system. They are responsible for those basic inputs of human capital, in the jargon of economics, through which their offspring will be qualified as *Homo oeconomicus*. Quite reasonably, the educational economist worries about how to get the mother to inject the largest possible unpaid capital input into her child. In an economist's words: ". . . By the time the children enter the first grade, significant differences in verbal and mathematical competence exist among them. These differences reflect, first, variations in native ability and, second, the amount of human capital acquired before the child reaches the age of six. The stocks of acquired human capital reflect, in turn, varying inputs of time and of other resources by parents, teachers, siblings, and the child itself. The process of acquiring pre-school human capital is analogous to the acquisition, later on, of human capital through schooling and on-the-job training."[39] Quite correctly, the mother's unrewarded time-*cum*-effort inputs into the capitalization of her child are here described as the prime source of human capital formation. Even if one considers such expressions grotesque, it is necessary to concede the truth of their substance in a society in which competence is assumed to be

39 The passage is quoted from p. 451 in A. Leibowitz, "Home Investment in Children" in T.W. Schultz, ed., *Economics of the Family: Marriage, Children & Human Capital* (Chicago: University of Chicago Press, 1974): 432–51. Frank Stafford (*Ibid.*, pp. 453–56) comments: "The efficacy of public policy as a vehicle for altering the income distribution is limited since, it is said, income is so strongly influenced by parental background that opening better schooling opportunities will not have any appreciable effect on earnings for those born into low-income families. In this light, do different forms of income maintenance, by allowing more home-time to the mother, result in a larger home-investment in children?" (See literature in FNs 26, 27.) One probable model for the *post-welfare* state is obviously a state-sponsored *caring society* brought into existence by the social engineering of conditions that call for and induce *unpaid care*. Sweden, which early on had become a model of the welfare state, seems now to be the first society explicitly aiming at this transformation. Since the autumn of 1977, the Secretariat for Future Studies (Box 6710 S-113 85 Stockholm, Sweden), in a major policy study, *Care in Society*, clearly reflects this trend: the ideal of a nation in which, by the year 2006, all citizens will be drafted as care-providers from age five to the grave.

scarce and must be economically produced. The mother's shadow work constitutes an economic activity on which the cash flow, salaries, and surplus value for capital formation all ultimately depend. And the state-sponsored, professional "operationalization" of shadow work, at the center and in the economic peripheries, constitutes a new development strategy best called the *colonization of the informal sector.*[40]

Shadow work, however, cannot be measured in units of currency, although it is possible to transform a specific activity now exacted as shadow work into labor done for wages. This has been tried in the case of commuters. Some Austrian unions, following the lead of a Swedish union, obtained recognition by the employers that commuting was part of their employees' work. Commuting, they argued, is a burdensome task imposed on each worker. It becomes necessary because factories are located not where workers live, but where property is cheap, highways numerous, and sites for executive residential areas close. Commuting constitutes that shadow work by which the worker picks up his own labor force each morning, puts it into a car, and then, acting as the chauffeur of the commodity the employer has contracted to rent during the eight-hour workday, drives this commodity to the workplace. In addition, this shadow work requires a high level of capital investment. A significant percentage of each workday's wages must be spent by the worker for the purchase and maintenance of the car, and to pay the taxes that finance the construction of the highways on which the car runs. And commuting remains shadow work, whether the vehicle is a car, a bus, or a bicycle. Some small unions won their point. Their members then acted each morning as the chauffeurs employed by the

40 The distinction between policies that foster *totalitarian mutual care* and those that foster *personal conviviality* is, in my opinion, a priority issue for social ethics in the 1980s. A well-annotated, lively, comprehensive bibliography on means vs. ends in US civilization is now available: S.H. Cutliff, et al., *Technology and Values in American Civilization: A Guide to Information Sources* (Detroit: Gale Research, 1980). For a phenomenology of the various styles in which total care can be pursued, consult Valentina Borremans, *"The Inverse of Managed Health," Social Development Issues* 1, no. 2 (Uppsala, Sweden: Fall 1977): 88–103, expanded into "L'envers de la santé médicalisée," *Zeitschrift der Schweizerischen Gesellschaft für Sozial und Preventivmedizin* 2/3 (1979).

factory to transport their own bodies to work. If, however, this kind of argument were generally accepted and workers were paid for the now unpaid toil expended on "capitalizing themselves" for the job and then transporting themselves to and from it, the industrial system would cease to function.[41]

As these men have done, women can also demand that their shadow work be transformed into paid labor. But as soon as the shadow price of shadow work and the cost of wage labor are compared, the paradoxical nature of the former becomes evident. At least in the non-militarized sector of every modern economy, the shadow-work input required is arguably greater than that of wage labor.[42] The industrial system is based on the assumption that most basic needs must be satisfied for an increasing majority of society's members by the consumption of a bill of goods. Hence, the toil that is connected with the consumption of these commodities is anthropologically more fundamental than the toil connected with their production. This has been hidden, as long as technical imperfections made human hands or memories necessary ingredients in the production process: Consistently productive labor was identified with legitimate work, and toil that was associated with consumption was passed over in silence or associated with satisfaction. Now, the time input in production decreases sharply, while the growing commodity intensity of society increases the time input necessary for consumption. At the same time, more different forms of consumption have become "musts"—not satisfactory but instrumental forms of time use: John drives, not because he likes driving, nor because he wants to drive like the Joneses, but because he cannot avoid it. It would

41 For a formal statement of this, see Jean Robert, *Le temps qu'on nous vole: Contre la société chronophage* (Paris: Le Seuil, 1980). My ideas on shadow work owe much precision to ten years of frequent conversations with the author.

42 In the military sector of a modern economy, unreported activities are relatively minor. The international trade in arms is kept secret by, but not unreported to, governments. Only from Italy do we hear that major arms factories subcontract production to the black market. The current trend toward the militarization of late-industrial economies must also be understood as an attempt to protect the "reported" from the "unreported" economy.

Economic Sex

be mislabeling most acts of consumption, if we called them "satisfaction"—they constitute unadulterated toil, full-blown shadow work. The total volume of shadow work rapidly surpasses the total volume of available production-associated work or ritual. No matter how you compute a money equivalent to housework, its total value exceeds the volume of wage labor.

When feminists argue that women should be paid for what they do to ready for consumption what the family income buys, they are mistaken when they ask for wages. The best they can hope for is not a shadow price but a consolation prize. The gratis performance of shadow work is the single most fundamental condition for the family's dependence upon commodities. Even if these commodities were to be produced increasingly by robots, industrial society could not function without shadow work. It is to money what the neutron is to the electron. It is as unlike productive "employment," in which commodities for others are produced, as it is unlike homesteading and traditional household activities, which are performed neither for nor with much money.

Shadow work today hides behind much that passes for self-help. Self-help is a modern term: Not so long ago, it was used to suggest masturbation. Self-help divides the acting subject into two parts: One hand washes the other. The term became current in international development through its widespread use by U.S. agencies for international assistance. Through this term, the economist's traditional distinction of all activities into either production or consumption, either productive or reproductive "relations," is projected right onto the consumer: With his right hand he is taught to produce what his left hand supposedly needs. He is taught to do as much with as little as possible, to perfect the most deficient commodities with the greatest possible amount of shadow work. Not only are new products continually being designed for shadow work, for self-help, but microprocessors are increasingly taking over certain jobs, and those people no longer needed in wage labor are then pushed into shadow work.[43] Thus,

43 THE SELF-SERVICE ECONOMY

The impact of the current transition toward a self-service economy on the economic status of women has been touched upon only marginally in the literature on women's work. In the unreported economy women are

shadow work ceases to be predominantly womain's domain. With every year that passes, shadow work becomes more obviously genderless, and so turns from being an arena of women's oppression into the main arena of the economic discrimination against her.[44]

Now middle-class fathers increasingly claim for themselves the experience of the kitchen and of childcare. They want to "do the steaks" for the guests, to spend an hour playing with their infant son. But under the guise of shouldering some of the

---

handicapped, even more than in the reported economy, when they try to compete with men for jobs that generate income, status, or other social claims. In the nether economy, to which unemployed men are now also condemned, men compete with women for the least burdensome and most ego-supporting forms of so-called self-help. Attali (*op. cit.* FN 38) describes the last phase of the industrial system, the industrialization of services that each consumer renders unto himself. The organization of this unpaid production takes up an increasing percentage of paid activities. Paid activities come to have as their goal the boosting of demand for self-produced services, while reducing the cost of the direct service. I see this reflected in a new family ideal: the redefinition of the family as an economic "intermediary" structure. The household becomes a self-service unit. Before industrialization, it was to a large degree subsistent. With industrialization, it became the place where the proceeds of wage labor were upgraded through women's shadow work. Now it tends to become the place to which society channels industrial products to have them transformed through the family's shadow work into a bill of goods that satisfies the household members and keeps them busy, dependent on each other, and disciplined. This model can accommodate not only traditional family styles but also new kinds of marriages and communes; the model can be combined with ecological, libertarian, and, it seems, decentralist ideals. This new, late-industrial family is no longer organized around the wage labor of one, or even of several, of its members but around genderless togetherness in sexist shadow work.

44 DISCRIMINATION IN SELF-HELP

Gerda R. Wekerle, "Women House Themselves," *Heresies* 11, vol. 3, no. 3 (1981): 14–16 reviews programs of self-help housing and urban homesteading conducted under public sponsorship, and argues for the need to extend equal opportunity laws to self-help. She finds constant discrimination against women by agencies set up to promote various kinds of self-help projects. Werkgroep Kollektivering, *Kollektivering van Huishoudelijke Arbeid* (Amsterdam, 1981) finds that wherever, over a three-generation span, housework had been collectivized, women got a bad deal.

"housework," they open a new field for competition and resentment between the sexes. Formerly, women felt forced to compete
for equal opportunities in wage labor. Now men begin to demand
special considerations in the shadow work of the home. During the
last twenty years, as women have gained legal protection for
equal opportunities, on-the-job discrimination has become more
widespread and more acutely felt. Now, with more men being
forced into shadow work as employment becomes ever more
scarce, discrimination against women, right in their homes, will
become more pronounced.

This, then, is the picture suggested by recent studies.[45] Discrimination against women in formal employment and in shadow
work is worldwide, and the same is probably true, although seldom discussed, for women in the unreported or submerged
market. Discrimination both on and off the job spreads with a
rising GNP, as do other side effects like stress, pollution, and
frustration. None of these forms of discrimination is seriously
affected by cultural background, politics, climate, or religion. Re-

45 WOMEN'S STUDIES

A sophisticated summary of the state of the art in women's studies that
reads with great ease is Ann Oakley, *Subject Women: Where Women
Stand Today—Politically, Economically, Socially, Emotionally* (New
York: Pantheon, 1981). This is a history and a sociology of late-twentieth-
century industrialized society, with the spotlight on women, their world and
experience. She attempts to develop a taxonomy of tendencies within women's studies and liberation movements (pp. 317–41). "If the anthropology
of women is not coming of age in the English-speaking world, it is at
least hitting an adolescent growth spurt," says Rayna Rapp, "Review Essay:
Anthropology," *Signs* 4, no. 3 (Spring 1979): 497–513. This essay complements Oakley. An emerging stage of the critical perspective is documented by Margrit Eichler, *The Double Standard: A Feminist Critique of
Feminist Social Science* (New York: St. Martin's Press, 1980). For a
mapping of the discipline as it touches my arguments: Jane Williamson,
New Feminist Scholarship: A Guide to Bibliographies (Old Westbury,
CT: Feminist Press, 1979), which is selective, scholarly, and critical; Mary
Anne Warren, *The Nature of Woman: An Encyclopedia and Guide to the
Literature* (New York: Edgepress, 1980), which is discursive and lively;
Cynthia E. Harrison, *Women in American History: A Bibliography* (Santa
Barbara, CA: Clio American Bibliographic Center, 1979), which gives
about 3,400 abstracts from 550 periodicals, 1963–76. For special-area
bibliographies on women's studies, see the corresponding titled footnote.

ports on discrimination follow a pattern not unlike that of reports on cancer of the breast and uterus: When the per-capita GNPs are equivalent, geography influences the way in which the malady is discussed and recognized, rather than the way it occurs. Australian women keep splendid statistics and Italian women cultivate abrasive cynicism. The barriers that keep women from privileged wage labor and the traps that lock them into the kitchen are explained in different ways in Japan and in the USSR, but everywhere they are comparable in height and depth. Again, the educational process provides a good example. Even when, in different countries, it is of equal length, even if the curricula are the same, its consistent result everywhere is a lower lifetime salary for women than for men. Indeed, the more advanced the levels of education scaled, the more tightly are women locked into their place, for they then have less chance than men for a new start on a different track. The battles of the seventies may have opened the executive suite to women, or have weakened the springs on the traps of the kitchen, but this change has disproportionately benefited "sisters" from privileged backgrounds. A few more women behind the operating table or on the university faculty, an occasional husband domesticated for washing the dishes—these rare tokens only highlight the persistent discrimination against women as a group. At the same time, off-the-job resentment has sharpened its sex-related edge.

The Feminization of Poverty

Although sex discrimination is worldwide, it looks different in underdeveloped countries. Neither income nor economic discrimination is distributed equally in societies of the Third World. There, sex discrimination is primarily an experience reserved to those women who have somehow benefited from economic growth. The dentist's wife in Oaxaca has learned to appreciate the advantages of the new economic put-down. Unlike the New York doctor's wife, the Mexican woman with the two-car garage leaves the house in charge of a domestic when she escapes to a feminist gathering. Only the capitalist Third World still provides a propitious environment for the cultivation of the sex parasite—which

Economic Sex

South African feminist Olive Schreiner foresaw in 1911—for, unlike her counterpart in New York, she can flourish as a *house* wife. Her experience is totally beyond that of her distant cousin who lives with the tooth puller in the village. Each Tuesday, this woman walks behind her man to the market and peddles her tomatoes, while he pulls teeth and sells charms. She defers to her husband but is not economically dependent upon him. The tooth puller's concubine still knows by magic and gossip how to keep men in their place. The bourgeois latina has traded both for the servant plus car, and the right to flirt with feminist rhetoric. The New York teacher has neither magic nor servant nor words to tell the market woman what she has lost. The social science sexist gibberish forces her into genderless thought.[46]

46 STEREOSCOPIC SCIENCE

For orientation to the study of women in Latin America, see June Nash and Helen I. Safa, eds., *Sex and Class in Latin America: Women's Perspective on Politics, Economics, and the Family in the Third World* (New York: Bergin, 1980). In the introduction J. Nash states: "We are now in a liminal state of the social sciences. The values on which our selective criteria are premised are being questioned by people who were never before a significant enough part of the *profession* to challenge them. These include women and natives of the cultures scrutinized" (p. 15). The sixteen studies collected in this anthology illustrate three typical attempts to combine a new focus on women with the conventional central perspective of established science. From this emerges something the author calls *stereoscopic science*, within which I suggest that three currents should be recognized: (1) *complementary* research, in which conventional concepts and methods are applied to subjects that had been hitherto selectively omitted (for instance, the labor-force participation of high-school-graduated mestizo women); (2) *compensatory* research, in which the male/white/capitalist/northern/etc. theoretical bias incorporated into conventional categories is recognized and compensated for (characteristically, compensatory research uses the standard hand-me-down categories of conventional history or social science—production, productivity, exploitation—but uses them in a perspective "from below"); and (3) *contrasting* research. Not infrequently, during this laundering, a new, strong color is added to the concepts analyzed: a "fem" or "latino" or "black is beautiful" emphasis. The resulting research then easily becomes overcompensatory, or *contrasting*: For instance, unpaid activities are recognized as exploitative work only when they are performed by women. These three forms of stereoscopic science illustrate the fact that the characteristic central perspective of science can be stereoscopic as well as monocular. Gender eludes both

In Latin America the immense majority of people, men as well as women, now live unlike either the Mexican doctor's wife or the tooth puller's woman. Most live in the modernized poverty of the slum. Their household depends largely on income. But income has grown at a much slower rate than that by which progress has destroyed the utilization value of their surroundings. For a generation, development has swallowed those environmental resources that had allowed people to meet most of their needs without recourse to the marketplace, and in the process they have unlearned most of the skills necessary for subsistence. Unlike their cousins who went as wetbacks to Texas and who then moved into the ruins of the South Bronx, the Third World slum dweller still finds shared progress credible; these people still believe in the rhetoric of the Brandt Report and Castro. They cannot yet understand why Latinos in the South Bronx organize against the modernization of poverty and try to keep teachers, social workers,[47]

equally. The result of such stereoscopic research is complementary, compensatory, or contrasting epistemological sexism (see FN 54). I have argued elsewhere ["Research by People," *Shadow Work* (*op. cit.*, pp. 75–96, FN 8)] that the researcher who wants to avoid the bias implicit in a central perspective ought to identify himself clearly as one engaged in research that is disciplined, critical, well documented, and public, but emphatically non-scientific. Only non-scientific research that uses analogy, metaphor, and poetry can reach for gendered reality.

47 MODERNIZATION OF POVERTY

Like "work" (see FN 13, esp. Mollat), "poverty" went through a semantic discontinuity as it became a modern key word. Modernized poverty is a different kind of social reality than the poverty of the past; it implies conditions of scarcity. Referring to a millionaire's sick wife as a *poor* woman constitutes a metaphorical, not a proper, use of the term. Today "poor" is opposed to "rich." This was certainly not true in the Middle Ages. The poor were opposed to the powerful. See Karl Bosl, "Potens und Pauper: Begriffsgeschichtliche Studien zur gesellschaftlichen Differenzierung im frühen Mittelalter und zum Pauperismus des Hochmittelalters," *Festschrift O. Brunner* (Göttingen: 1963): 601–87. Poverty—not just in India, but also in Europe—was at certain times an ideal, a sign of prestige, a virtue. G. Ladner, "*Homo Viator*: Medieval Ideas on Alienation and Order," *Speculum* 42, no. 2 (April 1967): 233–59 masterfully described the pilgrim, *Homo viator*, placed between "ordo" and "abalienatio." "Convegni del Centro di Studi Sulla Spiritualita Medievale," *Povertá e*

or hospital care out of their neighborhood. Without any economic distinction on the basis of sex, they have become commodity-dependent in a world that has no employment to offer. They are denied the traditional opportunities for subsistence and find themselves unwanted in the good jobs that development begrudgingly provides.[48] Thus, both men and women share the double bind of

---

richezza nella spiritualitá del secolo XI⁰ e XII⁰, vol. 3 (Todi: Italia, 1969) collects a dozen contributions dealing with the spirituality of poverty. These medieval attitudes seem absurd only to people who forget that modern societies pride themselves in their ability to pauperize the largest number of citizens by defining them as recipients of some kind of service they can no longer provide for themselves. This mechanism has been described, for instance, by Robert A. Scott, *The Making of Blind Men: A Study of Adult Socialization* (New York: Russel Sage Foundation, 1969). The author finds that "being accepted among the blind and behaving like a blind person are both to a great extent independent of the degree of optical impairment. The status of most of the *blind* in the contemporary USA results above all from their successful client relationship to an agency that is concerned with blindness."

48 WOMEN AND ECONOMIC DEVELOPMENT

In Esther Boserup, *Women's Role in Economic Development* (New York: St. Martin's Press, 1974), see especially "Male and Female Farming Systems," pp. 15–35. Here Boserup tries to show what happens to women during the transition from a traditional rural culture to a modernized and urban economy. Far from incorporating women into the production process, the growth of the cash economy becomes an obstacle to their participation as equals in the creation of material culture. This book effectively compares the economic degradation of women throughout the process of development of Latin America, Asia, and Africa. See also, Laurel Bossen, "Women in Modernizing Societies," *American Ethnologist* 2, no. 4 (November 1975): 587–91. For Africa only, Denise Paulme, *Women in Tropical Africa* (Berkeley: University of California, 1971) demonstrates that colonialism has consistently destroyed the complementarity of male and female roles in all four of the societies she has selected for study. In all of them the transition to a cash economy has led to previously unknown status gaps between the sexes. Jane I. Guyer, "Food, Cocoa, and the Division of Labour by Sex in Two West African Societies," *Comparative Studies in Society and History* 22, no. 3 (1980): 355–73 gives in the first few footnotes a summary of the status on the discussion of the sexual division of productive labor during the seventies. Though she quotes principally literature on Africa, the theoretical issues involved come clearly into view. In the two societies she then studies, she finds that women's

the New York housewife: exclusion from decent employment *and* from subsistence. For these modernized poor in poor countries, economic development has become equivalent to the feminization of their genderless poverty.

The export of shadow work from rich to poor countries has been consistently overlooked. This occurs because students of economics find themselves crippled by the terminological impotence of their discipline: Their concepts cannot distinguish shadow work as an entity *sui generis.* Just as the "new home economics" cannot distinguish the activities of a homesteading woman from the upgrading of packaged junk carried out by the

---

incorporation into the cash nexus confirmed and aggravated on the income level their former segregation at the level of cultural definition. Useful in identifying older French literature on the subject is Gabriel Gosselin, "Pour une anthropologie du travail rural en Afrique noire," *Cahiers d'Etudes africaines* 3, no. 12 (1963): 512–49. Modernization, for women as opposed to men, narrows the choice of available jobs. In socialist countries it acerbates the double burden of job-*cum*-housework. In capitalist countries it drives women to compete with each other for paid housework. For the situation in Lima, Peru, see Elsa M. Chaney, *Domestic Service and Its Implications for Development* (Washington, D.C.: Agency of International Development, 1977). Also, these women increasingly work for other poor women because, in all seventy-eight developing countries surveyed, the number of households that depend mainly on the earnings of an adult woman are on the increase; see Mary Buvinic and Nadia Youssef, *Women-Headed Households: The Ignored Factor in Development Planning* (Washington, D.C.: International Center for Research on Women, 1978). Bibliographic guide: M. Buvinic, *Women and World Development: An Annotated Bibliography* (Washington D.C.: Washington Overseas Development Council, 1976). In Mona Etienne and Eleanor Leacock, eds., *Women and Colonization: Anthropological Perspectives* (New York: Praeger, 1980), anthropologists with an historical perspective attempt to reconstruct the position of women in a dozen societies prior to the emergence of the capitalist system. Valentina Borremans, *"Technique and Women's Toil," forthcoming in *Bulletin of Science Technology and Society* (University Park: Penn State University, 11/82) argues that *research for women* aimed at providing them with new technologies has been part of development-oriented policies and has always increased the total toil of women. Only *research by women,* conducted by those who themselves use the new tools and techniques can reduce women's toil, decrease women's dependence on the cash nexus and consequently the severity of sexism.

American housewife, so it is incapable of differentiating between
use-value-oriented subsistence activities and the economy of
trash, in which the slum dweller recycles other people's crates and
refuse to make his shelter. Claudia von Werlhof calls the production generated by this kind of nether existence the blind spot of
economics, into which modern society pushes the wage earner's
dependent partner in order to turn him or her into the invisible
"source of primitive accumulation." A question concerning this
ideal type of consort immediately arises: Is the shadow-working
housewife made in the image of the Latin American slum dweller,
or is the latter, within the world economy, the new genderless
housekeeper of the northern partner?[49]

Economic discrimination against women appears when development sets in. It does not then go away; nothing indicates that
it ever will. In conversation with Frank Hubeny, I came to the

49 DEVELOPMENT OF
INTERNATIONAL HOUSEWORK

In the perspective of Claudia von Werlhof, *Las mujeres y la periferia*
(Bielefeld: University of Bielefeld, 1981), economic development can be
understood as the result of the bondage of women and other marginal
laborers to a kind of activity for which housework in rich countries is the
paradigm. She notices the tendency to divide work between those who
produce commodities and those who put them to use (p. 21), parallel to
the tendency to commercialize and monetarize the former (those who
produce) but not the latter (those who only use the commodities) (p. 17).
The current restructuring of the world economy, its adaptation to costly
energy, microprocessors, and the rising need for social controls seems to
amount to an attempt to instill in and impose on the male part of the
population a kind of working ability that so far had been considered
characteristic and natural only for women. Henceforth, "development"
will mean the creation of a huge sector where people living economically
marginal lives must, in order to survive, become adept at recycling the junk
(that is, substandard or discarded commodities) that the industrialized
sector has defined as trash. The majorities in underdeveloped nations increasingly assume a function that is analogous to the "housewife" of the
"wage earner" (the industrialized world). Therefore, one can talk about
what goes on at the periphery of industrial society as an international *Ver-
hausfraulichung* (housewiferization). A parallel argument, brilliant but
mostly blind to the issue of sex discrimination within this new international
housework, has been made by André Gorz, *Adieux au prolétariat: Au delà
du socialisme* (Paris: Editions Galilée, 1980): 127–46.

conclusion that the struggle to create economic equality between genderless humans of two different sexes resembles the efforts made to square the circle with ruler and straight edge. Eudoxus tried and learned how to compare irrational numbers. The problem remained unsolved until Lindemann, in the nineteenth century, showed that there could be no solution to it. He demonstrated that π was not an algebraic number, and thus increased our awareness of the incommensurability among real numbers. Political economy is still in a state comparable to mathematics before Lindemann. Faced by the evidence of its consistent failure to create economic equality between the sexes, we might now entertain a long overlooked possibility: The paradigm of *Homo oeconomicus* does not square with what men and women actually are. Perhaps they cannot be reduced to humans, to economic neuters of either male or female sex. Economic existence and gender might be literally incomparable.

III. Vernacular Gender

Outside industrial societies, uni-sex work is the rare exception, if it exists at all. Few things can be done by women and also by men. The latter, as a rule, just cannot do women's work. In early eighteenth-century Paris, you could recognize the bachelor from afar by his stench and gloomy looks. From notaries' records, we know that solitary men left no sheets or shirts when they died. In the time of Louis XIV, a man without a woman to keep house could barely survive. Without wife, sister, mother, or daughter he had no way to make, wash, and mend his clothes; it was impossible for him to keep chickens or to milk a goat; if he was poor, he could not eat butter, milk, or eggs. He could not cook certain foods even if he had the ingredients.[50] And today, in the rural Mexico I know so well, a woman would rather die of embarrassment than let a man cook the beans.

From afar, the native can tell whether women or men are at work, even if he cannot distinguish their figures. The time of year and day, the crop, and the tools reveal to him who they are. Whether they carry a load on their head or shoulder will tell him

See Micheline Baulant, "La famille en miettes: Sur un aspect de la démographie du XVIIe siècle," *Annales, ESC* 27, nos. 4–5 (July–October 1972): 959–68, translated into English by Patricia M. Ranum as *"The Scattered Family: Another Aspect of Seventeenth-Century Demography," in *Family and Society*, eds. Robert Forster and Orest Ranum (Baltimore and London: Johns Hopkins University Press, 1976): 104–16.

their gender. If he notices geese loose in the harvested field, he
knows a girl must be nearby to tend them. If he comes across
sheep, he knows he will find a boy. To *belong* means to know
what befits *our* kind of woman, *our* kind of man. If someone does
what *we* consider the other gender's work, that person must be a
stranger. Or a slave, deprived of all dignity. Gender is in every
step, in every gesture, not just between the legs. Puerto Rico is
only three hours from New York. Two-thirds of its people have
been to the mainland. Yet even today, in the interior of the island,
there is no such thing as a Puerto Rican gait; women sail down a
path like sloops chopping in the tradewinds, and men swagger
and roll to the rhythm of the machete, but both in the unmistakably *jíbaro* fashion. One knows that they could not be from
nearby Santo Domingo, much less be gringos from the States. In
many Puerto Ricans, vernacular gender has survived for decades,
not only in the Harlem barrio but even when they have lived
mixed up with hillbillies and blacks in the South Bronx.[51]

Gender is something other and much more than sex. It
bespeaks a social polarity that is fundamental and in no two
places the same. What a man cannot or must do is different from
valley to valley. But the social anthropologist has missed the point,
and his terminology has become a unisex mask for a reality that has

---

51 VERNACULAR

This is a technical term that comes from Roman law. It can be found there
from the earliest records up to the codification by Theodosius. It designates
the inverse of a commodity: "*Vernaculum, quidquid domi nascitur,
domestici fructus; res quae alicui nata est, et quam non emit*": Du Cange,
Glossarium Mediae et Infimae Latinitatis 8 : 283. "Vernacular" means
those things that are homemade, homespun, home-grown, not destined for
the marketplace, but that are for home use only. The term has come into
English principally to refer to one's native tongue. For lack of a better
term, I would like to breathe new life into the old word. I will deal with its
history in my forthcoming book *Vernacular Values*. I will refer to the
whole of any set that is made up of two gendered subsets as "vernacular."
For example, I shall speak of a *vernacular language* when I refer to the
complement of male and female speech (FN 101), of a *vernacular universe* (FN 89) when I refer to the complementary grasp of a social reality
by that society's men and women, or of *vernacular tools* when I want to
designate a group's tool kit that is more or less clearly divided by gender
(FN 70).

two sides. What Bohr and Heisenberg have done for the epistemology of physics has not yet been done for the social sciences. That light fits the paradigms of both particle and wave, that neither theory alone conveys its complex reality, and that no broader framework allows us to grasp it more clearly are today everyman's truths. But that a similar approach is demanded for most social-science concepts is still news for many.[52]

"Culture," like "behavior," is a typical term that is used when "the" Puerto Rican becomes an object of study. The social worker

52 COMPLEMENTARITY AND
SOCIAL SCIENCE

Modern physics has learned to deal with the complementarity of two perspectives. Light can be reduced neither to a wave phenomenon nor to a particle phenomenon. In either case, too much is left out. To call it both seems a paradox. The complementarity is meaningful only by virtue of the mathematical form given to the theory in which it appears. The underlying idea of epistemological complementarity is not new. Following Euclid, who conceived of the eye as sending out rays whose ends probed the object, Ptolemy and then the great scholastics distinguished *lumen* from *lux*. Lux is light when it is subjectively perceived; *lumen* is a stream coming from the eye to light up the object. Vernacular reality can be thought of as a huge quilt, each patch having at its own, iridescent color, its *lux*. In the *lumen* of gender analysis, each culture appears as a metaphor, a metaphoric complementarity (FNs 55–57) relating two distinct sets of tools (FN 70), two types of space-time (FNs 78, 79), two domains (FNs 86, 87). These find expression in different but related styles in which the world is understood or grasped (FN 89) and spoken about (FNs 94–101). Science, both mono- and stereoscopic (FN 46), is a filter that screens from the observer's eye the ambiguity of gendered light. But this same screen is permeable in both directions for the genderless lumen the observer projects on his object and in which he or she observes the object. The symbolic asymmetry that constitutes the social reality of each vernacular is effaced by the central perspective of cultural anthropology. The *Eigenvalue* of each and every vernacular reality cannot be seized in the monochromatic, genderless lumen of such concepts as *role* (FNs 62, 63), *exchange* (FN 33), and *structure* (FNs 76, 77). What the scientific observer then sees through his diagnostic spectacles are not men and women who really act in a gendered subsistence society but sexual deviants from an abstract, genderless cultural norm who have to be operationalized, measured, ranked, and structured into hierarchies. Cultural anthropology that operates with genderless concepts is inevitably sexist (see my comment on Rubin, FN 7). This sexism is much more blinding than old-style ethnocentric arrogance.

makes efforts to deal with "him." The delicate and always dual nuances contained within each aspect of vernacular culture are ignored, jammed together, violating the traditions of millennia. The teacher in the New York school tries to help the Puerto Rican "child." He or she does not realize that childhood only came into being as gender vanished. The teacher seldom reflects on the fact that the symbiosis of the social sciences and modern institutions is an effective device for reducing gender to sex. I shall later argue that this breakdown constitutes the decisive anthropological characteristic that sets the contemporary age apart from any other. But before launching an initial exploration of gender, I shall outline three shoals on which it would be easy to run aground before reaching deep water. These preliminary remarks will also provide a perspective on economic sex.

Ambiguous Complementarity

Only the newcomer perceives culture. For the insider there are men and women and then a third reality: outsiders who might be foreigners, slaves, domestic animals, untouchables, or freaks. If the outsider is perceived as a sexed being, his sex or, more properly, gender is seen in some analogy to that of "our" men and women. Kinship is possible only between what we conceive as men and women; it only specifies the fit between gendered people. What we perceive as men and what we perceive as women can meet and fit not only because but in spite of the unique contrast between them. They fit like the right fits the left.[53] The analogy between male and female and the duality of right and left is useful

53 RIGHT AND LEFT

Right and *left* have recently become labels for biological and neurological scientific research and for popular myth. For literature on this, see Hubbard, FN 58. The following literature deals with the use of "right" and "left" as shorthand terms referring not to biological but to *symbolic dualism*. For the assessment and history of ethnographic evidence on symbolic dualism, see Rodney Needham, ed., *Right and Left: Essays on Symbolic Classification* (Chicago: University of Chicago Press, 1973; Phoenix pbk., 1978). The author provides a major introduction to seventeen articles written by as many authors between 1909 and 1971. Of the many possible interpreta-

at this point, principally because it allows me to explore some of the dangers of misunderstanding. In many cultures the left hand is the weak and powerless one; it has been subject to millennia of mutilation. Right-handedness is not just accepted or submitted to: It has become the inculcated norm. The child who would use the left hand is reprimanded, the hand slapped, tied behind the child's back, or crippled. Organic asymmetry has become the fact. A neurological preponderance that manifests itself in greater sensibility, strength, or aptitude has been turned into the ideal of right dominance. The left has become adaptive to the right as its ever needed and cherished assistant. The analogy can be and is constantly used to support the idea that the "female sex is socio-biologically male adaptive."[54]

However, this is precisely *not* the point I want to make. The

---

tions given to R/L symbolism, one particular view of this complementarity has penetrated the Western intellectual tradition. On this, see Otto Nussbaum, "Die Bewertung von Rechts und Links in der Römischen Liturgie," *Jahrbuch für Antike und Christentum* 5 (1962): 158–71 and Ursula Deitmaringen, "Die Bedeutung von Rechts und Links in theologischen und literarischen Texten bis um 1200," *Zeitschrift für deutsches Altertum und deutsche literatur* 98 (November 1969): 265–92.

54 SEXISM: MORAL AND EPISTEMOLOGICAL

Science is doubly sexist: It is a male-dominated enterprise and it is a construct of genderless (objective) categories and procedures (see FN 52). When gender crops up among academic subjects, it is in the humanities, e.g., religious studies along the line of Mircea Eliade, *Myth and Reality* (New York: Harper and Row, 1963) or literary criticism such as Carolyn G. Heilbrun, *Toward a Recognition of Androgyny* (New York: Knopf, 1973). The first kind of sexism, I would call moral and impute it to the character of the practitioners, individually or collectively. *Moral sexism* has been pilloried in recent feminist writings, both for what it does and for what it leaves out: Men predominate among scientists; men determine what shall be considered as science; most women scientists are disciples of these men; and on every level male prejudices are incorporated into scientific categories. As a result of this criticism, female sexism has become a trendy perspective, adopted increasingly also by men. The second kind of sexism is more fundamental. I call it *epistemological sexism*. It filters gender—both male and female—out of the concepts and methods of legitimate science (see FNs 46, 52). It is implicit in any scientific discourse that confuses gender with sex, as well as in ordinary speech when the

analogy means something different. Each man and woman outside of a push-button society depends for survival on the interplay
of two hands. In some societies, right-handedness is more pronounced than in others. In other societies, as in the Chinese,
etiquette, good taste, and world view demand that the left and the
right predominate alternately in a delicate, detailed orchestra-
tion.[55] In some societies, as among the Nyoro of Africa, to be left-
handed destines one to the sacred group of diviners. But, regard-

---

conversation is dominated by a web of key words (FN 2). Moral sexism
has been effectively challenged during the seventies. But this challenge to
moral sexism in science has all too often only deepened the hold of
epistemological sexism on the challengers themselves. For instance, an
obvious instance of moral sexism consists in interpreting everything relating to sexual difference (e.g., Right/Left) that has a correlation to biology
as innate. This tendency has become so dominant that it threatened in the
late seventies to become trivial, and scientific language came to express the
male scientists' wish fulfillment about right/male dominance and left/
female adaptation. This interpretation was challenged. For the literature,
see FN 58. However, the challenge usually took either of two forms, both
epistemologically sexist: (1) Typically, the criticism was explicitly fem-
sexist on a moral level (the critic points out that the title of FN 53 should
have read "Left/Right"); (2) more seriously, the critic points out that
Right/Left does indeed stand for duality, but duality in the abstract, and
then ranges male/female as just one more among many dualities, confirm-
ing via structuralism the non-existence of gender as a duality sui generis
(see more on structuralism, FN 76). For recent trends in women's studies
that, in my opinion, tend toward the recognition of epistemological sexism
in science, see Lynda M. Glennon (op. cit. FN 12). She distinguishes four
often overlapping types of feminist endeavor to deal with the sexism implicit in the most common dualities used as analytic concepts by the social
sciences.

55 YIN AND YANG

Marcel Granet, *"Right and Left in China," trans. Rodney Needham, in
Rodney Needham, ed., Right and Left (op. cit., pp. 43–58, FN 53).
Never does one find absolute oppositions in China: A left-hander is not
sinister and neither is a right-hander. A multitude of rules show that left
and right predominate alternatively. Diversity of time and place imposes,
at any point, a delicate choice between left and right, but this choice is
inspired by a very coherent system of representations. The alternative pre-
eminence, however, does not alter the fact that the right hand is the more
widely used. It is for this very reason, probably, that the left hand pre-
ponderates. This is shown by a number of important rules of etiquette. A

Vernacular Gender

less of the greater power, skill, or dignity attributed to one hand, more often the right than the left, the two hands are used for complementary actions and gestures. Tradition rigorously instructs the left-handed shaman which hand he must use for the offering. The two hands always act together according to two programs that are never the other's mirror image. Thus, this unique kind of duality is always ambiguous.

The oldest traditions place the fundamental trait of our existence into this singular kind of bifurcation. It constitutes an ambiguous complementarity, different from both a mirror image and a shadow. As duality, it is distinct from the positive copy of a negative and from the deterministic match of DNA's double helix. I assume it to be the foundation of metaphor and poetic speech— the only appropriate mode to express it. Twins, the navel/umbilical cord, yin/yang are among the mythological representations through which this duality seeks expression.[56] One of the difficulties in the kind of opposition that exists between gender and

---

classical and delicate description of this ambiguity in Africa can be found in Marcel Griaule, *Conversations with Ogotemmeli* (London: Oxford University Press, 1965). In various writings, R. Panikkar has explored the issue in respect to India. He interprets the Western "search for Christ" as a *homeomorphic equivalent* (a non-identical term that performs a similar function) to the brahminical search for poles that are fused without being intermingled. See R. Panikkar, *The Unknown Christ of Hinduism* (New York: Orbis, 1981). In recent literary criticism, "androgyny" is a key word under which the issue is touched upon. See N.T. Bazin, "The Concept of Androgyny: A Working Bibliography," *Women's Studies* 2 (1974): 217–35.

56 METAPHORS FOR THE OTHER

When I speak in metaphors, I engage in a deviant discourse; I am alert to my special, odd, and startling combination of words. I know that I cannot be understood unless he who listens to me is wide-awake to my intentional use of a term that carries other than literal meanings. Every vernacular language is the result of two different speech forms corresponding to two gender domains in each of which the world is grasped in a gender-specific way (see FN 101). Each gender is muted in relation to the other. When using common vernacular words to speak not *into* but *about* the opposite domain, the vernacular speaker intuitively uses a kind of metaphor. For ideas on metaphor, see Warren A. Shibles, *Metaphor: An Annotated Bibliography and History* (Whitewater, WI: Language Press,

sex should now be less obscure. It may be appropriate to consider vernacular gender as the foundation of ambiguous complementarity, and the sex of economic neuters as the modern experiment to deny or transcend this foundation. By reducing all interaction to exchange, the social sciences have laid the groundwork for this denial and for the legitimacy of an *economic* analysis of the relations between men and women. *This is why I speak about eco-*

1971): 10–17. For me, the most impressive modern texts exposing the near impossibility of using twentieth-century language to speak about gender (and what survives of it) is Luce Irigaray, *"La tache aveugle d'un vieux rêve de symétrie," Speculum de l'autre femme* (Paris: Editions de Minuit, 1974): 9–161. See "Women's Exile," *Ideology and Consciousness* 1 (1977): 71–75, an interview with Irigaray that touches on *Speculum*; also see Elaine Marks and Isabelle de Courtivron, eds., "This Sex Which Is Not One" and "When the Goods Get Together," *New French Feminism* (Amherst, MA: University of Massachusetts Press, 1980): 99–106 and 107–10. For a masterly introduction, see William Empson, *Seven Types of Ambiguity* (New York: New Directions, 1947). The metaphorical relationship itself can be expressed in a metaphor. This is what religious symbols frequently do. Ludwig Wittgenstein, "Bemerkungen über Frazer's *The Golden Bough," Synthèse* 17 (1967): 233–53 speaks about this: ". . . Putting magic into parenthesis in this case is the magic. . . . Metaphysics becomes a kind of magic." The *gorgone*, for instance, is a metaphor of this kind. It is always facing you, with its neither-nor features swallowing your eyelight in its empty sockets: looking at yourself as the mask that fits your face. Jean-Pierre Vernant, "L'autre de l'homme: La face de Gorgo," *Le Racisme: Pour Léon Poliakov, sous la direction de Maurice Olender* (Brussels: Editions Complexe SPRL, 1981): 141–56. By the same author, "Figuration de l'invisible et catégorie psychologique du double: le Colossos," *Mythe et pensée chez les Grecs* (Paris: Maspero Petite Collection, 1971–74): 251–64. Twins are equally frightening. See, for instance, Aidan Southall, "Twinship and Symbolic Structure" in J.S. La Fontaine, ed., *The Interpretation of Ritual* (London: Tavistock, 1972): 73–114. When I use the term "gender" I am aware that I give it meaning on three distinct levels: (1) Descriptively, I refer to one of the two strong subsets of any vernacular reality (speech forms, tools, spaces, symbols) that are more or less related to male or female genital characteristics; (2) I refer to the vernacular whole insofar as it is constituted by the complementarity of these two subsets; (3) and, on the level of epistemology, I am aware that "gender" in the second sense is a metaphor for the ambiguous symbolic complementarity that constitutes each of the two genders (in the first sense) as metaphors for each other. My thinking on this point is nourished by the scholastic concept of *relatio subsistens.*

nomic sex. It should therefore be clear that two distinct types of language are required for speaking about what once existed and what now obtains.[57]

Socio-Biological Sexism

I have chosen to begin this introduction to gender and sex with a reference to the right and left hands because the analogy is effective. Further, the analogy immediately suggests a second diffi-

5 7 AMBIGUOUS COMPLEMENTARITY

The complementarity between genders is both asymmetric and ambiguous. Asymmetry implies a disproportion of size or value or power or weight; ambiguity does not. Asymmetry indicates a relative position; ambiguity, the fact that the two do not congruously fit. Explicit reference to the asymmetry of genders is made in the footnotes on patriarchy (FN 21), on relative power (FN 84), and throughout the entire text. Here I deal with ambiguity. The ambiguity that characterizes gender is unique. It is two-sided: Men symbolize the mutual relationship differently than do women (see FN 56). Robert Hertz, *"The Pre-Eminence of the Right Hand: A Study in Religious Polarity," now in Rodney Needham, ed. (*op. cit.*, pp. 3–31, FN 53), tried to incorporate this notion of complementarity into the social sciences at a time when the concept had begun to be fruitful in the physical sciences. He was a genius and recognized that in the social sciences the fundamental polarity implied both asymmetry and ambiguity. He died in the trenches of World War I and since then has been misinterpreted. First, his editor, Marcel Mauss, domesticated the disconcerting asymmetry and ambiguity contained in Hertz's idea of complementarity, harnessing the unfamiliar and anomalous duality by defining it as the foundation of all "exchange." See M. Mauss, *The Gift: Forms and Functions of Exchange in Archaic Societies* (New York: Norton, pbk., 1967). (The original French version was published in 1925.) Then Levi-Strauss proclaimed Mauss the first to have treated the total social fact as a symbolic system of exchanges between individuals and groups, and identified Hertz as Mauss's teacher. The *fuzzy, partly incongruous* complementarity that can be understood only by means of metaphors, which Hertz had begun to recognize as the root of culture, was repressed in the social sciences in favor of operational concepts such as role, class, exchange, and, ultimately, "system" (see FN 76). Here I want to compare the complementarity that constitutes the relationship between the genders to the process of exchange between constituted partners. The former tends, ideally, toward "subsistent relations":

culty that, unlike the first, is not fundamental but contingent on current academic fads. In the United States, it is now almost impossible to analyze gender related to behavior without provoking a response from two quarters—feminist Marxists and socio-biologists. I want to keep my argument free from both these distorting repercussions. A discussion of gender with feminist Marxists is impossible. Their sex-conscious use of political economics eliminates the ambiguities of gender by means of a double filter. However, I want even more carefully to avoid stooping to engage in any argument with those who are taken in by the fashionable rhetoric of Lionel Tiger, E.O. Wilson, A. de Benoist, and their like. They start from the postulate of biological determinism and assume that culture is built on it; for me, what is unique about *Homo sapiens* as a human phenomenon is the constant *incarnation* of the symbolic duality of gender. I do not quarrel with the observations made by the new ethologists; however, the fact that genderless modern humans behave almost as apes confirms my thesis that the regime of sex is inhumane. Further, biological determinists need not be answered by me; that task I can leave to what, in the USA, is called the *liberal establishment*. The legitimacy of social planning and the management of care within a liberal society depends on the credibility of the expert's claim that he is anti-fascist and anti-racist. It is for him to point out that the new socio-biology of sex is replacing the socio-biology of race launched by Count Gobineau. When one sees what sexism reveals, racism then seems more like an early homologous groping. As nineteenth-century racist theories served to buttress European colonial pretensions, so contemporary sexist thought ministers to a worldwide regime of latter-day unisex humbug. The new sexism fits the colorful elites who govern post-colonial economies today.

---

meanings metaphorically and not antithetically related. Exchange, in contrast, implies a relationship between social actors, and a common bond that is independent of their actual interchange. Exchange drives partners toward an ever *clearer fit*, (homogeneity and not ambiguity) whose asymmetry therefore tends toward *hierarchy* and *dependence*. Where exchange structures relationships, a common denominator defines the fit. Where ambiguity constitutes the two entities that it also relates, ambiguity engenders new partial incongruities between men and women, constantly upsetting any tendency toward hierarchy and dependence.

The contention of all socio-biologists is the same.[58] And the structure of their argument is ingenuously simple, the source of its seductive strength. Most readers of their books are not prepared to see that behind the complex discussions woven of mathematical algorithms and risky statistics nothing more lies hidden. The argu-

5 8 S O C I O - B I O L O G I C A L   M Y T H O L O G Y

In part, at least, science is a gusty and faddish intellectual enterprise that focuses on issues that trouble scientists emotionally or politically. This is particularly clear in the scientific attempts to link human, intraspecific, organic differences to behavior. Stephen Jay Gould, *The Mismeasure of Man* (New York: Norton, 1981) deals directly with the history of the scientific attempt to abstract intelligence as a single quantifiable entity, located within the brain, that permits the ranking of people. The book, however, can also serve as an introduction to the ups and downs of the ideology of biological determinism from craniometry to Peter J. Wilson. Already, in 1944, Gunnar Myrdal spoke of the "tendency to assume biological causation without question, and to accept social explanation only under the duress of a siege," as an ideology that allows one to take the current status of groups as a measure of the position in which its normal individuals *should* be. Gould focuses on this bio-determinism, which is rising in popularity again as it regularly has in times of political retrenchment. Since the mid-seventies, millions of people have learned to suspect that their social prejudice and their inferiority are after all scientific facts, that they fit politically into the ranks intraspecific specialization has assigned them. For criticisms of the attempt to reduce the social and human sciences to subdisciplines of socio-biology by magnifying the effects of heredity on human behavior, see William M. Dugger, "Sociobiology for Social Scientists: A Critical Introduction to E.O. Wilson's Evolutionary Paradigm," *Social Science Quarterly* 62, no. 2 (June 1981): 221–46, and Clifford Geertz's critique of D. Symons's *The Evolution of Human Sexuality* (New York: Oxford University Press, 1980) in *The New York Review of Books* (January 24, 1980): 3–4. For specific literature on the issue discussed here, see: Helen H. Lambert, "Biology and Equality: A Perspective on Sex Differences," *Signs* 4, no. 1 (Autumn 1978): 97–117, and the major, thorough, and many-faceted analysis of the sexist perspective on scholarship in human biology: M.S.H. Hubbard and Barbara Friend, eds., *Women Look at Biology Looking at Women* (Cambridge, MA: Schenkman, 1979). Note, however, that there are some very articulate feminists who now argue that males and females are like separate subspecies of humanity whose behavioral style is inherently different, irrespective of their cultures: Alice Rossi, "A Biosocial Perspective on Parenting," *Daedalus* 106, no. 2 (Spring 1977): 1–31. The well-intentioned profession of feminist egalitarianism may camouflage the prick of racism that is implied in bio-social determinism—no good intentions can expunge it.

ment runs as follows: Among primates, the female is already male-adaptive.[59] Primitive men dominate their women; high culture institutionalizes this dominance; hence, it is scientifically legitimate to speculate that genes must account for the regularity of this pattern of primacy in men and submissiveness in women. Genetic male dominance accounts for sex roles then and now.

It is not, however, because of the weakness of the argument that I consider a controversy with academic sexism out of place, but rather because of the style in which the claims of the theoretical "biocrats" are presented. This style has much in common with racism from Gobineau to Rosenberg—"scientific" argumentation that addresses itself only to the true believer. Racism and sexism are alike not only in argument and style; their image of men is woven out of the same stuff. For both racist and sexist suppositions, humans can be scientifically put into categories and then arranged according to rank. Dark skin, low IQ, female sex, and other genetic deficiences fall close to the bottom. Both the racist and the service professional presume the existence of an objective perspective by which they can operationally rank people's claims to scarce privileges. Both rankings are based on the assumption of genderless individuals acting under conditions of growing scarcity. Therefore, the perspective of the racist or that of the modern educator fits only into modern Western culture. However, the legitimacy of the service professional depends on a believable rhetoric that effectively obfuscates the racism hidden in professional diagnosis. The task of arguing with the new, crude socio-biocrats I can therefore leave to those of my colleagues whose professional spectacles direct them to impute "needs" rather

59 ANIMAL SOCIOLOGY

Animal sociology is a kind of science fiction in reverse. While SF attributes meaningful and purposeful behavior to constructs of the fantasy, AS, animal sociology, attributes society to sub-humans. Both have in common with SS, social science, the fact that they operate with genderless terms. The occasional predictive value of SF scenarios or the confirmation of behaviorist theories by animal experiment simply demonstrate that SS categories are blind to what is characteristically and exclusively human: gendered culture. For critical access to the literature, see Donna Haraway, "Animal Sociology and a Natural Economy of the Body Politic," *Signs* 4, no. 1 (1978): 21–60, and other contributions in the same issue.

than to measure "inferiorities," to those teachers, medical men, gynecologists, and social workers who are trained to degrade others into consumers of their services through their scientific diagnoses. Their self-interest combined with their optimism impel them to see that their careers, based on much more subtle ranking, are threatened should they be publicly identified with the cruder socio-biological sexists.[60]

60 THE RACIST AND THE PROFESSIONAL

The comparison between racists and service-oriented professionals is intentional, although I know that many of my readers identify themselves as professionals, and few as racists. I cannot, however, avoid the comparison. Those interested in my reasons should read Ivan Illich, *The Right to Useful Unemployment* (London: Marion Boyars, 1978), especially the second part. A growing number of historical studies of the nineteenth century show that the service professions invented their diagnosis of needs to create demands for the therapies they then came to monopolize. Burton S. Bledstein, *The Culture of Professionalism* (New York: Norton, 1976) is well documented. Within the framework of the nation state, which tended to monopolize service production even where the production and commerce of goods was left in private hands, the professionals "played on public fears of disorder and disease, adopted deliberately mystifying jargon, ridiculed popular traditions of self-help as backward and unscientific, and in this way created or intensified . . . a demand for their services," Christopher Lasch, *The New York Review of Books* (November 24, 1977): 15–18. In this context, the professional establishments acquired the ability to define "deficiencies" by scientific opinion; to conduct research that would confirm this opinion; to impute these deficiencies to concrete individuals by "diagnosis"; to subject entire population groups to compulsory testing; to impose therapy on those found to be in need of correction, cure, or upgrading. The logic of this process has been described with inimitable incisiveness by John L. McKnight, *The Mask of Love: Professional Care in the Service Economy* (Boston and London: Marion Boyars, 1982). The professional and the racist ethos converge. They are both based, albeit with different subtleties, on the same assumption: Biological diagnosis entitles the biocracy to social grading. Nowhere can this convergence of professional ethos with biological discrimination be seen more clearly than through the history of gynecology (see FNs 80, 87). Maurice Olender, ed., *Le Racisme: Pour Léon Poliakov* (op. cit. FN 56) contains several contributions that link the anti-feminine to the anti-Judaic prejudice in the tradition of the Enlightenment.

Social-Science Sexism

A notion called the sex role[61] has become very popular during the last fifteen years. Games people play, scientific treatises, pedagogical methods, and political rhetoric are all built on the assumption of its existence. Concern with sex roles seems to rise with GNP. In rich countries, how to choose, assume, and transmit sex roles has become a major worry for many people. Sociological role theory is a much more stubborn obstacle to the analysis of gender than the newly fabricated concepts of socio-biology. However, any recourse to role concepts will blind one to the perception of gender in speech as well as in action.

Gender is substantive. This is not true with sex in the economic neuter. In the perspective of the neuter, sex is a secondary attribute, a property of an individual, an adjective characteristic of a human being. The concept of sex role could not come into being until society's institutions were structured to meet the genderless needs of genderless clients with genderless commodities produced in a genderless world. The sex role builds on the existence of genderless *man*. One's sex, however, is not perceived as

61 ROLE

"Role" is a concept by which, since Ralph Linton, *The Study of Man: An Introduction* (New York: Appleton-Century Crofts, 1936), sociology links the social order to the characteristic behavior of the individuals who comprise it. Role is the device by which people become part of a plural that can then be analyzed by genderless concepts. Further, the use of role as a category of the social sciences precludes the possibility of introducing gender into the discussion. Gender relates two persons to each other who are more profoundly *other* than role-playing individuals ever could be. Sociology has borrowed the concept of role from the theater, where it first appeared as a technical term when European actors began to perform on an elevated stage that made scenes a sequence of "entrance," "performance," and "exit," on a "set." Thus, as a concept, role was as new to the sixteenth-century theater as it is to twentieth-century sociology. See Richard Southern, *"Fourth Phase: The Organized Stage," The Seven Ages of the Theatre* (New York: Hill and Wang, 1963): 155–215. On the impact of the role concept on methodology, consult W.H. Dray, "Holism and Individualism in History and Social Science," *Encyclopedia of Philosophy* 4, ed. Paul Edwards (New York: Macmillan, 1967): 53–58.

just one more role, one more outfit to don, one more well-fitting or ill-tailored suit for special occasions, like the role of parent, academic, or plumber. Most people consider the sex role less changeable; women know that they are stuck with it in an oppressive way. But, like it or not, to have a sex role—be it assumed, imposed, or resented—is something other than belonging to a gender. It is one thing to say that you are a man or a woman, and something quite different that you are a human being of male or female sex. Unlike gender, which means that you are either a square or a circle, the sex role is like a foundation on which other roles can be built. Some people wear their own skin as if it were chosen like either lingerie or skivvies, and beneath it feel skinned, plastic selves. Others view their sex role as a corset into which their genderless libido was forced by their parents, a foundation onto which they can layer any uniform or dress and then change or occasionally discard it. As with the vernacular, one is born and bred into gender; the sex role is something acquired. One can blame parents or society for an "assigned" sex role or a taught mother tongue; there is no way to complain about vernacular speech or gender.

The distinction between vernacular gender and sex role is comparable to that between vernacular speech and taught mother tongue, between subsistence and economic, existence. Therefore, the fundamental assumptions about the one and the other are distinct. Vernacular speech, gender, and subsistence are characteristics of a morphological closure of community life on the assumption, implicit and often ritually expressed and mythologically represented, that a community like a body cannot outgrow its size. Taught mother tongue, sex, and a life-style based on the consumption of commodities all rest on the assumption of an open universe in which scarcity underlies all correlations between needs and means. Gender implies a complementarity within the world that is fundamental and closes the world in on "us," however ambiguous and fragile this closure might be. Sex, on the contrary, implies unlimited openness, a universe in which there is always more.

Strictly speaking, discourse about gender must therefore be expressed in metaphorical language; in no two worlds does it mean univocally the same thing. And the dual, specific whole that the complementarity of concrete genders brings into being—a "world," a "society," a "community"—is both shaped and limited, asymmetrically, by its components. Gender can be grasped only by means of morphology; its existence depends in turn on the size and shape of the dual world it structures.[62] A snail, after adding a number of widening rings to the delicate structure of its shell, suddenly brings its accustomed building activities to a stop. A single additional ring would increase the size of the shell sixteen times. Instead of contributing to the welfare of the snail, it would burden the creature with such an excess of weight that any increase in its productivity would henceforth be literally outweighed by the task of coping with the difficulties created by enlarging the shell beyond the limits set by its purpose. At that point, the problems of overgrowth begin to multiply geometrically, while the snail's biological capacity can at best be extended arithmetically. So gender sets limits to the social structure it forms, a structure expressed in every aspect of life-style, but first of all in kinship.

62 SOCIAL MORPHOLOGY

I believe that in each vernacular milieu gender is the source of a social form that can take its shape only within limited parameters. In biology a characteristic form can exist only within a narrow range of size. Mouselike beings range from an inch in length to the size of a rat; an elephant with mouselike feet cannot exist. Some of the most beautiful pages on this are in J.B.S. Haldane, *"On Being the Right Size," in James R. Newman, *The World of Mathematics: A Small Library of the Literature of Mathematics from A'h-mose the Scribe to Albert Einstein* 2 (New York: Simon and Schuster, 1956): 952–57. D'Arcy Wentworth Thompson, *On Growth and Form*, an abridged edition edited by J.T. Bonner (Cambridge: Cambridge University Press, 1971), concentrated his attention on the morphological relationship of anatomical form and size. Leopold Kohr, *The Breakdown of Nations* (London, 1941; reprint ed. available) has pioneered social morphology, correlating social form and size. E.F. Schumacher, Kohr's pupil, summed up his teacher's axiom to his satisfaction in *Small Is Beautiful: Economics as if People Mattered* (New York; Harper and Row, Torchbooks, 1973). I argue that *social beauty* appears when the material elements of a culture are of the size that is appropriate to its concrete, gendered complementarity. Maintaining this "milieu" within parameters of size that correspond to the form (in Greek, "morphé") is necessary for the existence and preservation of a gendered relationship between men's and women's domains.

The idea behind the term "sex role," as this term is generally used, implies exactly the opposite. The carrier of the sex role is tacitly assumed to be a plastic individual having a genderless existence that is more or less shaped by "sex." Most studies that have been done during the last hundred years on the differences in men's and women's activities all over the world were carried out by observers interested in primitive, traditional, exotic sex roles, even at a time when the term was still unknown.[63] Thus, where gender was observed it was reported as some kind of sex.

The confusion is nicely illustrated in a 1947 statement by M. Herskovits: "No phase of the economic life of non-literate people has attracted more attention than has the sex division of labor, and many attempts have been made to explain it."[64] The sen-

6 3 / 6 4   SEX   ROLE

On the term "sex," see FN 7; on "role," FN 61. The term "sex role," in ordinary speech, is of post–World War II origin. *Sex differences* fascinated the Victorians (see FN 67). During the first two decades of the twentieth century, scientific interest fastened particularly on the difference in measurable intelligence between men and women (see Gould, FN 58). In the late twenties, the creation of scales for the measurement of femininity and masculinity that manifest themselves in non-intellectual characteristics became good business. For orientation to the literature, see Julia Ann Sherman, *On the Psychology of Women: A Survey of Empirical Studies* (Springfield, MA: C. Thomas, 1971) and a critical complement to Sherman's work: Joyce J. Walstedt, *The Psychology of Women: A Partially Annotated Bibliography* (Pittsburgh: KNOW, 1972); this also lists non-professional studies. Under the influence of psychoanalysis in the thirties, differential emotional needs were scientifically identified and operationalized for use by therapists, social workers, and educators. By the fifties, it was particularly the differential tendency toward homosexuality that seemed important to researchers. For the historiography of sex differences, see Eleanor E. Maccoby and Carol N. Jacklin, *The Psychology of Sex Differences* (Palo Alto, CA: Stanford University Press, 1974). To get a perspective on the importance that the sex role has acquired in the social sciences, see H.A.D. Astin, *Sex Roles: A Research Bibliography* (Rockville, MD: National Institute of Mental Health, 1975).

64 Melville J. Herskovits, *Economic Anthropology* (New York: Norton, pbk., 1965). The original title was *Economic Life of Primitive Peoples*, 1935. For the thirty succeeding years, most quotations on the sexual division of labor in handbooks of sociology written in English and other languages were nothing but passages lifted from the seventh chapter of this book.

tence abounds with assumptions: The frontier dividing *them* from *us* is *our* literacy; all people live an *economic* life—*Homo sapiens* is always *Homo oeconomicus*—and thus act under the assumption of scarcity; the author knows what "work" is; finally, the pre-rational *sex* division of labor is the great mystery modern anthropology must attempt to explain. In the meantime, the vast literature Herskovits mentions has grown tremendously, but only a tiny fraction of it clarifies the distinction between gender and sex.

How the study of sex roles has muddled the issue of gender can be easily understood by looking at the literature of three periods during which "women's work" was in vogue: Victorian ethnography, New Deal cultural anthropology, and recent feminist studies. The Victorians believed in social evolution, and they hunted for data in the writings of travelers and missionaries. Strange, unexpected behavior fascinated them as much as the extraordinary life forms that Darwin discovered on the Galapagos Islands. But, unlike their informants, they had an urge to classify what they found. Like bones, behavior had to be fitted into categories that could be arranged according to evolutionary steps, and whose culmination was England's Victorian middle class, the ultimate civilization, the fittest to survive. In the United States, an alliance of women and clergymen read into these reports proof for the timeless quality of woman's role as a homemaker, of woman's *nature* as a gift to the menfolk, who must venture out into a rough life to subdue *nature* for their sake. Anthropology of the sex role began as a scientific proof for what Ann Douglas has called "the sentimental lie." In this context, women's work could now be understood as a mark of the harsh treatment inflicted on the weaker sex by primitive cultures. Progress could be seen as the enclosure of women into genteel domesticity, and a progressive specialization of status and vocation between the hardworking provider and his woman, liberated from the burdens of production.[65]

For the next two generations, interest in women's work was

65 VICTORIAN FEMINISM

Victorian feminism succeeded in making the relations between men and women in primitive societies a fascinating topic of conversation. But the evidence they found of a great variety of savage behavior was construed by Victorian anthropologists as proof of an evolutionary pattern that led to the universal norm of the bourgeois family. See Elizabeth Fee, "The Sexual

low, but between 1935 and 1937 it exploded again. Within less than two years three classic studies were published. Margaret Mead stressed that biological sex alone cannot possibly account for the socio-cultural differences in personality structure between male and female that we observe everywhere.[66] She sought to

---

Politics of Victorian Social Anthropology," *Feminist Studies* 1 (1973): 23ff. For further recent studies on Victorian sexism, see Jill Roe, "Modernization and Sexism: Recent Writings on Victorian Women," *Victorian Studies* 20 (Winter 1977): 179–92; Marlene LeGates, "The Cult of Womanhood in Eighteenth-Century Thought," *Eighteenth-Century Studies* 10, no. 1 (1976): 21–39; B. Didier, *"L'Exotisme et la mise en question du système familial et moral dans le roman à la fin du XVIIIe siècle: Beckford, Sade, Potocki," *Studies on Voltaire* 152 (1976): 571–86. The recognition that the ensuing polarization of sexual attributes represents a new type of social classification that uses character rather than status as its key parameter (a classification that would have been unthinkable before the Enlightenment), I owe to Karin Hausen, *"Family and Role Division: The Polarisation of Sexual Stereotypes in the Nineteenth Century—An Aspect of the Dissociation of Work and Family Life," in Richard J. Evans and W.R. Lee, eds., *The German Family: Essays on the Social History of the Family in Nineteenth-and Twentieth-Century Germany* (London: Croom, Helm; Totowa, New Jersey: Barnes and Noble Books, 1981): 51–83. Also fundamental to my understanding has been Barbara Welter, "The Cult of True Womanhood, 1820–1860" in *American Quarterly* 18 (1966): 151–74. The polarization of sexual characteristics led both to a new social perception of the female body (FNs 80, 87) and to a new perception of the domestic sphere as the sole domain appropriate to the feminine citizen. On the steps by which the ideological value of domesticity was propagated in the USA—aided by the collusion of women and clergy, both "disestablished" with independence—and on the absolute need for the existence of *redeeming domesticity* in an industrializing society, see the brilliant and complex interpretation by Ann Douglas, *The Feminization of American Culture* (New York: Discus Books/Avon, 1977). For the status of current discussions of Victorian feminism, see Jill Roe, "Modernization and Sexism: Recent Writings on Victorian Women" in *Victorian Studies* 20 (1976/77): 179–92. On Victorian literature *by* women *for* women that expresses a definition of success divergent from Victorian assumptions about women and work, see Elaine Rose Ognibene, "Women to Women: The Rhetoric of Success for Women, 1860–1920" (New York: Rensselaer Polytechnic Institute Dissertation, 1979).

66 SEX AND TEMPERAMENT

Margaret Mead, *Sex & Temperament in Three Primitive Societies* (New York: Morrow, pbk., 1963) and Erich Fromm and Michael Macoby,

elucidate these differences by recourse to the psychological concepts of her time, all ultimately founded on a Freudian reading of American family life. In the same year Ralph Linton focused on the contrast between male and female behavior. He was the first to use the term role (in 1932) and described the almost limitless plasticity of the sex roles that a culture can provide for its members. Behavior rather than personality was his interest. Finally, George Murdock[67] began to publish his *Ethnographical Atlas*.

Social Character in a Mexican Village (Englewood Cliffs, NJ: Prentice Hall, 1970) mark the beginning and probably the end of the attempt to use the genderless categories of psychoanalysis (Fromm in conjunction with Marx) to explain how *temperament* or *social character* shape the relationship between men and women under very different social conditions.

67   ROLE COMPLEMENTARITY

Whereas Victorians focused their attention on the opposite spheres for which nature has destined masculine and feminine humans (FN 65), Americans during the Great Depression were particularly concerned about the division of productive labor by sex. True to form, many thousands of societal traits from many hundreds of societies were tabulated and tested for cross-associations, erecting structures of conjecture upon the foundation of significance tests that produced invalid hypotheses despite the fact that all data presented were, statistically, significant; see A.D. Coult and R. Haberstein, *Cross-Tabulations of Murdock's Ethnographic Sample* (Columbia, MO: University of Missouri Press, 1965). For a simple introduction to the data collected, see George P. Murdock, "Comparative Data on the Division of Labor by Sex," *Social Forces* 15 (1937): 551–53; and, for quick reference to the opus, the same author's, "Ethnographic Atlas: A Summary," *Ethnology* 6, no. 2 (1967): 109–236. Dry, shredded, but sometimes useful information on who does what, where, can be found in his epigones, Joel Aronoff and William D. Crano, "A Re-examination of the Cross-Cultural Principles of Task Segregation and Sex-Role Differentiation in the Family," *American Sociological Review* 40 (February 1975): 12–20; Alain Lomax and Conrad M. Arensberg, "A Worldwide Evolutionary Classification of Cultures by Subsistence Systems," *Current Anthropology* 18, no. 4 (December 1977): 659–708; and William D. Crano and Joel Aronoff, "A Cross-Cultural Study of Expressive and Instrumental Role Complementarity in the Family," *American Sociological Review* 43, no. 4 (August 1978): 463–71. The attempt to discover universal tendencies to associate certain types of tasks with one or the other sex, cross-culturally, has led to invalid or to trivial results as often as it has been attempted. Women are associated statistically with work the anthropologists perceive as "repetitive, interruptible, non-dangerous, and

He was primarily concerned with "work" and how it is divided between men and women. Glancing at his charts, you can learn that Okinawans of both sexes participate in the making of pots, but males do appreciably more than females; among Druzes, only women are potters; and among the Koreans, only men. For eleven types of activity among hundreds of different cultures, nine different degrees of male-female participation are given. But Mead's insistence on personality, Linton's on behavior, and Murdock's on work only blur the distinction between gender and sex role, which must be made intelligible.

Around the middle of the century, interest in women's distinctive activities fell dormant again. Modernization was on the agenda. For the first time, anthropologists were on the payroll of policy makers, employed to identify obstacles to progress. Precisely during those decades when participant observation was refined as a method for reporting in detail and with delicacy on who does what in a village or hut, gender-bound behavior was treated mostly as a barrier to development, a sex-role stereotype, a cause of low productivity and an essential ingredient of poverty. Anglo-American women's studies of the early seventies thoroughly altered this situation and organized a third wave of interest in women, this time from a feminist perspective.[68] In fact, the male

---

based on simple techniques," "tasks implying low risk and performed close to home," "of low social value," "tasks whose relative values are more resistant to change than the techniques used in their performance." Finally, the search for statistical associations has led to the "discovery" of exceptions. Where Murdock arrived at a "world equal interchangeability rate" of tasks between men and women of 16 percent, this rate rises to 81 percent among two sub-groups of the Western Bontoc Igorot in Luzon: Albert S. Bacdayan, "Mechanistic Cooperation and Sexual Equality Among the Western Bontoc," in Alice Schlegel, ed., *Sexual Stratification* (New York: Columbia University Press, 1977): 270–91. Still the most readable and lively critique of the myths generating these hypotheses is Ann Oakley, *Woman's Work: the Housewife, Past and Present* (*op. cit.* FN 32).

68 FEMININE SUBORDINATION

Many of the studies on differences between men and women outside industrial society made during the first half of the seventies infer that the lack of publicly recognized power and authority for women is a sign of their

bias in women's contribution to the first two bodies of research
became a field of study. Soon, the work of several generations of
anthropologists provided abundant evidence of an almost grotesque
inability even to suspect what women do. But so far, most of these
new studies have only reinforced, albeit from a female perspective,

---

subordination. For orientation on the literature, see Susan Carol Rogers,
*"Woman's Place: A Critical Review of Anthropological Theory," *Comparative Studies in Society and History* 20 no. 1 (1978): 123–62. This is
a very helpful guide to the treatment of sex-related differences and relative
status of men and women in British and US anthropology. Naomi Quinn,
"Anthropological Studies on Women's Status," *Annual Review of Anthropology* 6 (1977): 181–225. Evalyn Jacobson Michaelson and Walter
Goldschmidt, "Female Roles and Male Dominance Among Peasants,"
Southwestern Journal of Anthropology 27 (1971): 330-52 is useful as an
index to forty-six monographs published between 1940 and 1965 that
analyze peasant societies and address relative sex role and status. Ruby
Rohrlich-Leavitt, ed., *Women, Cross-Culturally: Chance and Challenge*
(The Hague: Mouton, 1975) and an entire issue called "Sex Roles in
Cross-Cultural Perspective," *American Ethnologist* 2, no. 4 (November
1975) contain a representative sample of approaches to the cross-cultural
study of women; for a Marxist-feminist perspective, see the Women's
Issue, *Critique of Anthropology* 3, no. 9/10 (1977). These studies overwhelmingly use analytic categories that implicitly deny the distinction
between gender and sex, between patriarchy and sexism (FN 21),
and between asymmetric influence and hierarchic power distribution
(FN 84). Further, in doing so, most of these studies give primacy to the
public sphere, accept the modern male-orientated definition of cultural
importance, and make the reader blind to the asymmetry of power that
characterized gendered existence. Louise A. Tilly, "The Social Sciencies
and the Study of Woman: A *Review Article*," *Comparative Studies in
Society and History* 20, no. 1 (1978): 163–73, commenting on Michelle
Zimbalist Rosaldo and Louise Lamphere, eds., *Woman, Culture, and Society* (Palo Alto, CA: Stanford University Press, 1974), makes this very
clear. However, perhaps significantly, the only two major studies on primitive women published during the decline of interest in sociological and
anthropological research on women (from about 1945 to 1970) are both
concerned with the asymmetry of power between the genders: P.M.
Karberry, *Women of the Grassfields* (London: HMSO, 1952; reprint by
Gregg International, 1970) and Audrey Richards, *Chisungu, A Girl's Initiation Ceremony Among the Bemba of Northern Rhodesia* (London:
Faber & Faber, 1951). In Ernestine Friedl, *"The Position of Women:
Appearance and Reality," *Anthropological Quarterly* 40 (1967): 97–105
the question about power asymmetry is reopened in a delightful way: In a

the same fundamental assumptions about gender as a primitive form of sex role, an assumption that, at first implicitly and then explicitly, had guided the earlier anthropologists.[68] For the most part, then, women's studies have acted as a further camouflage of gender.

---

life-style centered on the household, the power that counts seems to be the power in the house. My distinction between gender and sex, and their relative dominance in different societies, could dispel much of the confusion so far inevitable when the "subordination of women" is discussed. See especially the literature in FNs 21, 84.

IV. Vernacular Culture

Tools are intrinsic to social relationships. Each person relates to society through actions and the tools effectively mastered to carry out those actions. To the degree that one actively masters one's tools, their shape determines his/her self-image. In all pre-industrial societies, a set of gender-specific tasks is reflected in a set of gender-specific tools. Even tools that are there for *common* use can be touched by only half the people. By grasping and using a tool, one relates primarily to the appropriate gender. As a result, intercourse between genders is primarily social. Separate tool kits determine the material complementarity of life.

The separateness of tool kits can lead to an extreme division of domains. In a moving chapter, Pierre Clastres, who has lived among the Guayaki, reports on such a split world in the Amazon jungle. Women's domain is here organized around the basket each one has woven for herself at the time of her first menses, and the men's world turns around the bow. No personal authority stands above the two domains.[69] The division, which is constantly experienced, engenders the tension that holds this society

The example can be found in Pierre Clastres, *Society Against the State,* trans. Robert Hurley (New York: Urizen Books, 1977). There are other cultures peopled by even more reluctantly social beings. The Siriono men and women of South America believe they are related to one another only through the moon: John Ingham, "Are the Siriono Raw or Cooked?" *American Anthropologist* 73 (1971): 1092–99.

together. If ever a woman touches the bow of a hunter, he loses his manhood and becomes *"pané."* His arrows become useless, his sexual powers are lost, he is excluded from the hunt, and, if he does not just shrivel and die, he lives out his life behind women's huts, gathering food in a discarded basket.

Gender and Tools

There is, however, no need to look into the exotic for cultural knots that tie gender to tool. It is both more convincing and less distracting to look into our own recent past. On close inspection, many of our grandparents' tools still smell of gender. While working on a draft of this chapter, I was the guest of a Quebec baker, a nationalist and artist working with her traditional kitchen tools. She runs a shop near Sherbrooke, and along with her cakes offers patrons a milieu that is a modern version of a medieval studium, a place of reflection and discussion. She invited me to read these pages to an interested audience in the dining room. The walls were decorated with a dozen rusty farm tools. They had been collected because they were beautifully shaped and locally made. Together, we inspected these remains from households and farms, none older than the century. Originally, they must have had their proper names, but most were forgotten by now. No one could even guess the use or purpose of some of the tools. Others were obviously made for digging or sawing, but nobody knew the crop or wood for which they had been crafted. And, with the exception of one old woman, no one in this group of French-Americans knew anything about the gender to which the different tools had been bounded, whether they had been destined for the hands of woman or man.

While in North America, even in Quebec, gender has been laundered from tools, it still survives in the tools of many pockets of rural Europe, and in some places more than in others. Here, men use the scythe and women the sickle. There, both use a sickle, but there are two sickles, each of a different design; the handle and blade betray the gender. In Styria, for example, men's sickles are clean-edged for cutting, and women's are indented, curved, made for the gathering of stalks. Wiegelmann's great inventory of peasant work[70] reports hundreds of such stories for a confusing variety of places. In one valley in the Alps, both genders use the scythe, but she only to cut the fodder, and he for the rye. Here, only she touches the knives in the kitchen; there, both cut the bread, but one cuts down and away, and the other draws the blade toward the chest. Almost everywhere, men plant grain. But in one area on the upper Danube, women harrow and sow, and that is the one place

70 TOOLS AND GENDER

The association of gender with simple tools has a privileged position in research on gender: The association is directly observable. This is not so, for instance, in the association of gender with tasks. The list, or taxonomy, of all tasks "assigned" in a given culture is always at least partly a creation of the observer. Tools are concrete entities, and the observer can directly record whether they are handled by men or by women. The lack of studies that focus directly on the association between tools and gender is therefore a most surprising lacuna. Most observations made on this association have been recorded in the course of studies having a different focus. A good introduction to the theme for English readers is Michael Roberts, *"Sickles and Scythes: Women's Work and Men's Work at Harvest Time," *History Workshop* 7 (1979): 3–28. Rich and detailed, and with a good bibliography, are Günter Wiegelmann, *"Zum Problem der bäuerlichen Arbeitsteilung in Mitteleuropa," *Geschichte und Landeskunde, Franz Steinbach zum 65. Geburtstag* (Bonn: 1960): 637–71 and, by the same author, "Erste Ergebnisse der ADV-Umfragen zur alten bäuerlichen Arbeit," *Rheinische Vierteljahresblätter* 33 (1969): 208–62. A useful complement to the above is Maria Bidlingmaier, *Die Bäuerin in zwei Gemeinden Württembergs* (Stuttgart: Kohlhammer, 1918), for its time an exceptional study in which the author carefully compares the daily work of peasant women before World War I in a traditional and in a modernizing village. Also, see Ingeborg Man, *Erntegebrauch in der ländlichen Arbeitswelt des 19. Jahrhunderts. Auf Grund der Mannhardtbefragung in Deutschland von 1865* (Marburg: 1965). For Hungary, see Edit Fél and Tamás Hofer, *Proper Peasants: Traditional Life in a Hungarian Village*, Viking Fund Publications in Anthropology, 46 (Chicago: Aldine, 1969): 101–37 and, by the same authors, *Bäuerliche Denkweise in Wirtschaft und Haushalt: Eine ethnographische Untersuchung über das ungarische Dorf Atány Schwartz* (Göttingen: 1972): esp. 149ff, which includes sayings, jokes, and ridicule by which gender trespasses are censured. Where rules are strict, exceptions are clearly stated. The author reports that, even after World War II, a widow forced to do her husband's work would be helped: The blacksmith, for instance, would sharpen her tools without charge. A beautiful and rich study on the subject—focusing, however, only indirectly on

where men do not handle the seed stock. Animals are tied to gender, even more than plants. In one place, women feed cows but never the draught animals. Farther East, women milk cows that belong to the homestead, while the herd on the manor grounds is milked by men. Only a few hours' walk away, the same job is done only by maids. Tenaciously, the ties between gender and tool have survived, while wars have destroyed cities as they swept over Europe, and economic growth has transformed rural life. In the midst of synthetic pesticides, combines, and TV, certain old tools have anachronistically preserved the trappings of gender.

When the tie between tool and gender has been broken, it has happened more frequently and more purposefully in Eastern Europe than in the West. At best, it survives in the memories of the old. A decade ago, I listened to a Serbian peasant telling how haying had been done a generation back. He described gathering, loading, and storing the hay as if the work had been a ballet in which men and women each danced their appropriate parts. While he spoke, we were watching how things are done now. Haymaking has turned into a unisex job under workers' control, which any hired hand can do. With a mixture of sadness and pride, the old man looked at the young woman who was driving the tractor of the village commune. The gender that disappears on a tractor had adapted to ever new conditions over millennia. The tie between gender and ox in some well-documented cases has survived from prehistoric times. No woman ancestor of this young driver would have yoked or fed an ox. This gender trait can be traced back in her people to a time when they neither spoke a Slavonic language nor lived in the same part of Europe.

---

tools—is O. Löfgren, *"Arbeitsteilung und Geschlechtsrollen in Schweden,"* *Ethnologia Scandinavia* (1975): 49–72. B. Huppertz, *Räume und Schichten bäuerlicher Kulturformen in Deutschland* (Bonn: 1939): esp. 191ff and 281ff argues that the ties between tools and gender, and even more those between animals or plants and gender, have remained unchanged in certain areas of Germany since the Neolithicum. On the Catholic saints appointed as guardians over the correct gender assignment of sickles and scythes, see Leopold Schmidt, *Gestaltheiligkeit im bäuerlichen Arbeitsmythos: Studien zu den Ernteschnittgeräten und ihre Stellung im europäischen Volksglauben und Volksbrauch* (Wien: Verlag des Österreichischen Museums für Volkskunde, 1952): esp. 108–77.

Gender, Rent, Trade, and Crafts

"Primitive" life is always built on a split set of tools. The life of the hunter and gatherer is so divided, but so is the life of planter and shepherd, as it has been from neolithic to modern times. With few exceptions, the gender divide is neat and obvious in non-urban society. Subsistence economy coincides with gendered existence. Thus, there is a strong temptation to consider gender as a distinctive sign of tribal and peasant life. If social gender is studied at all, it has remained a subject for anthropologists. Historians have overlooked the fact that gender is equally dominant in all historical periods, is constitutive of all urban civilizations, and basic to simple commodity production. If its rule was relaxed, this happened only among decadent elites, and then for only short periods. Only the rise of commodity-intensive industrial society led to the loss of gender. As a result, the history of gender's demise in the nineteenth and twentieth century still remains to be written. Only when gender is recognized as a key historical subject will its breakdown in industrial society become visible. To give some examples of historical gender, I shall briefly refer to gender in rent, trade, and crafts.[71]

7 1   DIVISION OF LABOR

In English, the function of key words can also be assumed by a compound term. One is the *division of labor*. At first sight the use of the term in ordinary conversation seems unproblematic. When inspecting the way in which the term is explained in dictionary and handbook, however, it becomes immediately obvious that three *unrelated taxonomies* of human activities are confused and consolidated by this "division": (1) the functional division of productive tasks (urban/rural, shoemaker/carpenter, the seventeen steps needed to make a needle); (2) the gender-specific assignment of tasks in traditional societies; and (3) the distinct and opposite roles assigned to the wage earner and to his or her dependents. The term cannot be used for historical or anthropological description without inducing confusion among these three meanings. See Barbara Duden and Karin Hausen, "Gesellschaftliche Arbeit—Geschlechtsspezifische Arbeitsteilung" in Annette Kuhn and Gerhard Schneider, eds., *Frauen in der Geschichte* (Düsseldorf: Pädagogischer Verlag Schwann, 1979): 11–13. This is the reason I avoid speaking about the "division of labor."

Medieval tenants and freeholders owed rent to a lord.[72] Since they ordinarily lived outside the money economy, their rent constituted the only significant surplus, the only exchangeable good they produced. Designating their other activities as "production" would be a mistake, since today this term implies some form of value transfer and consumption that, for the medieval peasant, applied only to rent. This lack of distinction between production and consumption functions is the clearest characteristic of the difference between subsistence and an economic existence.

Hundreds of contracts between peasants and their lords from the ninth to the twelfth centuries tell us what rents were: partly produce and partly servitude. And traditional rent was frequently paid in a gender-specific way. A large number of contracts carefully determined not only the amount of rent due for the land but also the gender from whom it was due. For instance, Ingmar paid the abbey fifteen days' labor, presenting himself each day with two draught animals, and also owed one sheep every second year; his wife—and in the case of her death, a maid—delivered five chickens each fall. The language makes it obvious that two irreconcilable competencies are involved in the payment of the rent and that there is no common denominator uniting them. "Women's products" and "men's products" are clearly distinct. Church law did not forbid any and all general "servile work" on feast days. Rather, it clearly specified that *men* were to abstain from the hunt, from tree-felling, from the building of stockades; and *women*, from hoeing, shearing lambs, and pruning trees. The two could not

---

7 2   T H E   E L I T E   A N D   G E N D E R

Production—that is, the creation of surplus for others—remained a matter of gender into the nineteenth century. And the consumption of its surplus also remained overwhelmingly gendered. To live off rent did not usually imply an economic existence based on the satisfaction of the genderless needs typical of the modern consumer. High status did not blur the gender line. Status, if anything, made the divide even more visible and conscious because lords and ladies had the leisure to "show off" their gender. And sometimes it sanctioned specific transgressions (FN 106). Löfgren (FN 70) reports on noblewomen in the saddle in a society where usually only men rode.

produce the surplus to pay the rent interchangeably. Both the product and the exacted service were gender-bound.[73]

As with rent, so trade can have gender. And the trader is not always the man. Nor is there much substance to the belief that women trade in the village square and men roam afar. In Malaysia, the western Sahel, and the non-Hispanic Caribbean, it is the women who conduct the household's activities, and the pattern is deeply ingrained. The trade is based on the women's contacts with kin, and men have no chance to break into their circuits. Whether the trade is in pottery or jewelry, the woman is the one who deals with distant villages, while the man takes care of the house. To keep the husband in the home, a woman trader might force a second wife on him under the threat that otherwise she would leave him—a threat that even today holds good in Senegal. The man knows that what she trades no one would buy from him, and that her income is needed for the house. Like rent, trade goods also have gender. In northern Burma, no one in his right mind would buy jewelry in the market from a man; it would undoubtedly be fake for the tourist.[74]

Crafts also have gender, often an intricately developed one. Not only the crafts of subsistence—potting and cooking in one's own hut, or spinning and weaving to outfit one's camel—but also arts and crafts organized for sale and trade possess gender. A tailor in the North African *bazaar* cannot be replaced with a

73 RENT AND GENDER

The evidence that in the early Middle Ages different agricultural products were expected as rental payments from men and women of the same household comes from Ludolf Kuchenbuch, "Bäuerliche Gesellschaft und Klosterherrschaft im 9. Jh. Studien zur Sozialstruktur der Familie der Abtei Prüm," *Vierteljahresschrift für Sozial- und Wirtschaftsgeschichte*, 2 vols. Beiheft 66 (Wiesbaden: 1978). It is also quite clear that during the ninth century, individuals, irrespective of their sex, were granted tenancies in exchange for specified rents to be contributed by their households. The history of gendered rent and its demise during the Middle Ages remains to be written. On the history of servile work prescribed on the Lord's day, see Otto Neurath, "Beiträge zur Geschichte der Opera Servilia," *Archiv für Sozialwissenschaften und Sozialpolitik* 41, no. 2 (1915): 438–65. On work taboos and holidays, see Pierre Braun, "Les tabous des 'Feriae,'" *L'Année sociologique* 3rd series (1959): 49–125. To understand the ideological difficulties in the study of the sexual division of labor in past times, see Christopher Middleton, "The Sexual Division of Labor in Feudal En-

seamstress; or, where would one find a shoe repair *woman?* When the eye is sharpened for the perception of gender, an everyday dish or an ordinary piece of cloth can reveal a pattern as subtle but as real as fine filigree. Fulling, dyeing, weaving, cutting, finishing —each stage requires several distinct contributions, some made only by women, some only by men, until a four-handed opus has been completed.

A couple of recent studies on medieval trades have made much of the fact that many guilds allowed women to become masters. The silk-spinning and -weaving guild in fourteenth-century Cologne was made up solely of women. But, more surprisingly, we find women in guilds that were decidedly men's domain: In one case, a woman headed a fourteenth-century smithy, which had two dozen workers and a heavy investment in water-mill–driven hammers. But such women were widows of guild members, and by being in the guild, they could keep the shop in the family. They were appointed the shops' guardians, as their men had been before them. But to jump from evidence of this guardianship of town or family interests to a conclusion that

---

gland," *New Left Review* 113/114 (January–April 1979): 147–68. On women in the medieval village in general, see Rodney H. Hilton, *The English Peasantry in the Later Middle Ages* (Oxford: Clarendon Press, 1975): 95–110.

74 TRADE AND GENDER

On trade and gender, see Sidney W. Mintz, "Men, Women and Trade," *Comparative Studies in Society and History* 13 (1971): 247–69. A husband could never tamper with his wife's trading business in the way he can lay claim to the money she brings home. Mintz reviews social science literature on women traders and finds that his colleagues just cannot describe such women with equanimity; they cannot avoid associating their behavior with child neglect and prostitution. Gloria Marshall (pseudonym: N. Sudarksa), "Where Women Work: A Study of Yoruba Women in the Marketplace and the Home," *Anthropological Papers, Museum of Antropology*, no. 53 (Ann Arbor, MI: University of Michigan, 1973). Rich, detailed, her study describes a topsy-turvy world: Men who are dependent on their wives' incomes exercise authority over their women in household affairs. A lively description of women traders in San Juan Evangelista, Mexico, is B. Chinas, *The Isthmus Zapotecs (Case Studies in Cultural Anthropology)* (New York: Holt, Rinehart & Winston, 1973). She observes a strict division of tasks and a high level of complementarity.

women worked iron ore side by side with the apprentices, in competition with them, would be ludicrous.[75] Rent, trade, and craft are only examples of areas that must be studied to evolve a history of gender in advanced or high civilization.

Gender is not a concept that can be viewed as merely a quaint aspect of primitive life-style, something that town life, simple commodity production, or complex marketing can wash from society's texture. Gender thrives in high civilizations. In the urban life of the Middle Ages it combined with the division of labor into crafts and arts to bring about new and complex configurations that are far more difficult to disentangle than the primitive divide on which anthropologists have fastened.

Gender is not confined to the present, to the actions and tools that sustain life in the present of any historical period. Each culture also assigns some tasks to men and others to women when it celebrates its own past. In Minot, in central France, the same woman who washes the newborn of the village also washes and lays out the dead. Ceremonial custom preserves gender from a distant past. Memory, too, is as dual. To this very day in Thrace, men speak about the dead and their deeds, but only women can address them. Only the women can shriek, lamenting those who have passed away and invoking their protection. Gendered action stretches into the past, into the beyond.

75 CRAFT AND GENDER

Michael Mitterauer, "Zur familienbetrieblichen Struktur im zünftischen Handwerk" in H. Knittler, ed., Wirtschafts- und Sozialhistorische Beiträge. Festschrift für Alfred Hoffmann zum 75. Geburtstag (Munich: 1979): 190–219. And, by the same author, "Geschlechtsspezifische Arbeitsteilung in vorindustrieller Zeit," Beiträge zur historischen Sozialkunde 3 (1981): 77–78. The legal status of women in the guilds and workships of pre-industrial Europe has been recently studied, but there is little available on the gender-specific assignment of artisans' tools. Some information can be gleaned from the literature mentioned in Edith Ennen, "Die Frau in der mittelalterlichen Stadtgesellschaft Mitteleuropas" (ms., 1980); Luise Hess, Die deutschen Frauenberufe des Mittelalters (Munich: Neuer Filser Verlag, 1940), and, especially on semi-tabooed professions, Werner Danckert, Unehrliche Leute: die verfemten Berufe (Bern and Munich: Francke Verlag, 1963).

Gender and Kinship

Historians avoid discussing gender by consigning its reign to prehistory alone. And prehistory they leave to anthropology. But anthropologists possess their own avoidance mechanisms. Like physicians who lose sight of the sick by concentrating on the disease, they overlook gender by focusing on kinship. Henry Morgan himself, the man who launched kinship studies in the middle of the last century, described kinship systems as complex relationships among individuals sexually polarized into men and women. Morgan and later anthropologists tend to de-emphasize the clear truth that kinship primarily structures gender domains in their complementarity. Kin are those who in precisely defined terms can reach one another across the gender divide. Kinship essentially organizes the rules of who is who to whom, which is much more significant than the establishment of a regime that gives some men power over some women. Kinship presupposes the two genders, which it relates to one another. Gender not only tells who is who, but it also defines who is when, where, and with which tools and words; it divides space, time, and technique. It would appear that the fascination the incest taboo exercises over scientists born into decent families distracts their vision from the gender divide that underlies kinship. To explain gender by using kinship as one's point of departure is an undertaking not unlike the reconstruction of a body from its own X-rays. Gender can neither be elicited from kinship nor, in a structuralist fashion, reduced to one aspect of a cosmic duality.[76]

76 STRUCTURALISM

The immediate material object of gender studies is the correspondence between two sets of places, tools, tasks, gestures, and symbols on the one hand, and between what in any given society are called men and women. Structuralism can be understood as a particular attempt to avoid or de-emphasize the study of this singular correspondence and complementarity by jumbling it on one shelf with a host of dualities—hot/cold, right/left, sacred/profane—that are basic to the rules that govern the internal relations in a system. According to the tenets of structuralism, the system of signs and tokens that constitutes a culture is generated by a central core, which cannot be identified with a society's institutional framework of

I cannot avoid, however, thinking that this urge to rank gender with other dualities has as its principal purpose the preclusion of the search for sources. Robert Graves talks about the poet's necessary search for his sources "in the nests of the White Goddess, the Night Mare's nest lined with the plumage of prophetic birds and littered with the jawbones and entrails of poets." A fright-filled and risky task awaits both the poet and the genderless modern. The former must cross the trackless expanse of thickets and moors; the latter, the wastelands and ruins that lie beyond highway and conventional key words.

Gender and Wedlock

Anthropologists uncritically place the conjugal couple at the center of "the new science," albeit often in disguises that are hard to see through. Behind every ego they postulate procreators joined in wedlock, like their own mothers and fathers. They patently fail to realize that the sexed perception of their own

power and subsistence. Through the analysis of myths and ritual, the structural anthropologist tries to explore this core that remains hidden from sociological analysis of the society's institutional framework. For an introduction to the history of structuralism, see the anthology edited by Roger Bastide, *Sens et usages du terme "structure" dans les sciences humaines et sociales* (The Hague and Paris: Mouton 1962) and, more succinctly, Ernest Gellner, "What is Structuralism?" *The Times Literary Supplement* (July 31, 1981): 881–83. In a subtle but consequential fashion, structuralists' analyses reinforce the genderless categories of *role* (FN 61) and *exchange* (FN 57) to the extent that, for Lévi-Strauss, "Women, like words, are meant for exchange."

A second reason structuralism is incapable of relating gender to kin is implied in the criticism of Leach, who points out that the system of kinship that is central to structuralist analysis fits neither culture nor a society's institutional framework as conceived by those making the analysis. I submit that this weakness is the result of the structuralist mania to consider the male/female polarity as just one among many dualities, thereby perpetuating the confusion between analogical complementarity and exchange. The difficulties of criticizing structuralism from a point of view that is both Marxist and feminist appear clearly in the brilliant article by Gayle Rubin, *"The Traffic in Women: Notes on the 'Political Economy' of Sex," in Rayna Reiter (*op. cit.*, pp. 157–210, FN 22) and in Felicity Edholm, Olivia Harris, and Kate Young (*op. cit.* FN 22).

origins, an ethnocentric bias, distorts what they study. This prejudice disables both the historians and the anthropologist, prevent-
ing them from seeing what makes the modern couple unique.
Therefore, the recognition that "marriage" is as much a genderless key word as "role" or "exchange" is a necessary first step
toward the study of gender and genital activity.

Starting with the twelfth century, Western societies developed
economies based on the surplus product that could be expropri-
ated from households comprised of conjugal couples. We know
that surplus can be collected and exchanged in many ways; Karl
Polanyi and his students have proposed typologies to distinguish
the forms. But the wedded couple as the unit for surplus production creates a singular type. The important and essential new
factor was neither the size of the family living under one roof
nor the ability to organize kin, servants, guests, or slaves in this
unit but the *economic* function of the couple. Ethnology knows no
parallel for this kind of household, which became the anthropological condition *sine qua non* for the unique productivity of the
Westernized world. Anthropologically, Westernization can be
understood as the convergence of many different kinship patterns
toward the model of the conjugal household.

In the process of this merging, the two meanings of the word
"marriage" gradually coalesced. Marriage designates, on the one
hand, the festive wedding and ritual nuptials that can be recognized in one form or another in almost every known society and,
on the other, the state of matrimony, a situation difficult to find in
many societies. In medieval Europe, the state of matrimony
began to assume ever greater importance. What had been principally a ceremony to tie together two families related by complex
lines of kinship became the event by which two individuals were
joined for life in the new economic unit of the couple, an entity
that could be taxed. This shift from a tie creating knots between
two webs of genders toward the welding of two individuals into a
taxable unit was masked by the fact that "marriage" became a
term meaning indistinctly the feast and the ongoing jointly productive lifespan of a conjugal couple.

In retrospect, it is important to note that in this early period
of conjugal production the daily activities that created surplus
remained strictly gendered. In fact, Church law sometimes interpreted and reinforced the divide. But as the conjugal couple

gradually became the fundamental unit of taxation, most of the created surplus lost its traditional gender. The woman was no longer responsible for delivering her eggs to the lord; the man of the house became the household's representative for the payment of rent. It is true that, even into the nineteenth century, work on the lord's manor or on public roads was levied by gender. But rent was increasingly monetized, local currencies were replaced by the modern state's money, and the conjugal couple proved itself as a flexible productive unit, superior to any previous form of household. Its continued reliance on gender kept it to a large extent subsistent, while the growing ability of state and Church to assign new gendered functions beyond and against traditional gendered proprieties made the couple adaptable to rapid technological change. Tasks remained gendered, but first the Church and much later secular powers presumed to define gender domains: For half a millennium the economy rested on the household of broken gender. The emergence of conjugal household production was the anthropological condition for the formation of early European peasantry and urban life—which distinguishes the European from farmers, merchants, and craftsmen elsewhere in the world.

The spread of gendered but conjugal production was only the first stage in the process that set Europe apart from all other cultures. The couple provided a fundamental homogeneity for Christian Europe, although the social step into this state was not taken without hesitation. There were variations in time and place, and many communities remained out of step until after World War II. This economically productive wedlock was a *first* stage in the evolution of the couple; it did not immediately imply any loss of gender. Thus, for five hundred years, from the thirteenth to the early nineteenth centuries, a kind of wedlock spread in which men and women yoked in matrimonial production were kept to their respective gendered tasks. Both feudal and mercantilist organization of state power is predicated on the surplus that was produced by the conjugally wedded but still gendered couple.[77]

77 ECONOMIC WEDLOCK

I believe it is possible to distinguish three steps that led to the paradigm of partnership that is currently called marriage: (1) the institution of the rent-

Then, quite abruptly during the nineteenth century, the gendered assignment of household tasks was replaced by the *economic* division of wage and shadow work, discriminatingly assigned according to the newly discovered sexual characteristics of the consorts. The age of broken gender had served in Europe as

paying individual household; (2) the increasing dominance of the couple within this taxable household during the Renaissance and period of rising mercantilism; and (3) the economic polarization of the sexes during the nineteenth century. The trend toward sexual partnership during the twentieth century presupposes these steps, which were taken at different times by different classes in different regions as they joined the West. This is the conclusion I drew from a series of conversations in Berlin with Barbara Duden and Ludolf Kuchenbuch, and which Uwe Pörksen later joined. We began with a critique of present-day theories of feudalism by Kuchenbuch: Ludolf Kuchenbuch, *"Bäuerliche Ökonomie und feudale Produktionsweise: Ein Beiträge zur Welt system Debatte aus mediaevistischer Sicht" in *Perspektiven des Weltsystems: Materialien zu E. Wallerstein "Das moderne Weltsystem,"* ed. J. Blaschke, Berliner Institut für vergleichende Sozialforschung (Frankfurt: 1982). The idea that during the Middle Ages kinship began to fade and to be replaced by a new social reality, economic matrimony, has been suggested to me at several points in Jack Goody, J. Thirsk, and E.P. Thomson, eds., *Family and Inheritance, Rural Society in Western Europe, 1200–1900* (Cambridge: Cambridge University Press, 1976). I also got many ideas from a seminar paper by Hans Medick and David Sabean, *"Call for Papers: Family and Kinship: Material Interest and Emotion," *Peasant Studies* 8, no. 2 (Spring 1979): 139–60. Etymology can serve as a starting point for reflection on the issue. Emile Benveniste, *Indo-European Language and Society,* trans. Elizabeth Palmer, Miami Linguistics Series 12 (Miami: University of Miami Press, 1973). Volume 1, chapter 4 explains that in earlier stages of Indo-European languages there were no common terms for designating a man's and woman's relation arising from their wedding. The kinship terms describing their relation to one another were also derived from different roots. Aristotle in *Politics* Bk 1, Ch. 2, 3–1253b, states explicitly that "the union between man and woman has no name—it is *a-nonymós.* The terms bespeaking the male are generally verbs, those for the woman nouns. *Maritare* as a verb means nothing but 'to join,' and *marriage* is its derivative. The derivation of *matri-monium* has nothing to do with *maritare.* It is composed of the term for mother, *mater,* and the suffix *-monium,* which always conveys a juridical status, in this case the legal status of motherhood. The term expressing the social or economic unit constituted by the couple had to evolve. A legal reform enacted by Emperor Nero probably contributed decisively to the doctrine elaborated by the Church fathers on the transition "d'une bisexualité de sabrage à une hétérosexualité de reproduction." On this, see Paul Veyne,

a transition from vernacular subsistence to economic sex. Only in this curious *second* stage did economically distinct and genderless sex partners become the foundation of industrial production. And such couples provided the norm for the "libidinal structure and perception" of anthropologists born to them. For such people, gender must at least be meaningless, if not deeply frightening. They cannot but prefer to study theories of kinship rules rather than the local habits of gender.

"La famille et l'amour sous le Haut Empire romain," *Annales, ESC* 33, no. 1 (January–February 1978): 35–63. For the Church's medieval contribution to society's move into wedlock, see Georges Duby, *Medieval Marriage: Two Models from Twelth-Century France.* (Baltimore: Johns Hopkins University Press, 1978), which was a draft for Georges Duby, **Le Chevalier, la femme et le prêtre: le mariage dans la France féodale* (Paris: Hachette, 1981). The surprise, perplexities, and confusions generated by this new social form are recorded by Marie-Odile Métral, *Le mariage: les hésitations de l'occident,* preface by P. Ariès (Paris: Aubier, 1977). My curiosity about the slow economic merger of genders into conjugal productivity was first stimulated by David Herlihy, "Land, Family and Women in Continental Europe, 701–1200," *Traditio: Studies in Ancient and Medieval History* 18 (New York: Fordham University Press, 1962): 89–113. On the adaptation of language to the new reproductive unit, see Giovan-Battista Pellegrini, "Terminologia matrimoniale," *Settimane di Studio del Centro Italiano di Studi sull Alto Medioevo, Il matrimonio nella societá alto medievale* (Spoleto: 1977): 43–102. On the evolution of weddings, see Jean-Baptiste Molin and Protais Mutembe, *Le rituel du mariage en France du XIIe au XVIe siècle* (Paris: Beauchesne, 1974). On the new ways of recording the lives of couples, see Diane Owen Hughes, "Toward Historical Ethnography: Notarial Records and Family History in the Middle Ages," *Historical Methods Newsletter* 7 (1973–74): 61–71. A good introduction to recent literature on the history of Western marriage since Roman times is the collection of fifteen studies by Jean Gaudemet, *Sociétés et mariage* (Strasbourg: CERDIC-Publication, 1980). A splendid new guide to the literature is now available: Derek Baker, ed., *Medieval Women* (published for the Ecclesiastical History Society) (Oxford: Blackwell, 1978). See also FNs 110–113, 120.

V. Gender Domains and Vernacular Milieu

Gender is vernacular. It is both as tough and adaptable, as precarious and vulnerable, as vernacular speech. As happens with the latter, gender is obliterated by education, and its existence is soon forgotten or even denied. Thus, many people today have lost the ability to remember or even imagine either gender or vernacular speech. For the high school graduate, his parents' vernacular has become a substandard dialect of the mother tongue he has been taught. For the daughter who returns to rural Mexico, equipped with her university degree, the gender of her old mother can easily appear as a bondage that *she* has escaped.

The profound contrast between vernacular speech and taught mother tongue is often obvious for the parents and elusive for the son. The parents realize that the two modes of language belong to irreconcilable worlds, that the children have lost the vernacular. The children are taught that they speak it correctly. The differentiation between gender and sex is even more slippery than that between vernacular speech and taught mother tongue.

Space/Time and Gender

The contours of spaces and schedules determine who does and who uses what and when. Gender demands that the Berber woman lean on the inside of the east wall of a house, while the outside of the wall is for man. The way the gender divide runs determines how closely the two genders mingle, and on which territories and occasions. In one valley of the Alps, they meet on the threshing floor, he with the flail and she with the sieve. Farther down the river, this place is men's exclusive domain. As they are divided, so genders are also interwoven differently in each culture and time.[78] They can rule separate territories and rarely inter-

7 8 MILIEU AND DOMAIN

André Leroi-Gourhan, Le geste et la parole: Technique et language (Paris Albin Michel, 1964): 241 insists that "unlike territory, human gender has no parallel in the world of primates." This assertion requires some elaboration. The space occupied by men and women in a given society is not the same. Pierre Bourdieu, *Outline of a Theory of Practice, trans. Richard Nice (Cambridge and New York: Cambridge University Press, 1977). Only in the haram in the depth of the Berber hut can the couple share space, Bourdieu comments (p. 67). Every other spot of the house is strictly gendered. The space occupied by men is perceived as a different kind of space than that occupied by women; each kind of space requires the movement and the temporal rhythm that corresponds to it. Space and time are both gendered, like tools and tasks. It is a grave mistake to confuse this milieu, woven out of the two separate, gendered spatial and temporal domains, with the territory of animals. Different cultures cut up the landscape in different ways. And, since vernacular space is porous, several cultures can share the same landscape. At the center of the milieu stands the house, the spatial duality that transmits culture: Clark E. Cunningham, *"Order in the Antoni House," in Rodney Needham, (op. cit., pp. 204–38, FN 53). The vernacular milieu is thus in contrast both to the animal territory and to the homogeneous space of economics. On the evolution of theories that attempt to define this economic space, see Pierre Dockes, L'Espace dans la pensée économique du 16e au 18e siècle (Paris: Flammarion, 1969). The vernacular milieu is gendered space, the cultural reality that results from the asymmetric and ambiguous complementarity between two spatial gender domains. This fact, however, seems to have escaped Western philosophers almost completely, as is evident in the monumental survey of their doctrines on space: Alexander Gosztonyi, Der Raum: Geschichte seiner Probleme in Philosophie und Wissenschaft, 2 vols. (Freiburg: Alber, 1976). Vernacular space must be understood as a hierarchy of milieus, each gendered. C. Karnoch, "L'étranger, ou le faux inconnu: Essai sur la définition spatiale d'autrui dans un village lorrain," Ethnologie Française 1, no 2 (1972): 107–22 shows that until 1950 the inhabitants of a French village perceived the space surrounding them as three concentric circles: the village; the surrounding valley, with a diameter that could be crossed in three hours; and the pays, made up of several villages inhabited by densely intermarried

twine, or they can be knotted like the lines in the Book of Kells. Sometimes no basket can be plaited, no fire kindled, without the collaboration of two sets of hands. Each culture brings the genders together in its unique way. There are places where young men and women come together to live communally for just a few years and then move out again into territories separated by a yearly widening gap.

Yvonne Verdier's book[79] on cooking, washing, and sewing

"forains." Below this tripartition was the household; beyond it, the outside world. Depending on the periodic expansion of or decrease in the household's membership, it was more or less present in the various milieus: Alain Collomp, "Maison, manières d'habiter et famille en Haute Provence aux 17e et 18e siècles," *Ethnologie Française* 8, no. 4 (1978): 321–28.

79 SPACE / TIME

Each gender domain has its own landscape and its own rhythm. Domain extends over space and time (for which Einstein coined the term "spime"). I found two very impressive recent studies attempting to describe women's spime: Yvonne Verdier, *Façons de dire, façons de faire: La laveuse, la couturière, la cuisinière* (Paris: Gallimard, 1979). This book is the result of seven years of ethnographic participatory studies by the author and three of her students in a village of 360 inhabitants, hidden in the hills close to Dijon. The author interprets the language of present-day women, and with the help of local documents, surviving poetry, paintings, and old pictures, she reconstructs the history of those women who led the others: the women who wash (the newborn, laundry, the dead), the seamstress who initiates the young, and the cook who presides over and sets the rhythm of ceremonies such as weddings and funerals. Since I was first introduced to field studies of this kind through Sidney Mintz, *Worker in the Cane* (New York: Greenwood, 1974), no other book of this type has so impressed me with its perceptive delicacy—with the possible exception Richards (FN 88). Martine Segalen, *Mari et femme dans la société paysanne* (Paris: Flammarion, 1980) can be read as a complement to Verdier. In Segalen, the accent on the complementary rhythms of man and woman in a contemporary peasant household of central France is stronger. With the arrival of genderless, and therefore scarce, machine-produced clock time, gendered rhythms tend to subside: Women are often much more *pressured* by the unisex rhythm than men, as M. Bidlingmaier (*op. cit.* FN 70) observed in 1915 in Lauffen. For the impact of larger rhythms, see Evatar Zerubavel, "The French Republican Calendar: A Case Study in the Sociology of Time," *American Sociological Review* 42 (1977): 868–77. On the coming of clock time to a rural area, see Guy Thuillier, "Pour une histoire du temps en Nivernais au XIXe siècle,"

in an isolated village is a masterwork, describing from women's perspective the finely wrought tissue of such a web. It is delightful to read her report on the slaughtering of a pig. Only the woman can choose which animal will be slaughtered, addressing it as "Monsieur," but the man must set the day for the slaughter. They go through dozens of appointed steps, as if dancing a minuet. Women prepare the sausage and men salt the lard. But while, in Minot, only women beyond their menopause can pick up salted pork from the larder, a few miles down the road not even they may trespass into this male space. Each village does its own dance to the tune of its own regional music.

Martine Segalen, in a recent book on husband and wife in French peasant societies, has broken new ground in describing their complementary rhythms. She carefully analyzes gender-specific tasks and their counterpoint timing, and explicitly distin-

---

Ethnologie Française 6, no. 2 (1976): 149–62. As calendar and clock homogenized genderless time, D. Sabean, interpreting M. Bidlingmaier (see FN 125), finds evidence that time pressure, or *Eile*, was felt much more disturbingly by women than by men. Also see philosophical contributions on the relationship between culture and time in Paul Ricoeur, ed., *Les cultures et le temps* (Paris: Payot, 1975). My search through the vast modern literature on the sociology, anthropology, and ethnology of time has led me to the conclusion that explicit research on gender and time or gender and rhythm has so far been neglected. A careful description of men's space in a rural community of southern France is given by Lucienne A. Roubin, *"Male Space and Female Space Within the Provençale Community," trans. Patricia M. Ranum, in *Rural Society in France*, ed. Robert Forster and Orest Ranum (Baltimore and London: Johns Hopkins University Press, 1977): 152–80. This extract from a book was later extensively reviewed by Maurice Agulhon, "Les chambrées en Basse Provence: histoire et ethnologie," *Revue Historique* (April–June 1971): 337–68. The study deals with a local men's club, which functions as a material witness to the gulf that exists between men's and women's space. The wine shops, the circles that prepare the carnival, the sunny benches on the church square are clearly men's domains. Alone, the oldest man of the household clears with a special sickle the access to the field that will be harvested the next day. Though public space and men's domain are by no means synonymous, in Provence, in physical extension, they tend to coincide. For an understanding of traditional milieu, literature is often the only source. A major attempt to reconstruct old milieus, and thereby also to report on gendered nature, is Ina-Maria Greverus, *Der territoriale Mensch: ein literaturanthropologischer Versuch zum Heimatphänomen* (Frankfurt: Athenäum, 1972).

guishes these from roles, status, and rank. She examines, also from a woman's perspective, the "architecture" of farms and the farmers' schedules; she collects proverbs and photographs, interprets old paintings and ethnologists' reports in order to reconstruct from surviving patterns what things must have been like in the middle of the nineteenth century. What she finds is a relationship between men and women much less governed by family and kinship than by the demands of the household based on the matched interdependence of men's and women's hands. She describes how men and women did their daily work as members of their own gender rather than as individual constituents of a couple who are married to form a pair. The coupled pair carried little weight in the nineteenth-century French peasant household. Both the myth of rough male dominance and the idyll of a romantic peasant couple miss the mark completely. The body of gender still survived.[80]

According to Segalen, it is the household that mediates between the individual and the village community, not the twosome,

---

80 THE SEXED BODY

The body as a clinical entity is something other than the living flesh of men and of women that constitutes a social and vernacular reality. Some languages, like German and French, have distinct terms for the two: *Körper* and *Leib, le corps* and *la chair*. Since 1972, the new *Ethnologie Française* has published a series of essays that attempt a history of the vernacular body as a social reality: e.g., J.P. Desaive, "Le nu hurluberlu" 6, nos. 3 and 4 (1976): 219–26; Françoise Piponnier and Richard Bucaille, "La bête ou la belle? Remarques sur l'apparence corporelle de la paysannerie médiévale" 6, nos. 3–4 (1976): 227–32; Françoise Loux and Philippe Richard, "Alimentation et maladie dans les proverbes français: un exemple d'analyse de contenu" 2, nos. 3–4 (1972): 267–86. Also see F. Loux, *Le jeune enfant et son corps dans la medicine traditionelle* (Paris: Flammarion, 1978). For further access to the literature: John Blacking, *The Anthropology of the Body*, monograph 15 (London: Association of Social Anthropology, 1977; New York: Academic Press, 1978); Michel Foucault, *Birth of the Clinic: An Archeology of Medical Perception* (New York: Pantheon, 1973); and, by the same author, *A History of Sexuality 1, An Introduction* (New York: Random House, pbk., 1978) has pioneered the historical research on the process by which the body of the new subject of the welfare state has been constituted through the professional discourse about his or her body. The judicial attempt to observe and control men's sexual functioning precedes by more than a century clinical control over women's genital organs. Pierre Darmon, *Le tribunal de l'impuissance:*

the parents, the couple. If the household breaks down and its members do not act in accordance with the demands of their respective genders, then the village community will discipline the offending individual directly. For example, in northern France the kitchen garden ought to be hoed in April; and this is woman's work. If by the first of May the ground is still unbroken, a straw man with a mattock in its arms will appear in front of her kitchen window. Another example: Should a man beat his wife, he too will get rough music. He will be covered with mud and pushed around the village in a wheelbarrow, accompanied by teasing doggerel and the clang of pots and pans. Should he let himself be beaten by his wife, he will be singled out again, tied backward on an ass with the animal's tail in his hands.[81]

Virilité et défaillances conjugales dans l'ancienne France (Paris: Seuil, 1979) describes the collaboration between the police and special tribunals to verify male potency. For the medicalization of the womb, see FN 87. The process of medical normalization described by G. Canguilhem, *Le normal et le pathologique* (Paris: PUF, 1972), led to clinical research on sexual normality: the sexed body. G. J. Barker-Benfield, *The Horrors of the Half-Known Life: Male Attitudes Towards Women and Sexuality in Nineteenth-Century America* (New York: Harper and Row, 1976) gives a chilling report on this epistemological conquest of the body's insides. He tells the story of Dr. Sims, who at his own expense kept a stable of black slaves in order to conduct experimental operations on their vaginal fistulae. In 1845, he had the idea of placing a Mrs. Merril on all fours—a position since then termed "Sim's position"—and adapted a spoon handle for holding the vagina open. He reports in his diary: "Introducing the bent handle, I saw everything as no man had ever seen before . . . the speculum made it perfectly clear from the beginning. . . . I felt like an explorer in medicine who first views a new and important territory." A colleague, Dr. Baldwin, commented on this: "Sim's speculum has been to the diseases of the womb . . . what the compass is to the mariner." The vagina became the entrance to new territory for the exploration of nature. Within two decades it led to the "grande découverte que la femme n'est pas femme seulement par un endroit, mais par toutes les faces par lesquelles elle peut être envisagée," which has been described by Yvonne Knibiehler, "Les médecins et la 'nature féminine' au temps du Code Civil," *Annales, ESC* 31, no. 4 (July–August 1976): 824–45. See also FNs 60, 87.

81 ROUGH MUSIC

For a good introduction to the literature dealing with the procedures of popular justice as guardian of local custom, see Roger Pinon, "Qu'est-ce

Gender Domains and Vernacular Milieu

As long as the gender divide sets the pattern and the tone, this identifiable community will continue to survive. Various terms have been coined to designate such a commitment to a normative code that has been sanctioned by the proof of survival. Anthropologists studying the peasantry tend to speak of "subsistence ethics." E.P. Thompson uses the concept "moral economy" for populations generally more urbanized. These are good strong terms because they permit us to compare the sense of decency under the rule of gender with a possible modern norm, one that corresponds to the assumption of scarcity. Both terms affirm the right of every villager, of every member of the crowd, to make survival the supreme rule of *common* behavior, not the isolated right of an individual. Both terms bespeak an attitude, an orientation, that protects the weakest from ruin. Both terms claim a right to a decorous, a customary existence, even if this right is articulated only in the struggle to defend it. But "subsistence ethics," no less than "moral economy," is a modern concept for the defense

---

qu'un charivari? Essai en vue d'une définition opératoire," *Kontakte und Grenzen: Probleme der Volks-, Sozialforschung: Festschrift für Kultur- und G. Heilfurt* (Göttingen: Otto Schwartz, 1969): 393–405. Methods mentioned include uncovering the roof, cutting down trees, putting salt into the well, the pillory, freezing out, tar and feathering. Françoise Zonabend, *La mémoire longue: Temps et histoires au village* (Paris: PUF, 1980) describes the *embuscade*, a ritual visit of neighbors that, through its more or less intense roughness, guages the hosts' probity. A repertoire of folk songs expressing degrees of social approval can be found in Ilka Peter, *Gasselbrauch und Gasselspruch in Österreich.* (Salzburg: Alfred Winter, 1981). E.P. Thompson, "'Rough Music': Le Charivari anglais," *Annales, ESC* 27, no. 2 (March–April 1972): 285–312 describes and analyzes rituals vernacular society uses, often cruelly, to express its disapproval of individuals who break the traditional rules rooted in local "prejudice" rather than in the law. These rituals are structured by kinship and usually punish transgression of the gender divide. See Christiane Klapisch-Zuber, "The Medieval Italian Mattinata," trans. James Smith Allen, *Journal of Family History* 5, no. 1 (Spring 1980): 2–27. On the conflict between traditional forms of peer control and new attempts to police the encounters between young men and women, see Hans Medick, "Spinnstuben auf dem Dorf. Jugendliche Sexualkultur und Feierabendbrauch in der ländlichen Gesellschaft der frühen Neuzeit" in J. Reulecke and Wolfhard Weber, *Fabrik, Familie, Feierabend: Beiträge zur Sozialgeschichte im Industriezeitalter* (Wuppertal: Hammer, 1978).

of an appropriate behavioral pattern that throughout history has been gendered. Therefore, I would like to leave the current, non-gendered sense of the terms "morality" and "ethics" intact, and find a different expression to speak about the imperative that guards local gender.

What one feels when going against the gender divide is a sentiment that is difficult for people today to reconstruct, partly because it seems to be as vernacular and, therefore, as "ungrammatical" as that divide itself, and partly because it is an experience that faded with gender. Neither "shame" nor "guilt" is quite the word, at least in their present-day meaning. Yves Castan has studied what the people in the Languedoc called "honnêteté" between 1715 and 1780.[82] I shall translate the term as "probity."

8 2 P R O B I T Y

The OED defines *probity* 1514 (Fr. *probité* or Lat. *probitas*, f. *probus*, good, honest) as moral excellence, integrity, rectitude, uprightness; conscientiousness, honesty, sincerity. I propose using this term to designate the subject's perception of the gender line as a norm relevant for him or her. The choice of this term allows me to speak about the perception of this particular limit without implying a special motive, which would be the case if I used such terms as shame, guilt, sin, honor, etc. On these, see C.D. Buck (*op. cit.* FN 3) under the above-mentioned terms. For the process by which *honor* came to predominate in the sense of probity typical for Europe, see Julian Pitt-Rivers, "The Anthropology of Honour" and "Honour and Social Status in Andalusia," *Fate of Shechem or the Politics of Sex* (Cambridge: Cambridge University Press, 1977): 1–47 and P. Schneider, "Honor and Conflict in a Sicilian Town," *Anthropological Quarterly* 42, no. 3 (July 1969): 130–55. (See my comments on these in FN 21.) Also: Pierre Bourdieu, "Le sens de l'honneur. La dialectique du défi et de la riposte. Point d'honneur et honneur. L'éthos de l'honneur," *Esquisse d'une théorie* (*op. cit.*, pp. 13–44, FN 78) for observations on North Africa. (English translation in *op. cit.* FN 78.) For a classical reflection, see Max Weber, "Rechtsordnung, Konvention und Sitte," *Wirtschaft und Gesellschaft*, 5th ed. (Tübingen: 1976). For the transformation of probity and honor under the impact of the process of civilization (FN 120), see Yves Castan, "La famille: masculin et féminin," *Honnêteté et relations sociales en Languedoc, 1715–1780* (Paris: Plon, 1975): 162–207. In the eighteenth century, the law did not yet attempt to regulate lower-class family life; the law only protected it. The attempt of the state to impose marriage and regulate family life in a secular way was still three to five generations away (see FN 12). Instead, each gender's physical domain and appropriate behavior was guarded by its sense of probity or honor. This

His research was done on court records of disorderly behavior, one of the rare repositories for the actual speech of illiterate, lower-class people. Part of the study demonstrates how probity kept people acting according to their gender, down to the minutest details. For example, when guests came to the house, the *woman* had to fetch the glasses, prepare the salad, bring the wine, and listen to every word said without seeming curious and without getting involved in the conversation. This was expected of her; being one of the women, she was able to make known, in ways that are more powerful than the straight speech of men, what was in the interest of the household. She thus committed a fault against her own kind if she joined in men's talk; she would lose the effective power of whispering and gossip.[83] It was her task to

---

disappears by 1780: See Yves Castan, *"Pères et fils en Languedoc à l'époque classique," Le XVIIe siècle* (1974): 31–43. Nicole Castan, *"La criminalité familiale dans le ressort du Parlement de Toulouse (1690–1730)," Cahiers des Annales* 33 (Paris: Armand Colin, 1971): 91–107 focuses on feminine honor (probity) in contrast to that of men: The woman acts in solidarity with the house, and without being dishonored can say and do things that would never be forgiven of the man. Honor demands that she act as a screen for stolen goods; that she fight off the tax collector; that she threaten with revenge those who would bear witness against members of the household; that she be at home alone when the house is used for the purposes of prostitution. As codified law and a proliferation of court actions replaced gendered control with civic control, women lost their honor in exchange for a new status as citizens of the second sex. Useful material may be found in A. Poitrineau, "Aspects de la crise des justices seigneuriales dans l'Auvergne du 18e siècle," *Revue d'histoire de droit français et étranger* (1961): 552–70. For a general orientation, see M. Alliot, "L'acculturation juridique," *Ethnologie générale: Encyclopédie de la Pléiade* (Paris: 1968): 1180–247.

8 3 G O S S I P

The community's probity is not only guarded by occasional outbursts of rough music (FN 81) and periodic mockery during carnivals (FN 108). In a subtle and continuous way, it is safeguarded by the community's traditional sayings, its inherited riddles, its fireside stories, and above all by its gossip. These act like the "aegis," the shield of gendered probity. Gossip plays a key role in guarding community honor. John B. Haviland, *Gossip, Reputation and Knowledge in Zinacantan* (Chicago: University of Chicago Press, 1977) shows how gossip in a Mexican village allows people to examine the rules they live by and to manipulate them to their personal

shield the house from the tax collector, who was unable to enter if she claimed to be alone. She also had to take the part of her children in an argument, even if they were inexcusably wrong. Probity demanded that she go for the face of the enemy with nails and teeth, if that were necessary. From the *man*, probity required the opposite: In any incident in which the woman was expected to defend the offspring, he was supposed to correct or punish the child, sometimes rudely.[84]

---

ends. Gossip about the past is a way in which a group thrusts its roots back, creating history for its members in relation to each other. Gossip ties friends together. Gossip creates a kind of badge of membership, since any competent member must understand the group scandals and the unwritten rules as to what constitutes legitimate gossip. Max, Gluckman, *"Gossip and Scandal," *Current Anthropology* 4, no. 3 (June 1963): 307–16. The more exclusive a group, the more intense the gossiping. Gossip keeps members of one gender together and distinct from the other. Only when gender broke down did gossip become a woman: Alexander Rysman, "How the 'Gossip' Became a Woman," *Journal of Communication* 27, no. 1 (1977): 176–80. God sib refers to a relationship close enough to make a person a godparent for the family's children. It refers to an adoption into ritual kinship either into the house's men or women. For Chaucer, "A woman may in no lasse synne assemblen with hire godsib, than with hire owene flesshly brother." The *god sib* was bound into the house's male gender, one of the close men. In Elizabethan times, the *gossip* lost his ties to the whole family and became a friend. In A *Midsummer Night's Dream*, a gossip is a drinking companion. A gossip carries the feeling of warmth and good companionship. Only in the nineteenth century does *gossip* become an abstract noun and stand for idle talk. Today it is directly associated with women, and becomes a negative stereotype used against them. For a study of androphobic tendencies in joke, quip, and pun, see E. Moser-Rath, "Männerfeindliche Tendenzen in Witz und Schwank," *Zeitschrift für Volkskunde* 75, no. 1 (1979): 57–67. Competitions among women trying to determine who can tease and fool the men best have been observed as part of Spanish culture: Yolando Pino-Saavedra, "Wette der Frauen, wer den Mann am besten narrt," *Fabula* 15 (1974): 177–91.

84 ASYMMETRIC DOMINANCE

Susan Carol Rogers, "Female Forms of Power and the Myth of Male Dominance: A Model of Female-Male Interaction in Peasant Society," *American Ethnologist* 2, no. 4 (November 1975): 727–56 briefly explores the transformation of male dominance from myth to reality during the process of industrialization. According to Rogers, the generalization of

Gender Domains and Vernacular Milieu

Le Roy Ladurie has probed the relationship between house and gender in the same southern region of France, but his study's focus was earlier times. He analyzed the records kept by the future Pope Benedict XII when, as a young bishop and inquisitor, he submitted several dozen inhabitants of the small mountain

---

universal male dominance is based on male-oriented definitions and therefore is a myth. Much of the literature on peasant modernization rests on false assumptions regarding the role of women. Men are said to wield *formal* and women *informal* power. Only when we stop looking at male roles and forms of power as the norm and begin to look at female arrangements and perceive them as equally valid and significant—though perhaps different in form—can we see how male and female roles are intertwined, and begin to understand how human societies operate. Already thirty years ago, Gregory Bateson, *Step to an Ecology of Mind* (New York: Ballantine 1975): 97 insisted on the profound contrast between competitive societies and "those in which people respond to what others do by themselves doing something similar." The pendulum in women's research is beginning to move in the opposite direction: Alice Schlegel, ed., *Sexual Stratification: A Cross-Cultural View* (New York: Columbia University Press, 1977) contains twelve case studies of societies, from the Philippines to modern Israel, pulling together many threads in the discussion about the equality and inequality of sexual status, trying to disentangle three dimensions of sexual rank: reward, prestige, and power. The author believes that, under conditions of subsistence, *balance* is the key word to describe the interdependence of the separate male and female domains, at least in the case of the Hopi culture that she describes on pages 245–69. Traditional female-male equality is thus threatened by the growing similarity of male and female roles in the home and on the job, which becomes inevitable as the Hopi are integrated into the US economy. J. Harris, "The Position of Women in a Nigerian Society," *Transactions of the New York Academy of Sciences*, 2d. ser., vol. 2, no. 5 (1940) observed something analogous among the Ibo. He sees the balance between the nominal rights of husbands and the de facto corporate rights of wives disturbed by integration. Rayna Reiter, "Men and Women in the South of France: Public and Private Domains" (*op. cit.*, pp. 252–82, FNs 22, 76) studies a village of 185 people in the southern foothills of the French Alps. Women working and living within the realm of their households seem to consider their domain more important than the public sphere of men (see FN 79). However, to the extent the family is integrated into the modern state, it is women who are being defined by their role within the family, and their "separate sphere" can no longer be construed as an equal one. See Ernestine Friedl, *"The Position of Women: Appearance and Reality," *Anthropological Quarterly* 40 (1967): 97–105. The appearance of the man's prestige can obscure the realities of

village of Montaillou to rigorous and skillfull questioning on suspicion of heretical catharism. With great subtlety, he solicited innumerable details about their daily lives from these peasants and shepherds of the northern Pyrenees, and had verbatim records of their responses prepared. Le Roy Ladurie studied these responses, gathered for him 650 years ago. No other document I know gives such a comprehensive firsthand description of what a community of householders felt about the roofs and territory they shared, and about the behavior they expected from and tolerated in each

---

woman's power. This is the conclusion drawn from observations of family life in a contemporary Greek village. "It is possible to argue that male activities have more prestige than those of the females in all societies, and, if this is true, the discovery of the relative social power of men and women may require more careful investigation. . . . Where the family is the significant unit of social and economic structure of the entire community, power within that unit must have important consequences for power distribution within society as a whole. . . ." One check upon the power of men is women's ability to disrupt orderly relationships in the men's world. What is expressed by women to men in the privacy of the household is a constant reminder of the lengths to which women go in the toil and the trouble they take in the performance of those household tasks that enable the men of the family to preserve their public honor. The effect of these complaints, which are culturally sanctioned, is to keep men aware of their dependence on their womenfolk. This asymmetric dominance, however, cannot but break down when the predominance of the cash economy transforms the household into a "consuming unit" (see FN 122). The distance between gender and sex makes it possible to recognize the difference between the asymmetry in the dominance of genders and the hierarchic distribution of homogeneous power under the regime of sex. Dominance here is an ambiguous term, meaning something different when attributed to women than it does when attributed to men. Power refers to a homogeneous force (similar to other genderless forces: see p. 176) that can be controlled to different degrees and in different ways by the two sexes. Asymmetry is fundamental to the ambiguous complementarity of genders (FN 57). It is constitutive of their very existence and determines the character of their concrete relatedness. In contrast, power, which like a currency can circulate without respect to gender, ultimately tends toward symmetry. And while the asymmetry between genders has always inspired awe, the hierarchic distribution of power among theoretical equals inspires envy (FNs 5, 6). For this reason I consider the genderless key word *power* inadequate to express (1) either the mutual exclusion from their respective proper domains that is implicit in the concept of gender (FNs 78, 79), or (2) the relative dominance of male domains over that of females, a situation patriarchy in its various forms authorizes.

other. Each of the victims of this inquisition comes to life as a person, not only when behaving as the bishop would approve but particularly when following the dictates of his or her own gender's probity in ways that the inquisitor wants to check. And on every page the *domus*, the "house" in the strongest possible sense, means the roof under which and the place in which the two genders meet: the kitchen; the goods and land; the children and family as a whole, slaves and guests included.

The *domus*, not people, seems to be the subject of history, the basic social unit. The house, at once building and family, links men and women to their possessions, which relate them to each other. From these painstaking interviews between judge and Montaillou peasants of the late twelfth century, it appears that they—unlike the post-medieval, typically European peasant—are not yet obsessed by the land and its tenure; it is the *domus* that counts, even more than spouse or child. Not the naked family, but the *domus* is subsistent and autarchic; it reproduces itself in offspring. Here, in Montaillou, the women of the house are in charge of fire, cooking, gardening, greens for animals, and the fetching of water. The men look after the fields, the woods, and the sheep, getting occasional help from a woman belonging to the *domus*, or one hired from elsewhere. Material life is created by the home, the main acting subject, through its men and women.[85]

In the Etruscan lands of central Italy, a Latin word is used to designate both the central subject of history, the *domus*, and its

The example in the text is taken from Emmanuel Le Roy Ladurie, *Montaillou, Cathars and Catholics in a French Village, 1294–1324* (London: Scholar Press, 1978): 146ff. The *domus* of the Pyrenees is, however, just one characteristic form the ultimate subject of history has taken. Even within France it can take several other forms. Jean-Louis Flandrin, *Families in Former Times* (Oxford: Cambridge University Press, 1979) distinguishes three forms typical for rural France. The first of these is the southwestern *domus*. In feudal times it was the *domus* that was ennobled. The heir bore the title of the house; whether the heir was male or female was rather secondary. The main task of the heir was to produce a new heir for the house. It was the *domus* that owned the land. The *domus* plunged those who now lived within it into the house's past. Almost the opposite of a *domus*, according to Flandrin, is the peasant household of central France. Here, the community of those who work the land together is the group who will inherit it. Flandrin confirms the position of Segalen (see FN 79):

tutelary gods, the *lares*. These are old gods, with prominent phallus or vulva. Together they protect the boundaries of their common milieu. Traditionally they are venerated at the cross-roads, although their effigies are stored above the hearth. They are worshiped by day, keeping order in the house, even though they rise from the subsoil where the dead lie. And the dwelling itself, the home, the domestic establishment around the hearth, is also called the *lar*. Perhaps *lar* could serve as a technical term to designate that ultimate subject of history of which the *domus* is one specific example.

Gender and the Home

Gender shapes bodies as they shape space and are in turn shaped by its arrangements. And the body in action, with its movements and rhythms, its gestures and cadences, shapes the

---

It is not the couple, *le couple*, that constitutes the subject of a holding's history, but *le ménage*. A third pattern in which genders can be interwoven to form a subject of history is that typical for Normandy. It is a pattern probably brought and imposed on the land by the conquering Scandinavians. Here, the household is based on kinship ties between blood lines, and these are rooted in their respective soils. It is the blood that claims the land. The widow, when she leaves the dead man's household, takes with her the land she had brought to the wedding. Each of these three household types represents one pattern in which genders interweave to form a social fabric. In France the ultimate subject of history has for a long time been one or the other form of the household. Later feudal and state power was built on the assumption of economic wedlock (FNs 77, 121), and under different forms this was true for England and for Germany. Michael Mitterauer, *Grundtypen alteuropäischer Sozialformen: Haus und Gemeinde in vorindustriellen Gesellschaften* (Stuttgart: Frommann-Holzloog, 1979). For the subcastes of India, see Louis Dumont, *Homo Hierarchicus* (Paris: Gallimard, 1966; English translation, University of Chicago, 1974). On the Indonesian village community, see Clifford Geertz, *The Religion of Java* (Chicago: University of Chicago Press, Phoenix Books, 1976). I feel the need for a term that sets the subject of gendered histories apart from the subject of history in the Hegelian tradition. I propose for this purpose *lares*, because the term has no present technical use. From G. Radke, *Die Götter Altitaliens* (Münster: 1965): 166ff. I understand that, strictly speaking, I should talk about the "lares compitales"—those venerated in a chapel with as many windows as there were hearths within the community's boundaries.

home, the home as something more than a shelter, a tent, or a house. To live somewhere means to make a home, by bringing children into the world no less than by planting trees and building walls. Rare are the words that designate human actions—the verbs—that do not also refer to homemaking. In vernacular culture, dwelling and living coincide. With gender-bound tools, oriented by a gender-specific meaning, vernacular life weaves a gendered cocoon set in a biological niche. All living is dwelling, the shaping of a dwelling. To dwell means to live in the traces that past living has left. The traces of dwellings survive, as do the bones of people. Uninhabited space quickly becomes a desert.

To build a home means to encroach on the territories of other life, wildlife, to create fields, pastures, churns for domesticated forms of life—for grains, donkeys, and the bacteria that coagulates the butter. Among possible ecological niches, the home forms a distinct class, but its special character has been more obscured than illuminated by recent ecological talk. Although the ecological movement has fostered an important new common sense, it has also subtly encouraged sexism since it has enriched genderless—that is, sexist—language about space. The terms of ecology are the parvenues among key words of the late seventies and thus ought to be warily used.

A home is neither a nest nor a garage. The ecologist may call all three of these locations niches. For the philosopher, they are places in three kinds of space, each brought into existence by a distinct kind of action. Biological nesting, technical parking, and historical dwelling generate heterogeneous spaces. By instinct, the animal stakes out its territory. The nest is the spatial mode for the instinctive reproduction of its kind. A garage is the very opposite, designed for parking under the assumption of scarce space.

A modern apartment comes out of the same kind of space for which garages are designed. It is constructed out of economic—that is, genderless—modules of space-time, of "spime," and is made to meet the tenants' imputed needs. It is usually attached to transportation systems. Both the garage and the apartment are rationally and economically built for the overnight storage of a productive resource. Both are man-proof; the walls are insured against damage by bumpers or children, and both cars and children are insured against damage from accidents. The apartment is a repository that serves for the confinement of people, who are considered fragile and dangerous. It is impossible for the tenants to "make a home"; the place is structured and equipped for shadow work only. It is the address at which wires and traffic lanes, postmen and police can reach and service those who are healthy, sane, and civilian, those who survive outside institutions on Valium, TV, and supermarket deliveries. It is the specialized place for the practice of intimacy between genderless humans, the only place left where the two sexes can pee into the same pot.[86]

86 HOUSING AND DWELLING

John Turner, *Housing by People* (London: Marion Boyars, 1976) introduced the now classic distinction between housing as the provision of a commodity and housing as an activity. I prefer to call this activity *dwelling*. Words meaning "dwell" come from such notions as "be" or "exist" and, especially, from "live"; that is, "to be alive." They also come from the ideas "remain" or "abide," from "sit, delay, linger, go slowly." And some from "possess, be busy with, cultivate." Further, some are denominatives from words for "house" or "place." For Indo-European synonyms, see C.D. Buck, (*op. cit.* FNs 3, 82), all of chapter 7, esp. pp. 11–13: dwell, house, home. Also, Emile Benveniste (*op. cit.* FN 77), especially volume 1, chapter 4. At this point my text owes much to conversations with Sigmar Groeneveld (Göttingen) on space that is within and out of reach of those who shape it; to Franco La Cecla (Bologne) on the threshold that divides and orients in contrast to the boundaries that enclose the milieu, and to discussion with Jean Robert (Cuernavaca) while he wrote *Le temps qu'on nous vole* (Paris: Seuil, 1980). At present, independently of each other, all three are writing studies analyzing the conditions that would permit, in a modern society, the generation of living space. The opposition of *gendered* and *sexed spime* (FN 79) can be used to enlighten and enlarge the distinction between vernacular and professional architecture, to which Sir G. Gilbert Scott, *Secular and Domestic Architectures* (London, 1857) first explicitly referred, and to which Bernard Rudofsky, *Architecture Without Architects: A Short Introduction to Non-Pedigreed Architecture* (New York: Doubleday, 1969) and *The Prodigious Builders* (London: Secker and Warburg, 1977) has recently called attention. Where all tools are gendered (FN 70), houses are both the result of gendered tool use and the place where these gendered tools are used. This I read into a beautiful book that describes the private history of a culture as the economy, diversity, and permanence of its dwelling activities, which express themselves in the culture's building: Sibyl Moholy-Nagy, *Native Genius in Anonymous Architecture* (New York: Schocken, 1976). A third author who insists on the duality that opposes vernacular shelter and professionally planned housing is Paul Oliver, *Shelter, Sign, and Symbol*

Gender Domains and Vernacular Milieu

The home in Montaillou, Minot, or today's rural Mexico is neither a territory staked out by animals breeding in the harness of their genes nor a specialized residence for sexual partners, carved into the shadowy slopes of economic space. A home made *by* people, not *for* them, is a space engendered by the bodies of its inhabitants, the environmental trace of vernacular living. The home is neither a breeding ground nor a well-equipped safe; it is the reflection in the milieu of men and women. Therefore, *to be at home* must mean something different for the two of them.

(London: Overlook Press, 1977) whose introduction to this volume contains a further element that, properly elaborated, sheds light on the duality with which I am concerned: on the one hand, shelter for a milieu woven from gendered domains; on the other, sexed shelter for genderless people. Oliver considers all shelter as a *sign* that, through interpretation, becomes a *symbol*. I would characterize vernacular shelter as the ambiguous sign of a culture that by gendered interpretation speaks about the two domains from which it arises. Two bibliographies provide access to research and evidence for the neglect of gender: Lawrence Wodehouse, *Indigenous Architecture, Worldwide* (Detroit: Gale Research, 1979) and Robert de Zouche Hall, *A Bibliography on Vernacular Architecture* (Newton Abbot: David & Charles, 1972), a scholarly research tool on England. For Italian, especially rural, housing: Tina de Rocchi Storai, *Bibliografia degli studi sulla Casa Rurale Italiana* (Florence: Olschki, 1968). This is the twenty-fifth volume of a series of regional studies. For factual information on the policies that suppressed vernacular architecture in the USA, see David Handlin, *The American Home: Architecture and Society, 1815–1915* (Boston: Little, Brown, 1979) and Howard J. Boughey, *Blueprints for Behavior: The Intentions of Architects to Influence Social Action Through Design* (Ann Arbor, MI: University Microfilms, 1968). A French research project that focuses specifically on the transition from vernacular to state-administered space is J.M. Alliaume, et al., *Politique de l'habitat (1800–1850)* (Paris: Corda, 1977), containing an article of particular relevance to the theme by Anne Thalamy, "Réflexions sur la notion d'habitat aux XVIIIe et XIXe siècles." Just as different cultures speak with terms denoting different word fields about the relationship of people and communities to their own dwelling, they speak in different ways about the immediate space beyond the dwelling's threshold—the space in which the dwelling itself is embedded. On the variety of word fields available for this purpose in several European languages, the contrasts among these word fields, and their change from the nineteenth to the twentieth centuries, see Paul Osswald, *Frz. "campagne" und seine Nachbarwörter im Vergleich zur Wortfeldtheorie.* (Tübingen: Tübinger Beiträge zur Linguistik, 1970).

As the warp runs on and on lengthwise in the fabric, and the woof crisscrosses it at right angles to tie the threads together, so the actions that engender the home, the actions that engender life space, are necessarily different depending on whether they leave traces from men or traces from women. Both men and women make themselves at home through every move. But for women, who can engender the unbroken succession of life, phenomenologically the relationship to space takes on special significance. The culture may be matriarchal or patriarchal, the greater share of power in the hands of women or men, but only for women does to live and to dwell mean to engender bodies, to leave behind a trail of new life. In one culture men may build shelters, make fences, or terrace a hill; in another, these tasks are assigned to women. But only from women does bodily life come into the world. No matter how the local mythology depicts the creator of the world—as mother, father, or androgyne; no matter whose name the children carry—mother's, father's, or uncle's; the special space (and the time that corresponds to it) that sets the home apart from nest and garage is engendered *only* by women, because it is they who bear living bodies.

This reflection might sound poetic, obscure, or romantic until one recalls that women are doubly *out of place* in the space of the modern apartment, and that they clearly say so. The encroachment and usurpation of normative space frustrates the flesh of women as it does not and could not affect men's. Unisex architecture is necessarily male-sexist, as is the unisex ticking of watches. Such designs place women, in their flesh and rhythms, in double jeopardy: Their potential contribution to homemaking is frustrated, and they are yanked out of their proper gender context; in both respects, they suffer more than men.

By being turned into economic producers—paid or unpaid, on the job or at home—women, like men, are deprived of the environmental conditions that allow them to live by dwelling in a place and, by dwelling, to make a home. To the degree that they become more productive economically, both men and women become homeless. But the loss of a gendered home, and its replacement by specialized reproduction modules, deprives women of the kind of amplitude needed for new space-generating life. Each one alone, they deliver new individuals into genderless economic space, into a world made out of normalized spime blocks. Apartment space is just as hardened and genderless as hospital space in this respect; it, too, cannot be used for gendered lying in. Those who have tried home births in their apartments, and treasure them in comparison with hospital deliveries, know from their frustrating experiences that the topology of their bodies meshes neither with throwing a litter nor with reproducing the labor force; it fits neither a nest nor an assembly line: rather, it is shaped to bring forth vernacular space and time with a child.

Vernacular space not only shapes the landscape and the house, not only reaches into the past and beyond, it extends into the body itself, quite differently for women than for men. The result is that economic and genderless architecture forming well-governed international spime turns women inside out, transforming female gender into "the second sex." What Michel Foucault has called the clinical perspective, which developed in the course of the nineteenth century, washes gender itself out of the body.

Recently, the steps by which gender has been rubbed out of the body, thereby reconstructing women anatomically as a special kind of human endowed with sex organs but lacking sufficient hair, have been well studied. But the crucial innovation in this polarizing humanization of women is the new place assigned childbirth in its study and public regulation. Up to about 1780, medical treatises and public ordinances viewed childbirth as women's domain. The cessation of the menses, the suspicion of pregnancy, the swelling of the body, miscarriage, abortion, birth, lactation were no less women's affair than infanticide or the rearing of the in-fant (in Latin, literally, the non-speaker). These matters were neither private nor secret, but gendered. Generally, snuffing out its life by sleeping on it, by putting it on the window ledge in winter, or by withholding her breast from the monster would not be a concern of the authorities. In public language and discourse, both medical and legal, it is clearly women who bring children into the world.

The perception that women, in the plural and collectively, are the source of new life changed only during the last generation of the *ancien régime*. During that period, the language of the law overstepped the threshold of the vulva, much as the inquisitor had earlier overstepped that of the *domus*. The fetus began to be talked about as a citizen, albeit unborn. Legislation was passed to police the womb in order to protect the life it contained. The principal aggressor threatening the future citizen and soldier was now the mother, especially if she was poor or single. In 1735, the Prussian police begin to register unmarried women whose menses had ceased. The old herbal abortifacients were among the first drugs to be removed from the market by the authorities, or restricted by prescription to pharmacies; *thuya* trees were uprooted by the police in public gardens—as hemp is today.

The womb was declared public territory. The exercise of midwifery was made dependent on formal instruction and continual medical supervision. This transformation of the experienced neighbor into a licensed (and otherwise illegal), specialized *accoucheuse* was one of the key events in disabling professionalism. And this change was reflected in language. Childbirth ceased to be an event of and among women. The womb, in the language of the medical police, became the specialized organ that produces infants. Women were described as if they were wombs on two feet. Women no longer helped other women deliver; the doctor or midwife delivered the child.

By the middle of the nineteenth century, gynecologists had begun to penetrate into the new territory of the womb even before the onset of birth pangs. Toward the end of the century, they concentrated on disinfecting the birth canal in order to protect the newcomer against the diseases with which the possibly sullied mother menaced him. In the eighteenth century, the poorer the woman, the more she was suspected of a tendency to abort; in the nineteenth, she was believed especially prone to infect her child. Both earlier and later, her poverty served as the pretext for separating her from contact with other women and for institutionalizing her before she could give birth, a process conveniently serving to make her available as a training ground for future medicine men. Then at the turn of the twentieth century, in Massachusetts earlier than in Berlin or Milan, genderless hospital birth— hitherto viewed as a precaution against the wiles and diseases of women—began to be advertised as a benefit to the mother herself. Genderless medical care metamorphoses the womb into a kind of prenatal parking garage. Pregnancy under intensive professional care becomes, in my opinion, the ritual solemnizing the final victory of administered over vernacular spime.[87]

This essay deals with the contrast between gendered living and a sexist economy. But I have avoided any attempt to explain why a sexist regime ultimately and consistently works against

8 7 FROM THE DELIVERY OF THE MOTHER TO THE DELIVERY OF THE CHILD

In writing *Medical Nemesis*, I consecrated one whole chapter to the medicalization of death, which has meant the suppression of the vernacular *art of dying*. At that time Norma Swenson of the Boston Women's Health Collective pointed out to me that the jointly practiced art of giving birth was equally threatened by the medicalization of delivery. Access to an unfinished manuscript by Barbara Duden (Berlin) convinced me that, with the inversion of birth, gender (engendered by women) turns into sex reproduced by a new biocracy for which the womb is a natural resource. *Life* becomes a new guiding concept for science and administration; see K. Figlio, "The Metaphor of Organization: A Historiographical Perspective on the Biomedical Sciences of the Early Nineteenth Century," *History of Science* 14 (1976): 17–53, esp. 25–28. Enlightenment science designates nature as a woman to be unveiled, unclothed, and penetrated by the light of reason. Penetrated by this light kind of reason, woman, the epitome of nature, becomes when pregnant that mechanism whereby *life* is transmitted. The multiprofessional establishment, from which the modern state derives its legitimacy, hinges on the medical control of life at the point of its origin. For a study of expanding professionalism, at least in the USA, see Burton L. Bledstein, *The Culture of Professionalism: The Middle Class and the Development of Higher Education in America* (New York: Norton, 1978). On traditional ways of bearing children, I have found useful Jacques Gelis, Mireille Laget, and Marie Morel, **Entrer dans la vie: Naissance et enfance dans la France traditionelle* (Paris: Gallimard, 1978) and Jean-Louis Flandrin, "Contraception, mariage et relations amoureuses dans l'Occident *chrétien*," *Annales, ESC* 24, no. 12 (November–December 1969): 1370–90, or, in English, "Contraception, Marriage, and Sexual Relations in the Christian West," trans. Patricia M. Ranum, **Biology of Man in History*, ed. Robert Forster and Orest Ranum (Baltimore and London: Johns Hopkins University Press, 1975). Also see Alessandra Alimenti and Paola Falteri, "Donna e salute nella cultura tradizionale delle classi subalterne: Appunti di una ricera sulla medicina populare nell'Italia Centrale," *Donna-woman-femme* 5 (1977): 75–104, with bibliography. On traditional kinds of contraception, see Jean-Marie Gouesse, "En Basse Normandie aux 17e et 18e siècles: Le refus de l'enfant au tribunal de la pénitence," *Annales de démographie historique* (1973) describing the scandalized surprise of confessors at the contraceptive com-

women. The principal reason for this self-imposed limitation is
the belief that a satisfactory answer depends on a fleshed-out
philosophy of gender—and this remains to be written. But if I
should ever try to explain why the loss of gender does and must
degrade women even more than men, I would begin my search
with an analysis of the distinct and different effects imperial and
genderless environment has on the bodies of both men and
women.

---

petence of peasants. On abortion, Agnès Fine-Souriac, "La limitation des
naissances dans le Sud-Ouest de la France," *Annales du Midi* 40 (1978):
155–58. On traditional forms of infanticide, Regina Schulte, "Kindsmör-
derinnen auf dem Lande," in H. Medick, D. Sabean, eds., *Materielles
Interesse und Emotion.* (Göttingen: 1982) and Patricia Crawford, "Attitudes to Menstruation in Seventeenth-Century England," *Past and Present*
91 (May 1981): 46–73. On the extension of gynecological control,
Barbara Ehrenreich and Deirdre English, *For Her Own Good: 150 Years
of the Expert's Advice to Women* (New York: Anchor, 1978) gives a
general survey. On the creation of professional midwives (male and
female), and the medicalization of birth, see Ann Oakley, "Wise-
woman and Medicine Man: Changes in the Management of Childbirth" in Juliet Mitchell and Ann Oakley, *The Rights and Wrongs
of Women* (London: Penguin, 1976): 17–58. Frances E. Kobrin, "The
American Midwife Controversy: A Crisis of Professionalization," *Bulletin of the History of Medicine* 40 (1966): 350–63; J. Gélis, "Sages-femmes
et accoucheurs: L'obstétrique populaire aux XVIIe et XVIIIe siècles," *Annales, ESC* 32:5 (September/October 1977): 927–57: Gianna Pomata,
*"Madri illegittime tra Ottocento e Novecento: storie cliniche e storie di
vita," Quaderni Storici* 44 (1980): 497–552, a whole issue dedicated to
"parto e maternità, momenti della biografia femminile." On preventive
gynecology by the medicalization of contraception, see Linda Gordon,
Woman's Body, Woman's Rights: Birth Control in America (New York:
Grossman, 1976): 159–85. The hospitalization of birth went hand in hand
with a move toward a monopoly over sexual morality. No matter if the
day's fashion was for or against birth control, it implied a professional
competence over any decision regarding how and when women should, for
their own good, have intercourse. An especially perceptive study on the
medicalized discourse about women, as the new language began to shape
the new reality of women's bodies, is Jean-Pierre Peter, "Entre femmes et
médecins: Violence et singularités dans le discours du corps et sur le corps
d'après les manuscrits médicaux de la fin du XVIIIe siècle," *Ethnologie
Française* 6, nos. 3–4 (1976): 341–48. Analogous for the United States
is Carroll Smith-Rosenberg, "Puberty to Menopause: The Cycle of Fem-
inity in Nineteenth-Century America," *Clio's Consciousness Raised* (*op.
cit.*, pp. 25–37, FN 36). On motherhood, see also FN 127.

· 1 2 6 ·

Gender and the Grasp of Reality

Everywhere, girls and boys seem to grow into their respective genders early on. By the time they are weaned, they use unmistakably different gestures. In the Mashrik, the heartland of Islam from Egypt to Persia, where weaning takes place only after the second birthday (and later for boys than for girls), there are dozens of common sayings that instruct mothers on the different techniques for cuddling and handling the two genders. In some languages, where men and women use distinct kin-terms for the same uncle, the word fit for each gender's lips is often among the first to be learned. The duties befitting each gender are inculcated at an early age. By the time she is nine, a Bemba girl knows how to distinguish forty mushrooms, while the boy knows the calls of many birds. The most fundamental cognitive division in the evolution of concepts is that based on gender. However, psychological epistemologists of the last two generations seem to pay least heed to it. Identification and opposition in gender is part of a child's earliest empirical, but not yet verbal, growth. Piaget has coined a term for these primary distinctions; he calls them *infra-* and not just *pre-*logical. The most profound of these, gender, he seems to have overlooked.[88]

The infant begins to form concepts only by physically grasping what is "there." And unless it stretches out an arm, touches, holds, handles, and hugs other bodies, discernment can take no shape. These movements are not "spontaneous"; they are not mere biological reactions untouched by culture. The mother's eyes, which look differently at a girl and boy, already impress a distinct pattern on the eyes of the infant. Thus, the earliest touching and embracing of the world is done by the infant with its own body, instructed by vernacular gender. Where gender predominates, growing up can never mean becoming a logical neuter, a genderless human, a nonspecific pupil.

88 / 89 ASYMMETRY OF THE
SYMBOLIC UNIVERSE

The example comes from A.I. Richards, *Chisugu: A Girl's Initiation Ceremony Among the Bemba of Northern Rhodesia* (London: Faber & Faber, 1956). This is a tender and delightful study.

When, from infancy, men and women grasp the world from complementary sides, they develop two distinct models with which they conceptualize the universe. A gender-bound style of perception corresponds to each gender's domain of tools and tasks. Not only do they see the same things from different perspectives and in different hues, but early on they learn that there is always another side to a thing. And some things are always within reach for a boy but out of reach for girls—most of the time.

The genderless key words of contemporary discourse compel us to describe the ambiguous two-sidedness of vernacular reality as a sex war started by Adam and Eve. Invidious comparison now replaces awe as the reaction to otherness. The rituals that orchestrate the dance of life, marking bodies, intertwining genders, then pushing them apart again, are now dressed up as primitive sex education. The strange aberration, imagining mother when speaking about Clytemnestra, leads to a *monstrous* myth, no less an anomaly than attributing to Junior the passions of Oedipus.

Sex and gender are unfit to cohabit the same conceptual universe. The attempt to marry the two necessarily leads to the scientific sexism of anthropology, be it of a macho or a fem brand.

The most common sexist perspective by far is that of the *male* observer, a fact now well documented. Overwhelmingly, ethnographers are men. The rare women are either pupils or competitors of their male colleagues. It is tempting for the ethnographer to ask men what they think. Most researchers have linguistic difficulties and men, rather than women, are more likely to have learned some vehicular language—Haussa from market use, Arabic from Koranic school, or French from service in the army. This is the principal reason why, according to E. Ardener, ethnographers tend to report that women informants are a nuisance: "They giggle when young, snort when old, reject questions, laugh at topics proposed to them, and seem uninterested in speaking to a stranger." In addition, they are inaccessible much of the time because their men declare them to be dangerous, impure, or in need of protection. So ethnographers feed their models (embedded in questions) to male interlocutors, and these—changing, embroidering, or misunderstanding these axioms—fashion their responses to suit the occasion. Since the questions are posed in gender-blind language, gender obviously does not appear in the answers.

Women investigators have recently produced a "complementary" sexist description, a "fem-sexist" speculum in which they view a kind of mirror image of the male fantasies to which gendered reality has been diminished by "science." They have been primarily interested in the way women handle the symbols and levels of power. But since these newer studies, in large part, explore dominance and dependence in non-Western societies, they cannot but miss the complementary and ambiguous domains of gender. Ultimately, dominance and dependence are issues of a net transfer of power; they imply a competition for values or positions that are genderless. Once you view these values as scarce and equally desirable for men and women, you inevitably study the struggle for them in a sexist perspective.

Among the few anthropologists who have tried to unlink the study of male dominance from the analysis of conceptual universes that are asymmetric and only ambiguously complementary —and without denying the importance of the former—is Edwin Ardener. In his study of Bakweri women he found that they define the boundaries of their world in such a way that they live as women, but only up to a point, in what for men is "the wild" and for anthropologists is a seemingly impenetrable labyrinth. "Women do not readily see society bounded from nature; they will not necessarily provide a model for society as a unit that will contain both men and themselves. They may indeed provide a model in which women and nature are outside men and society."[89]

89 Under the heading "Complementarity and Social Science" (FN 52), I have pointed out the need to abandon concepts that impose a central perspective when the object to be described is a gendered reality. In FN 46, I warned that the various forms of "stereoscopic science" now being proposed should not be confused with the approach necessary to grasp gender; the practitioners of complementary, compensatory, and contrastive social science do not abandon the hypothesis of a genderless mode of cognition. Only explicitly non-scientific research that uses metaphor (FN 56) as its epistemological mode can bespeak the ambiguous and asymmetric complementarity (FN 57) that constitutes gender. I then pointed out that in a world of gender not only material culture—tools (FN 70), time (FN 79), space (FN 78)—but also dominance is gendered (FN 84). I have indicated the limits a terminology consistent with political economics imposes on an analysis of the imbalance between the two gendered domains. But I still have to stress the point that in a world of gender not only the material elements of

Unfortunately, Ardener used the terms "society," "the wild," and "nature" without insisting on the fact that for him these are metaphors. Therefore, his critics[90] expended a lot of effort showing that these terms have a heavy ideological charge defined by the way they were used during the Enlightenment. They failed to

culture but also the perceptions and symbolic inferences of that culture are gendered. The expanse, the perspective, the coloring, and the objects women see and grasp are different from what is seen and grasped by men. A first article by Edwin Ardener, *"Belief and the Problem of Women," in Shirley Ardener, ed., *Perceiving Women* (New York: Halsted Press, 1975): 1–17 was criticized by Nicole-Claude Mathieu, "Notes pour une définition sociologique des catégories de sexe," *Epistémologie sociologique* 11–16 (1971–73): 21–39. Edwin Ardener, "The 'Problem' Revisited," in Shirley Ardener, ed. (*op. cit.*) is a reply. In this second article Ardener establishes a conceptual framework according to which men are "muted" in certain expanses of women's domain: They can neither directly grasp them nor conceptually refer to them. Ardener assumes the same for women in relation to some parts of men's domain. The idea that such asymmetrical muting (impotence and silence) is constitutive of the symbolic complementarity of gender will be the subject of an essay on which I am working. On this topic Rodney Needham, *Reconnaissances* (Toronto: University of Toronto Press, 1980): 17–40 ("Unilateral Figures"). Charlotte Hardmann, "Can there be an Anthropology of Children?" *Journal of the Anthropological Society of Oxford* 4 (1973): 85–99 makes children into a paradigm for the existence of groups that are "muted" "unperceived," "elusive"—like women—living in an independent, autonomous but not totally incomprehensible segment of society with certain values and forms of interaction exclusive to them. She discusses the stratagems used in anthropological literature to exclude the need for recognizing this muted existence. The article suggests ideas applicable to the mutual mutedness of gender domains.

90 NATURE/CULTURE

A major task in the elaboration of *gender* as an analytic paradigm is that of disentangling it from the various dualities now current and even normative in social science research (see FNs 12, 76). By opposing the concept of *gender* to *culture*, "we have made nature herself an accomplice in the crime of political inequality"—(Condorcet). *On nature*, thus redefined, see Jean Erhard. *L'idée de nature en France à l'aube des Lumières* (Paris: Flammarion, 1970). Perhaps the most difficult contemporary duality to unravel is that of gender in relation to nature/culture. This is so because, since the Enlightenment, science is a human activity dedicated to the *naturalization* of both experience and ideology for the

grasp Ardener's point: We have no good words to express the asymmetry of gender-specific perceptions in prose.

Ultimately, the sexist bias of most anthropological studies is due to something more fundamental than the use of male informants, the focus of female researchers, or misunderstandings. The bias against gender is built into anthropology because anthropology tries to be a science. Its scientific logic makes it an analytical tool that studies men and women as "anthropoi," reduces gender

---

purpose of expressing that achievement in language (the argument comes from Figlio, *op. cit.* FN 87). Science must therefore be analyzed, in analogy to Roland Barthes's analysis of myth, as a collage whose persuasiveness is based on its assertion that what it expresses is natural. To paraphrase Barthes: What the world (or the assembly of empirical data) gives to myth (or to science) is an historical reality defined by the way in which men have produced or used it; and what myth (in this case, science) gives in return is a natural image of this reality. As a result, the "nature" studied becomes as mythical (scientifically genderless) as the genderless categories by which it is studied. The need to deal with this issue in the anthropologist's search for "women" was raised by Sherry B. Ortner, "Is Female to Male as Nature Is to Culture?" in Rosaldo and Lamphere (*op. cit.*, pp. 67–87, FN 68). She is less concerned than Ardener with the asymmetry of conceptual universes. Her main concern is that of finding an explanatory theory for the subordination of women to men which to her seems almost universal. She stresses, however, that any link-up between nature and women is a construct of culture rather than a fact of nature. Her article gave rise to a lively symposium: Carol P. MacCormack and Marilyn Strathern, eds., *Nature, Culture and Gender* (Cambridge: Cambridge University Press, 1980). This anthology contains several thought-provoking contributions that permit one to step back from the nature/culture paradigm so deeply embedded in science and popularized by the key words of ordinary language (FN 2). For an extreme example of a world view that cannot oppose culture to nature, see M. Strathern, "No Nature, No Culture: the Hagen case," (*Ibid.* pp. 174–222). Among the Hagen there is no culture in the sense of the cumulative works of man, and no nature to be tamed and made productive. When gender is used in a differentiating, dialectical manner, the distinction between male and female constantly creates the notion of humanity as a "background of common similarity." Neither male nor female can possibly stand for "humanity" as against "nature" because the distinction between them is used to valuate areas in which human action is creative and individuating. Among the Hagen all representations of domination and influence between the sexes are about precise forms of human interaction and not about humanity's project in relation to a less than human world.

GENDER

to sex, and makes of a metaphorical complementarity, which only
the culture's own poets can describe, a system of two homogeneous opposites. This raises a more basic question: If anthropology cannot get at gender as a subject, how can it explore anything
in the vernacular domain?[91]

Gender and Speech

The gender-distinctive grasp of reality finds its expression in
language.[92] At the age of five, boys and girls typically sound
different from one another, although no anatomical dissimilarity
has been found in their speech organs. Passing from babble to

91 ANTHROPOLOGY

Anthropology is a word that has a strange history. When Aristotle uses it
(*Nichomachean Ethics*, 1125 a 5), it means "gossip." When the term is
used by theologians, from Philo to Leibniz, it means something else: the
attribution of human feelings or motives to God, especially when the
reference is made by the speaker in deep humility and with the knowledge
that this metaphorical language is the only one that—though ambiguously
—fits the purpose. In the seventeenth century, the term was used for a
new, *natural* science that had as its object *man*. As a social science, anthropology was first recognized in the nineteenth century. For a summary of this
development, see O. Marquard, "Anthropologie—(philosophische)," *Historisches Wörterbuch der Philosophie*, ed. J. Ritter (*op. cit.*, pp. 362–74,
FN 3). I am inclined to join the opinion of Jürgen Habermas that, as a
distinct philosophical science, anthropology does not appear before the
First World War. Since then anthropology has consistently labored under
unisex terminology even when the anthropologist has tried to make the
distinction between women and men a central issue. What is needed more
than anything else is a modern epistemology of gender.

92–93 SEX DIFFERENCE IN LANGUAGE

A major attempt to record the language as it is actually spoken in southern
Germany has been under way for more than a decade. A preliminary
report is Arno Ruoff, *Grundlagen und Methoden der Untersuchung
gesprochener Sprache. Einführung in die Reihe Idiomatica* (Tübingen:
Niemeyer, 1973). The fact that the gender of the speaker was the major
variable encountered came as a great surprise to the investigators (p. 247).
"Die offenkundige Tatsache, dass sich zwischen Mann und Frau der in
allen Bestimmungen gleichen Gruppen die stärksten sprachlichen Unter-
schiede zeigen, war für uns die *unerwarteste* Feststellung" Barrie Thorne
and Nancy Henley, eds., *Language and Sex: Difference and Dominance*

· 132 ·

talk, they adopt the form and style appropriate to their gender, even when playing among themselves.[93]

As with "women's work," so-called women's language has also attracted scholarly interest in three successive waves.[94] Such curiosity was first aroused toward the end of the nineteenth century, a time when every possible evidence of women's consititu-

---

(Rowley, MA: Newbury House, 1975) does what the title says: It is an introduction to both difference and dominance. Nancy Faires Conklin, *"Toward a Feminist Analysis of Linguistic Behavior," *The University of Michigan Papers in Women's Studies* 1, no. 1 (1974): 51–73 gives access to earlier literature. Susan Philips, "Sex Differences and Language," *Annual Review of Anthropology* 9 (1980): 523–44 gives access to the newest literature. Good materials are assembled in J. Orasanu, M.K. Slater and L.L. Adler, "Language, Sex and Gender," *The Annual of the New York Academy of Sciences* 327 (1979) and by B.L. Dubois and I. Crouch, eds., *The Sociology of the Language of American Women: Proceedings of a Conference at San Antonio* (San Antonio, TX: Trinity University Press, 1979). My first introduction to the issue I owe to my now deceased young friend Larry M. Grimes, *El tabu linguistico: su naturaleza y función en el español popular de Mexico*, CIDOC Cuaderno no. 64 (Cuernavaca: CIDOC, 1971). His book is a mine of gender-specific taboo words in Mexican Spanish. A survey of the literature shows that most socio-linguists approach the difference between men's and women's speech "as a linguist would approach any variety of language." I am inclined toward the opposite prejudice. When analyzing vernacular speech opposition to taught mother tongue, I start from the assumption that the difference between the actual speech of women and the actual speech of men is unlike any other difference linguists otherwise explore. From intonation through grammar and lexicon; from the predominant topics to the style in which these are treated; from the rhythm of silences, sublinguistic noises, gestures, and glances to word order, I maintain that, from my own experience, vernacular language is made up of two distinct forms of speech. As a result of this bias based on observation, I have culled from the available literature mainly those items that fit my own hypothesis.

94 COMPLEMENTARITY IN SPEECH

I say "so-called" women's language as earlier I spoke about "so-called" women's work. We lack a linguistic term for the designation of gendered speech. For the available nomenclature, see Joshua A. Fishman, "Some Basic Sociolinguistic Concepts," *Sociology of Language* (Rowley, MA: Newbury House, 1972): 15–19. Gender-specific speech is not a variety of "the" language, but one of its two fundamental, constitutive complements. The moment you treat it as a variety, you have already introduced both a genderless, or "unisex," norm and, with it, the idea of

tional otherness was highly prized. Women's language was then one of those discoveries made by a clinical enterprise that had *a priori* defined a new, truly human anatomical, psychological, and behavioral reality and existence. This definition led women, as "the second sex," into a society of neuters, by now standardized according to a common norm. Every evidence of women's variance was grist for the professional mill: It could be turned to the profit of gynecologists, clergymen, home-economics teachers, and social workers who needed to define "needs" for which they alone could provide diagnostic language and normative therapy.

Nineteenth-century interest in women's speech was, however, short-lived.[95] While increasingly competent linguists have ex-

---

deviance. You also imply that, like a dialect, it could stand on its own feet, that either speech form could be spoken without the existence of its complement. Men's speech can be understood by the women who speak its complement; it will, however, be understood differently by the women than by the men (FNs 89, 97). A *vernacular language* as such can never be heard; it is a construct of the linguist who describes the behavior of statistical *humans*. The linguist's *lumen intellectualis* is that of the *scientific neuter* (FN 52). His conceptual searchlight and central perspective deaden the gender difference. Codification and orthography have consistently imposed the male form and thus have labeled what women continue to say as a deviant form. Even when standardization is the creation of a speech form through which men and women are made equals—in practice women remain less so. In vernacular cultures, occasions at which men and women speak to each other are rare. As a result, the occasions for dominance are rare. One reason for standardizing speech is the creation of one language with which men and women can talk to each other as *humans*. In practice, mixed conversation in unisex language turns each exchange into an occasion for dominance. See Don H. Zimmermann and Candace West, "Sex Roles, Interruption and Silence in Conversation," in M.A. Lowrie and N.F. Conklin, eds., *A Pluralistic Nation: The Language Issue in the United States* (Rowley, MA: Newbury House, 1978); also C. West, "Against Our Will: Male Interruptions of Females in Cross-Sex Conservation," in Orasanu (*op. cit.*, pp. 81–100, FN 92); M. Swacker, "Women's Verbal Behavior at Learned and Professional Conferences," in B.L. Dubois (*op. cit.*, pp. 155–60, FNs 92/93); B. Eakins and G. Eakins, "Verbal Turn Taking and Exchanges in Faculty Dialogue" (*Ibid.*, pp. 53–62).

95 ''WOMEN'S LANGUAGE''

Otto Jespersen, *Sproget, Barnet, kvinden slaegten* (Copenhagen: Gyldendal, 1941) is the major work of the epoch. In English, see Otto Jespersen,

plored all sorts of language variations—by age, status, education, or IQ—linguistic distinctions between the speech of women and men were relatively neglected until the late 1960s. Most studies of this second wave that adequately recorded the peculiarities of women's linguistic behavior tended to describe it as if it were a "dialect" peculiar to women, a thing subordinate to a superordinate entity that would be the "real" language. Then, during the 1970s, women's studies moved into this field. In every dimension and area of modern speech where such research has been carried out, an interminable amount of evidence for male domination has been looked for and found.[96]

Irrespective of the language—French, German, or English—statistical measurements show that men speak more loudly and more often than women; are more apt to interrupt, impose their views, and take over the conversation; and are more inclined to shout others down. Women tend to smile obligingly, excuse themselves and stutter, or in fits of insecurity attempt to imitate and

---

"The women," Chapter 13, in *Language: It's Nature, Development and Origin* (London: Allen & Unwin, 1922): 237–54. For representative research of the time, see A.M. Badia Margarit, "Note sur le langage des femmes et la méthode d'enquête dialectologique, domaine aragonais," *Orbis* 1 (1952): 15–18; Karl Bouda, "Die tschuktschische Frauensprache," *Orbis* 2 (1953): 33–34; Jacobus van Ginneken, "Mannen- en vrouwentaal," *Onze Taaltuin* 3 (1934/35): 289–92 (forms of address in the dialect of Drenthe).

96 SUBORDINATION IN SPEECH

Through the study of dominance some very fundamental observations on gender have been made. Nancy Faires Conklin, *"The Language of the Majority: Women and American English," in A *Pluralistic Nation* (*op. cit.*, pp. 222–37, FN 94) finds that in "any community there are separate norms for the behavior of men and women, and language behavior is no exception. Until recently, the traditional view of speech communities as uniform groups of speakers has masked the role of gender in language variation. In some cultures men and women have fairly distinct languages with different names for things and different word order. English at first sight appears relatively undifferentiated by sex—but, though more subtle, the differences are clear. Paradoxically those differences obvious to every child constitute at present a field for linguistic discovery. However, the question of which of these differences in contemporary English should be

outdo men. They then adopt men's vocabulary and syntax, men's strategies and rhetoric. But the more the words and themes are unisex, the more clear it becomes that both shrill pronouncements and silent reveries mark women as the second linguistic sex. The coeducational classroom and the union shop, the conference table and the cocktail party, have made language sexist, as the labor market has done for work.[97]

Even today, however, in many parts of the world men and women not only speak about different things, but do so because the language itself requires this. For example, outside office, factory, or politics, Japanese women rarely, more rarely than European women, take up the topics characteristic of men. But, when they do so, they say different things. And the difference is so great that it would be pointless to look for equivalent phrases in men's and women's speech, since in most situations the content will differ as much as the formal expression. Where women are obliged to devote five minutes to a conversation about a garden or a celebration, men, discussing the same subject, would lose face if they did

---

classified as *survival of gendered speech forms*, and which others as *sexist reflections in language* (see FN 101) has not, so far, been asked. In language, gender seems to survive *systematically* in spite of the growing imposition of unisex forms—in which, consistently, male speech dominates.

97 ROLE IN SPEECH AND ROLE IN LANGUAGE

Thorne (*op. cit.* FNs 92/93) points to the influence of *role* thinking on language studies. "The term role also, rather euphemistically, tends to gloss over power differences between men and women. It is significant that role terminology, which tends to imply 'different but equal,' is not applied to other cases of power differentials, e.g., we do not speak of racial roles or class roles. . . . Obviously a more accurate and flexible vocabulary for referring to social and cultural differentiation of the sexes is needed." This more accurate technical vocabulary would have to distinguish between two distinct situations: the use of vernacular speech and the use of taught mother tongue. In the first case, each speech-act resonates differently in the speaker's gender and in that of the corresponding other. In the second situation, the speaker uses the genderless "code" of a language, acquired like any commodity, in a way characteristic of his or her social sex. And in the genderless forum of taught mother tongue, male speech always places the male speaker on top.

more than make a three-word statement answered by a sublin-guistic grunt.[98]

The topical study of gender-specific language provides a par-tial view of the multidimensional domain of gender. Recently, this approach was used in a Spanish village and showed clearly that men talk about work in the fields, livestock, the shop, and the trade, while women's talk converges on observations about peo-ple, their motives, lives, and the needs of the household. But the topics discussed do not, any more than the tools used, adequately reveal how the world is grasped. Differences in phonology, in-tonation, syntax, vocabulary, and pronominal and nominal refer-ences distinguish masculine from feminine speech.[99] What these differences could reveal about symbolic complementarity, once they were accepted as constitutive of language rather than mar-

98 / 102 GENDERED SPEECH VS.
SEXIST LANGUAGE

J.J. Ottenheimer, "Culture and Contact and Musical Style: Ethno-musicology in the Comore Islands," *Ethnomusicology* 14 (1970): 458–62 discusses the fact that women sing different songs than men, and Karl Haiding, "Das Erzählen bei der Arbeit und die Arbeitsgruppe als Ort des Erzählens," in G. Heilfurth and I. Weber-Kellerman, eds. *Arbeit und Volksleben. Deutscher Volkskundekongress 1965 in Marburg* (Göttingen: Otto Schwartz, 1967): 292–302 notes that men and women traditionally tell different stories and jokes. The topics they can speak about are distinct. See Roy Miller, *Japanese Language* (Chicago: University of Chicago Press, 1967): 289. They use different systems of reference and of address, as Roy Miller points out in "Levels of Speech (*keigo*) and the Japanese Linguistic Response to Modernization," *Tradition and Modernization in Japanese Culture*, ed. Donald H. Shively (Princeton, NJ: Princeton Uni-versity Press, 1971): 661–67. A complicated line of demarcation contrasts male and female speech, involving different sentence final particles (fem. wa; m. za, ya). Women use the honorific o- before words that do not demand an honorific reference from men; for example, women say *o-mizu* for water. Some words referring to the same thing have etymologi-cally unconnected forms: delicious is *oishi* for women and *umai* for men. See J.F. Sherzer and R. Bauman, eds., *Exploration in the Ethnography of Speaking* (New York: Cambridge University Press, 1975).

99 S. Harding, "Women and Words in a Spanish Village," in R. Reiter, ed. (*op. cit.* FN 22) describes some characteristic strategies used by women in a Spanish village to penetrate the otherwise separate conversation of men.

ginal features, we can now only guess. In one Madagascar vernacular, men's language is considered prestigious precisely because it is indirect and avoids confrontation.[100] For a man to be considered a skillful speaker in that culture, he must use an allusive, formal style. What to a white New Yorker would sound like vacillating and spineless fuzziness, to the Merina sounds like dignified male speech. In this society, women are the marketers. They haggle aggressively, shout at children, keep everyone in their place by broadcasting their disgraceful behavior. Women are respected when, impulsively and angrily, they blurt out what they have to say. Feminine and masculine language can reveal the intricacies of relative gender dominance even better than the study of tools.[101]

100 Elionor Keenan, "Norm Makers, Norm Breakers: Use of Speech by Men and Women in a Malagasy Community," Joel Sherzer and Richard Bauman (*op. cit.*, pp. 125–43, FN 98).

101 Chapter 17 of Otto Jespersen, *The Philosophy of Grammar* (New York: Norton, 1965; orig. 1924): 224–26 suggests the use of the terms "feminine/masculine" to refer to gender (the grammatical classification of nouns), and "female/male" to refer to the sex of the object designated by the noun. A difficulty arises because (1) the grammatical gender (he/she/it) to which Jespersen refers, (2) the social gender (ambiguous complementarity that constitutes the main theme of this book, (3) social sex that results from the institutional polarization of homogenous human characteristics under assumptions of scarcity, and (4) genital or anatomic morphology are four classificatory notions with only a tenuous and often questionable connection. In the opening paragraphs of this book, I stated that anthropological (social) gender was the subject I wanted to name, to explore, and to distinguish from the social construct of (economic) sex. I now argue that the transition from the reign of gender to the regime of sex is reflected in ordinary speech. I propose that we refer to the complementary domains of vernacular speech by talking about *feminine* and *masculine* speech styles, and to the polarized divergence from the norm of a standardized (normed, written, advertized) language (taught mother tongue) by talking about *female* and *male* language. I insist on the distinction between gendered speech and sexed language. Gendered speech constantly breathes, whispers, and utters gendered duality (FNs 12, 56, 57), while sexed language imposes discrimination. Grammatical gender (genus), therefore, becomes in sexed language what it could not be in gendered speech: a constant device for a put-down. Two books that can be taken together as introductions to the literature on nominal classification

Gender Domains and Vernacular Milieu

Feminine and masculine features of language are its most tender and vulnerable aspects, even while the language is still very much alive. In the past, these features seem particularly to have been abandoned when a language became the instrument of empire, when it became a trade language, a language of administration that had to fit areas with very different gender divides. The feminine and masculine traits are the first to be threatened when language is standardized, and what tends to remain is mere grammatical gender, out of touch with old dualities and now mainly useful for discriminatory speech. When vernacular speech is destroyed by absorption into a taught national mother tongue, its linguistic duality is reduced merely to different patterns, intonations, and topics, and to male dominance in grammatical gender. Such has been the case wherever this process has been studied and wherever vernacular gender has been extinguished by the cash nexus, and vernacular speech by aphabetization, schooling, and TV. Formerly, Koasati was spoken (in southwestern Louisiana) with delicate and clear differences between feminine and masculine language.[102] But after World War II, only the elderly made the distinction, insisting that women's speech was attractive because it was easy, slow, and soft. Today, women use men's forms. Women's forms still survive as an oddity, only when women of the past are quoted in direct speech. The shift to male dominance—as in the new unisex "medium of communication," so perfectly adapted to industrial life-styles—has thus been observed, no matter how many grammatical "genders" the language possesses.

---

are Gerlach Royen, *Die nominalen Klassifikationssysteme in den Sprachen der Erde: historisch-kiritische Studie, mit besonderer Berücksichtigung des Indogermanischen.* (Linguistische Anthropos Bibliothek 4, Wien, 1930), which was critically reviewed by C.C. Uhlenbeck in *The International Journal of American Linguistics* 7, nos. 1–2 (1932): 94–96, and Götz Wienold, *Genus und Semantik* (Knonberg: Hain, Anton, Meisenheim, 1967), who analyzes the ambiguous position that places grammatical gender on the borderline between syntax and semantics. An admirable model of the approach needed to study complementary speech is Y. Verdier (*op. cit.* FN 79).

102 Mary R. Haas, "Men's and Women's Speech in Koasati," *Language* 20, no. 3 (1944): 141–49.

VI. Gender
Through Time

Culture evolves just as language does; it implies a *sui generis* evolution. If the term "culture" has any one meaning for all anthropologists, it says at least this.[108] There exists some form of behavior that is free from genetic programming, and that is not totally determined by instinct. Culture bespeaks a level of life that cannot be rendered in biological terms; genetic endowment and cultural heritage evolve according to opposite laws. Natural selection operates upon undirected variation that leads into genetic divergence; cultural evolution passes to the next generation traits that the present one has shaped. Biological evolution sprouts new branches that do not cross-fertilize, branches that never again unite once they have become solid. Culture evolves along another route; its form is anastomosis: Like a river, its waters divide, meander, and reunite. Biological evolution remains engraved; culture implies the memory of things past, which survive only in myth or history or custom.

103 ANASTOMOSIS

Such labels as "Lamarckian," "Darwinian," and "Mendelian" have become as useless as "Protestant" or "Marxist." I therefore avoid them when I speak about the transformation within vernacular culture that results from the changing configuration of the threshold between genders, and of the spime over which their complementary domains extend. On the difficulties of relating biological and cultural change, see Stephen Jay Gould, "The Ghost of Protagoras: A Review of *The Evolution of Culture in Animals*, by John Tyler Bonner, and *Man, the Promising Primate*, by Peter J. Wilson," *New York Review of Books* (January 22, 1981): 42–44. On the

At the Mexican National Museum there is a beautiful chart of such a river system, a river of *malacates*. Malacates are round, ceramic spindle-weights with a hole for the shaft in their middle; Mexican plows dig them up by the thousands each year, and they belong to different millennia. At the museum, an archaeologist has arranged these spindle weights into a circular system of rivers: Starting out from distant, archaic, and very different shapes, the *malacates* adapt, absorb each other's features, become more ornate and also more specialized. For centuries in some regions the *malacate* seems unchanged, and then suddenly it acquires a mestizo face by incorporating features characteristic of a distant valley. I like to stand in front of this chart and wonder who it was, man or woman, who contributed the new feature.[104]

In some cases, perhaps the change was a chance invention. The new notch in the spindle-weight resulted from an acccident that then proved practical. But, more probably, a stranger from the lowland passed through and left his *malacate*. Or a slave was captured, along with his different *malacate*. The new notch from the foreign model was seen, tested, and adopted. And so, the weight of the spindle changed. The hand that held and turned the shaft learned a new movement to which the other hand responded with a new twist of the yarn. A new motion in one hand necessitates a new response in the other. Knowing that the tools in such cultures fit the hands of only one gender, what is called "cultural change" always occurs first in one domain; a corresponding response then takes place in the other. As in a dance, so in cultural evolution: One always leads and the other follows, sometimes with a nod, sometimes with a change.

Millennia ago, on the southern slope of the Sierra Madre, a new corn began to be grown, the first kernels of which must have arrived from far away. The new corn was blue, and it produced

history and legitimacy of the term anastomosis, see the corresponding article in the *Trésor de la Langue Française* (Paris: CNRS, 1976). I found useful on the historiography of "Lamarck-ism" H. Graham Cannon, *Lamarck and Modern Genetics* (Manchester, Engl.: Greenwood, 1975).

104 A reproduction of such a meandering and looping, unfolding and ripening of plastic Mexican forms is in Eduardo Noguera, *La ceramica arqueológica de Mesoamerica* (Mexico City: UNAM, Instituto de Investigaciones Anthropologicas, 1975).

much more than the old variety. It had to be buried deeper in the ground, and the planting stick changed hands, from women to men. But the new grain, protected by a new god, also demanded a new *mecate*, a larger volcanic stone on which the women could grind it. Cultural anthropology, on the basis of data already gathered, could tell us much more about technical and cultural evolution if gender accommodation were taken into account.

Gender and Transgression

Over long time periods, the line dividing the two genders can change its course, and under certain conditions may or even must be transgressed. This fact clearly distinguishes gender infringement from animals' deviations from their sex-determined behavior. But at this point in my argument there is a distinction more important than that between animal sex and social gender: the difference between gender encroachment and the fading of the gender line itself. This disappearance of gender, *the* characteristic anthropological feature of industrial cultures, must be carefully differentiated from the transgression or infraction of gender.

Violation of the gender divide becomes clearly visible as tools change hands over various time intervals. But we can only speculate on many of the factors provoking such changes in the contours of gender. Certainly they are often the result of technological discovery: A tool or trait that had earlier been foreign but not tabooed became "gendered." For example, the donkey was an animal unknown to ancient Mexican cultures until it arrived in the company of the Spaniards. Its care could not have been restricted to either men or women; nor was it taboo—no rule forbade either to touch it. Quite rapidly, then, in the mountains of Guerrero, the activities associated with the care and use of donkeys became the responsibility of men, and thus the animal acquired a social male gender among the Indians, and was culturally discovered. Cultural discovery, often called technological change, outside industrial society has always been a process of gender-related gentling. Inevitably, the donkey was more than a change of equipment for men. Its use expanded the territorial province of one gender, introduced a new asymmetry between men's and women's domains, and, arguably, lightened women's work while diminishing their public status.

For these early Mexicans, the donkey was something very surprising but not taboo. I would reserve the term "taboo" for a prohibition that affects *both* genders, however differently, and by its absolute "No!" keeps the two genders within their *gens*. "Of every tree of the garden thou mayest freely eat. But of the tree of knowledge of good and evil, thou shalt not eat of it, for in the day that thou eatest thereof thou shalt surely die." (Genesis 2:16-17). The violation of a taboo entails frightful consequences for the entire community; extraordinary sacrifice and redemption are called for. Ideally, overstepping the gender divide is not a taboo. To distinguish this from taboo, I would call it *pané*. Gender informs Guayaki men, "Thou shalt not touch a basket; *that* is women's domain." What for her is appropriately gendered is *pané* for him.

Both *taboo* and *pané* designate a prohibition, but what they respectively forbid lies in different arenas. Taboo threatens the gendered duo from the outside; it makes the men and women of a *gens* speak together in the first person plural, "we." *Pané* bespeaks the other side of the moon, the other half of the world, that other, muted part of our reality I can know about only through its reflection in the opposite gender's words, looks, and actions.

In all times and places we find evidence that, without change in its contour or its magnitude, the barrier between genders has been trespassed. Public misfortune is often a cause for such a breach. During the Middle Ages, the heavy-wheeled plow drawn by a shod and harnessed horse was almost the symbol of male gender. Women would not dare to approach either the tool or the animal. But we find several late fourteenth-century miniatures from northern France depicting women handling the plow. The plague had decimated the population, and war had carried off most of the surviving men. Women had to work the fields until their boys became adults.[105]

105 DISREGARD FOR GENDER IN CALAMITY

That men do women's work and women men's is noted in many medieval chronicles as one of the key symptoms of cataclysmic disaster. It ranks

Not only public calamity but private misfortune too can induce an individual to neglect proprieties and take up work normally done by the other gender. Until recently, the cowshed was inaccessible to men in northern Sweden. It was a warm place where unmarried women lived and slept with the cattle, and women were certain to be among themselves during the long winter season. Daughterless widowers were, however, sometimes observed slipping into the shed to milk the cow, something they would never have done, while in public view. Occasional emergencies can also result in infringements. When haying is threatened by an approaching storm in a Tyrolean mountain meadow, the farmer and his sons may lend a hand to the women gathering the hay. But they could never demand this of a hired man. It seems that high status within a community brought with it more freedom to step beyond proprieties. But exceptions only confirm the general rule; they have been chronicled because they were considered noteworthy, and now they make up a privileged source for the study of gender.

Paradoxically, transvestism also functions to confirm the gender divide and to inform the historian. Spontaneous group violations of gender-related strictures are rare and have always been

---

with reports that survivors have had to eat cats, dogs, rats, and roots, and that man has turned on man as if he were a wolf. The collapse of the gender line, the transformation of inedibles into food, and the emergence of economic individualism, taken together, are manifestations of social breakdown and the appearance of the regime of scarcity. Raymond Firth, *Social Change in Tikopia* (New York: Macmillan 1959) has observed such a breakdown. In our century, famine on a Pacific island first strengthened social ties of solidarity between households. The general rules that govern primitive cultures observed by Chayanov and more recently by Marshall Sahlins, *Stone Age Economics* (Chicago: Aldine, 1972) remained intact: *Dirth*, in contrast to scarcity (see FN 11), re-enforces social ties and the rule that food can only be shared, never exchanged. In the first stage of famine, households rival one another more than what was deemed usual in generosity. In a second stage, the first signs of hypocrisy appear: Families begin to hoard, to share only with their own. When sharing ceases among family members, they cease to be part of their vernacular culture: The invidious individual *Homo oeconomicus* has come into being. Up to this third stage the *waiver of gender* is transitory; beyond it, sex encroaches on gender.

experienced as something frightening. During peasant wars, nothing would terrorize the nobility more than a wild crowd of women who had taken up arms. In some instances, men dressed up in skirts for battle and routed the enemy army without even having to resort to arms.[106]

Almost everywhere transvestism is ritualized into a seasonal participatory event. Carnivals from Sicily to Scandinavia have throughout the ages demanded that women play men, men play women, and men play women who play men. It has been argued that such "travesties" were occasionally used to inflame political passion. Especially during the eighteenth century, in fact, these traditional reversals became the occasion for ridiculing the "process of civilization" resented by the crowd; they became a tactic for resisting the teacher and the cleric. Satire and comedy freely utilized such gender violations. Recent studies on the cultural features of laughter, fairs, mummery, and riots rightly highlight the political uses to which travesty has been put in protecting the moral economy, the gendered existence of the crowds.[107] These

106 INTRUSION INTO THE OTHER DOMAIN

For examples, see the literature to FN 70. These individual transgressions, under the pressure of material necessity, must be distinguished from the neglect of gendered duty that is punished by "rough music" (FN 80) and from status-specific "deviance" of the gender line. In some places and times, riding with men makes a woman a lady. I want to note here that the ease with which one can occasionally violate the gender line seems to change with social status (see FN 72).

107 POLITICAL DEFIANCE OF THE GENDER LINE

Defiance is always a "political" act. Unlike the individual's *loss* of gender, e.g., the punishment that deprives the Guayaki of his gender, Clastres (*op. cit.* FN 69); unlike the *waver* of gender under the duress of war, famine, or plague; unlike the *breakdown* of gender that coincides with a culture's disappearance (FN 105); and unlike the occasional *invasion* of the opposite domain (FN 106); I classify as *political* those instances of infraction that constitute a symbolic attack on the established order. These acts of political defiance can be divided into three categories, each of which serves only as an ideal type. First (1) is the defiance of the other gender, by which Bemba women collectively leave their huts and infants in men's care, to bring the men back to their senses (see Richards, FN 68), or, under conditions of patriarchy, innumerable instances in which women

gender turnarounds also served to lampoon, thus keeping in check the relative domination of one gender: Putting women occasionally, publicly, and festively on top was a way of ridiculing men without seriously undermining their dominance. Inversely, in a Mexican village that is still today riddled by the fear of witches, the dance of men in drag as hags pursuing pre-adolescent boys dressed up as coyotes triggers an annual day-long celebration of laughter, putting simmering anguish in its proper place.[108]

But travesty has an even deeper function. In almost every culture we find that certain priests must dress as women, certain magical acts are connected with sodomitical rites, the pilloried are attired as the opposite sex, the culture hero must risk *pané*. The function of this pattern is to keep the gender divide crystal clear by reversing the public perspective on its outline. Magically, it may serve to surprise the guardian demons, keeping them satisfied and at bay. Ultimately, it reflects the rootedness of gender in the deepest mystical experiences.

---

imitate, lampoon, and shame men to redress a power imbalance. Good examples are found in Natalie Zemon Davis, *Society and Culture in Early Modern France* (Palo Alto, CA: Stanford University Press, 1975), especially chapter 5, "Women on Top," pp. 124–50. Second (2) is the act of ridiculing the invasion of bourgeois civilization into local culture. We see here a political use of travesty that occurs during the early period of capitalist development when the newly industrialized crowd, both men and women, attempt to defend their gendered economy by various forms of symbolic protest. Here the caricature and mockery of upper-class gentlemen and ladies, and of those who imitate them, can be interpreted as a plebeian defense of the moral economy. A third type (3) of political transgression is directed not against the gender line but against the division of the sexes. Pornography, at least since De Sade, and much of gay and feminist ceremonial behavior, seem to fit this category of travesty. Carnival and their dual travesty served until quite recently as a periodic insistence on the gulf between the moral economy of the people and the invasive commercial economy. An example from our time is Gerald Sider, "Christmas Mumming and the New Year in Outport, Newfoundland," *Past and Present* 71 (May 1976): 102–25.

108 MOCKING SANCTIONS

The study of travesty in the carnival is an excellent way to observe how the gender line is kept *intact* through ritual mockery. Jokes, sayings, proverbs, and riddles tend to serve the same function.

The Rise of the Heterosexual

Modern sexology clouds the historian's perspective on traditional travesty. Its categories are primarily sex-, not gender-, oriented.[109] This appears most clearly in the language used for sodomy. Only a limited number of societies have terms to classify their members on the basis of the gender to which they are *erotically* attracted. Among these, the particular style in which modern European societies stress this classification is unique. The fact that lovemaking among men or among women was more or less frequent in some places and times does not permit the historians to draw the conclusion that all societies have recognized "the homosexual" as a special kind of being. Before the European Renaissance, a person could not think of himself as a homosexual any more than as an author; he preferred boys to women, or he

109 THE LANGUAGE OF TRAVESTY

Modern language amalgamates gender and sex (see FN 7). Such language envisions genderless humans with genderless libidos that, in the course of their lives, take one of several characteristic forms. In this new language, we talk about the *transsexual,* an individual who believes himself to be miscast in the body with which he was born; or the *transvestite,* an individual who derives sexual satisfaction from dressing and/or behaving like a member of the opposite sex. The language lets us speak of a trend toward *unisex* behavioral patterns that are often adopted to mask unconscious male or female sexist fantasies. A history of transgression, which must describe the ideal types mentioned in FNs 105–108, is generally written from the perspective of the social sexologist; the available language makes his genderless language seem "natural." But such an outlook necessarily distorts the reality and meaning of the documents it attempts to interpret. For a survey of the largely confusing literature, see Vern Bullough, et al., *An Annotated Bibliography of Homosexuality,* 2 vols. (New York: Garland, 1976), esp. vol. 1, pp. 37–67 (on history) and vol. 2, pp. 351–84 (on transvestism and transsexualism), and Vern L. Bullough, "Transvestites in the Middle Ages," *The American Journal of Sociology* 79, no. 6 (1974): 1381–94. For the female transvestite in the Christian tradition, see John Anson, "The Female Transvestite in Early Monasticism: The Origin and Development of a Motive," *Viator* 5 (1974): 1–32; Marie Delcourt, "Le complexe de Diane dans l'hagiographie chrétienne," *Revue de l'Histoire des Religions* 153 (1958): 1–33; Marina Warner, *Joan of Arc* (New York: Knopf, 1981).

was skilled at writing verse. A man could be addicted to buggery much as he could have a violent temper. His contemporaries might refer to him as a bugger or a killer, but neither designation had the *diagnostic* power of the modern term. A man's making love to men did not make him intrinsically "other." Homosexual acts were recognized and each culture had its own way to appraise them— as child's play, as ritual inversion, as punishment for the Guayaki who had touched a woman's basket, as a vice to be ridiculed or to be violently repressed. As a special identity, the homosexual could not be imagined under the rule of gender. The Modern European deviant is as singular as the heterosexual conjugal partner.

Recently, two major studies have examined the history of homosexuality as a socially perceived propensity, as distinguished from the history of homosexual behavior. D.S. Baily shows that homosexuality as a sexual disorientation characteristic of some people but not of others went unremarked in pre-scholastic Christian tradition. Legislators, theologians, and moralists were concerned with venereal practices between people of the same sex and, following Paul the Apostle, execrated groups in which these practices were flaunted. John Boswell has critically sifted through and collected ample material for us to follow the establishment of homosexuals as a group endowed with a deviant nature.[110] It

110 THE HISTORY OF THE HETEROSEXUAL

The *homosexual* is in the *OED*, the *heterosexual* only in its supplements. Both terms are first mentioned in 1890. In 1957 the Wolfenden Report to the British Parliament drew a clear distinction between homosexuality as a propensity and homosexuality as a behavior. Both meanings have a history in Western societies, and were carefully distinguished for the first time by D.S. Baily, *Homosexuality and the Christian Western Tradition* (London: Longmans, 1955). In the interest of accuracy and clarity, Baily tried to coin "homosexualism" to designate the activity, and "homosexuality" the deviant constitution. The historical discovery of the homosexual as a special kind of human has recently been recounted by John Boswell, *Christianity, Social Tolerance and Homosexuality: Gay People in Western Europe from the Beginning of the Christian Era to the Fourteenth Century* (Chicago: University of Chicago Press, 1979). For a critical response to his thesis, see J.D. Adams, *Speculum* 56, no. 2 (1981): 350–55; Peter Linehan, *The Times Literary Supplement* (January 23, 1981): 73; Keith Thomas, *The New York Review of Books* (December 4, 1980): 26–29. On the history of the perception of some women as *lesbians*, see Lillian Faderman,

seems obvious that the new kind of constitutional deviance required the simultaneous emergence of the heterosexual norm on
which human consecration to conjugal production is based. But
so far no parallel history of "the heterosexual" has been written.
"The homosexual" must serve, therefore, as the mirror to trace
the conquest of the West by the heterosexual regime.

I can only suggest, here in these pages, the complex connection between the Church and the conversion of gender into sex.
The encounter between Arnaud, the subdeacon, and the inquisitor
of Montaillou can serve as our point of departure. Their discussion of the sodomy of which Arnaud stands accused brings out
two sharply etched divergent positions. Arnaud perceives the action in the perspective of gender; the inquisitor, from the nascent
outlook of *unnatural* sex.[111] The ecclesiastic's attempt to treat

---

*Surpassing the Love of Men: Romantic Friendship and Love Between
Women from the Renaissance to the Present* (New York: Morrow, 1981),
esp. the bibliography, pp. 417–80. Carrol Smith-Rosenberg, *"The Female
World of Love and Ritual: Relations Between Women in Nineteenth-
Century America," A Heritage of Her Own*, ed. N. Cott and E. Pleck (New
York: Simon and Schuster, 1979): 311–42 speculates that bodily contact
among American women crystallized into an aberrant kind of sexual activity
only at the turn of the current century. See also *Frontiers: A Journal of
Women's Studies* 4, no. 3 (1979), a special issue on lesbian history.
Parallel to the history of the emergence, constitution and destiny of the
explicitly *deviant*, marked for exclusion, a history of the *normal human*, the
heterosexual, is now needed. Without insight into the conceptual ortho-
pedics involved in his/her social construction, the *economic* character of
conjugal marriage and of our production-oriented society will not be
understood.

111 SODOMY AND HERESY

In the shift of "sodomy" from the category of *sin* against God or of *crime*
among men toward that of *heresy* (the breaking away from the body of the
Church), a new attitude toward deviance became visible. Up to this time,
heresy had simply meant the public denial of a doctrine formulated by the
Church, or a refusal to perform ritual acts prescribed by the Church. Not
infrequently, the term was confused with schism, the administrative sep-
aration from Rome. Heresy was directly opposed to orthodoxy, correct
faith or belief. Then heresy began to mean behavior contrary to ortho-
praxis, deviance from Church-standardized behavior. Henceforth, then,
any Christian who followed his traditional vernacular customs could be
accused of heresy, if these contradicted the behavioral norms of the

the sodomite as a heretic leaves the cleric baffled. He expresses his bewilderment in evident good faith: "I thought . . . in the simplicity of my heart that sodomy and ordinary fornication were indeed mortal sins, but much less serious than the deflowering of virgins, adultery, or incest." This Arnaud was of noble and urbane origin. He was sophisticated and literate in a worldly sense. At a time when it was extremely rare to own a book, he loaned books to others. Among the volumes he handled, one finds not only Bibles and calendars but also classics, among them a work by Ovid, an author transmitting detailed classical knowledge in the theory and practice of dalliance in lovemaking, which for a millennium the Church inveighed against. And, although Arnaud had never been ordained to the priesthood, he carried out his clerical duties with evident devotion. His confused responses still reflect a gendered point of view. Sodomy—interpreted as deviance by the inquisitor, the future Pope Benedict XII—remained beyond his grasp. For him, buggery was and remained just one of several ways of curing lust.

The history of the English word "bugger" illustrates the conflict. Originally, bugger was an ecclesiological term, a reference to Bulgarians who became Christians in the ninth century. They joined the Church of Constantinople, at that time separated from the Pope. Later, the term was transferred from these "separated" Christians to the Bogumils, a Gnostic sect that spread from Thrace through Bulgaria and into the Balkans, leaving its traces in the form of huge but simple sarcophagi. Coined for administratively separated Christians, the word now designated a foreign, non-Christian group. Three hundred years later, it was then shifted to the Bogumils' cousins, the Gnostic converts around Albi in southern France. These people, native to the heartland of

Church. On this transformation of heresy, see the report on a conference: "Sénéfiance 5," *Exclus et systèmes d'exclusion dans la littérature et la civilisation médiévales* (Aix-en-Provence: CUERMA; Paris: Champion, 1978) and V. Branca, *Studi sulle eresie del secolo XII* (Rome: Studi Storici 5, seconda ed accresciuta edizione, 1975): 293–327. On the current status of research on the participation of women in twelfth-century heresy, see Richard Abels and Ellen Harrison, "The Participation of Women in Languedocian Catharism," *Medieval Studies* 41 (1979): 215–251.

Christendom, were settled on the northern slope of the Pyrenees, Europe's bulwark against Islam. Among them, one household after another was attracted by the spirit of Gnosticism; the faith, rituals, and customs of these households were now called, indifferently, "heresy" or "buggery."

At this precise time, the Church had good reason to fear the spread of a spiritual adversary. Only during the centuries immediately preceding had the Church equipped itself with the doctrine, the personnel, the organization, and methods necessary for the *pastoral* care of households made up of individual souls. The permutation of churches from places of public worship and instruction into agencies for individualized care had begun under Charlemagne and was now perfected. One key element of this pastoral care was the cultivation and regulation of gendered, *conjugal* households. We forget that it was only during the High Middle Ages that matrimony slowly came to be considered a sacrament and thus a matter of ecclesiastical regulation. And this produced innumerable conflicts between the old vernacular and the new Catholic models of gender. The Church's pastoral care weakened the hold of local, self-limiting gender, while creating a mood of resistance against the clerical normalization of a *catholic* gender. The time was propitious for the spread of a "heresy" that could offer the villager a "Catholic" belief without a managerial imposition of gender-specific controls from Rome.[112]

112 CARE: PROFESSIONAL AND CLERICAL

Care is an insidious key word for a characteristically Western thing. John McKnight calls it the "mask of love." I have argued (in an article published in New York, summer 1982) that, precisely in the theological sense of "Christian charity" as an unprecedented ideal, its institutionalized corruption into "care" is historically unique. A commodity-intensive society is, above all, care-intensive. As such a society "develops," most of the individuals who make it up justify their existence by producing care. The fellow-citizen is needed mainly as an object of the care over which care providers have established a radical monopoly (FN 9). The need for care in such a society becomes the foundation of disabling professions (FN 60), and for the self-conscious partnerly "help" (FN 127) on which the modern family is built. Care is the ersatz of love and of hatred under the regime of sex. Care is a name for the pretense of genderless "love." I propose to call the producer of care the *curate*. The term was coined in the High Middle Ages to designate the caretaker of souls. The curate appears

The object of the fourteenth-century crusade against heretics in Languedoc was the network of households around Albi, which embraced attractive, *locally* ruled heterodox beliefs. "Cathar" households were perceived as forming infectious cancers within the body of the Church. The inquisition pried into the household to find out if the poison had spread throughout the channels of kinship from a related *domus*. Up until this time, members of vernacular-gendered households had come to the Church; now the Church moved in the opposite direction, overstepping the house's threshold. The deviant individual became the object of inquisitorial diagnosis and care. Within the heretical household, the theologian sniffed out the bugger, the person smelling of heresy. In this context, the term "bugger" was used in a doubly new way: It imputed a warped nature rather than mere criminal behavior, a monstrosity rather than nature's sinful enjoyment outside the bounds set by God.

The medieval shift from orthodox faith to Catholic behavior, the conversion of priests from men deputed to liturgical service

---

in the Western Church during the Carolingian reform; see Maria Bidlingmaier, *"Alkuin zwischen Antike und Mittelalter," *Zeitschrift für Katholische Theologie* 81 (1959): 306–50, 405–53. The priest never became a curate in the Christian East. There his central task remained the celebration of the Eucharist, not the administration of the sacraments. During the early Middle Ages the Western curate was still busy with blessings: A. Franz, *Die Kirchlichen Benediktionen im Mittelalter*, 2 vols. (Freiburg: 1909); H. Reifenberg, *Sakramente, Sakramentalien und Ritualien im Bistum Mainz seit dem Spätmittelalter: Unter besonderer Berücksichtigung der Diozösen Würzburg und Bamberg* (Münster: 1971–72). The evolution of sacramental theology (a theological technology), which set in with the eleventh century, runs parallel to the evolution of a positive attitude toward other new techniques; both these trends the Eastern Church resisted. For instance, in the West, incredibly complex new machines—the pipe organ in the church and the clock on the steeple—became symbolic of the new, curate-run Church; the East banned both. See Lynn White, Jr., *"Cultural Climates and Technological Advances in the Middle Ages," *Viator* 2 (1971): 171–201. Ernst Benz, "I fondamenti cristiani della Tecnica Occidentale" in *Tecnica, Escatologia e Casistica* makes a similar point. Western care designated canonically administered love under the regime of technique. On the transformation of attitudes toward technique in the second quarter of the twelfth century, see I. Illich, "Research by People," *Shadow Work* (*op. cit.*, pp. 75ff, FN 1).

into pastors and confessors of a flock standardized the two *sexes*, supported the new identification of sexual buggery with theological heresy. For the pastor, now represented by the image of the celibate cock on the steeple, watching over a flock that included two sexes, the bugger was the unredeemable enemy who had eventually to be burned.

The *plebanus* looking down from the steeple upon his people, the sheep entrusted to his care, is the prototype of the service professional. He is in charge of souls and equipped with the language to read their consciences. All the souls under his responsibility, he is taught, are of equal dignity and possess consciences to be examined and formed.

The inquisitorial bishop from Avignon speaks for the Church, for a new and rising Church that, later secularized and split, would take form in the contemporary professional establishment. He belongs to the Church that made over the ritual of penance into the yearly act of confession, a Church that only recently—as of the Lateran Council of 1215—had imposed on all her faithful the duty of telling their sins once a year to their own parish priest. This new law had been introduced with an original formula reflecting a novel perspective, the homogenizing perspective of sex: *Omnes utriusque sexus fideles*—all the faithful, men as well as women, are henceforth held to speak every year to their appointed pastor and reveal their sins. To enable the pastor to listen to these confessions, a new literature had come into being during the preceding century, a literature that had not yet fully washed Arnaud. Manuals advised the confessor on the sorts of questions to ask the faithful. Increasingly, the new manuals defined what this transgression meant for humans in general, independent of and sometimes contradictory to the local gender line. By restricting power, privilege, and ordination to men, Church law was not sexist; it simply reflected its sources. Church law *did* pioneer sexism by ruling on the consciences of equally immortal souls capable of committing the same sin with different bodies. By equating, in terms of sin, the transgressions of the same law by both men and women, it laid the foundation for sexist codes.

The compulsory confession of sins in the intimacy of the confessional was something radically new, the first and by far the most effective step toward the acceptance of written law and uni-

GENDER

versal education. It was almost the inverse of the public penance imposed as an irksome, prolonged ritual, frequently carried out in front of the church, that the Irish and Scotch were taught to practice at the time of their conversion during the early Middle Ages. The old penitential order was men's affair. It expressed the public and voluntary submission of recent converts to the new laws of the missionary. Ranulf had killed the murderer of his stepfather. He had done what it behooves a son to do; not to have taken vengeance would have been unforgivable under the old rules of the clan. But under the new rule of Christ, he ought to have forgiven. Ranulf stood for seventeen years outside the church door, in the heat of summer and the ice of winter. The new confessional order relocated penance from the outer into inner space; it compelled each "soul" to create this new space within itself, and to create it according to architectural rules laid down in Church law. Unlike public penance, done *once* over a period of years for a life's outstanding crime, confession meant a yearly accounting of secret transgressions against laws formulated by a catholic, that is, universal institution, Mother Church.[113] Confession creates an "inter-

1 1 3 A L M A M A T E R

The professional claim on monopolizing care (FN 112) went hand in hand with the development of a new definition for the care-providing institutions: Mother Church (*Alma*, i.e., breast-milk-dripping, *Mater*). The notion of one universal institution at whose breast all those who want to be saved must drink is of early Christian origin. It first appears in the writings of Marcion the Gnostic around A.D. 155. However, there is no influence of gnostic imagery or of pagan divinities in the formation of this concept: Joseph C. Plumpe, *Mater Ecclesia: An Inquiry into the Concept of the Church as Mother in Early Christianity* (Washington, D.C.: Catholic University of America Press, 1943). Neither does there seem to be a relation to the Roman imperial mater cult (*Ibid.*, pp. 9–14, 28–32). The Roman Church originally resisted identification with the mater image. Not the Church but Christian love was defined as motherly, as a love that engenders new life. However, by the late third and fourth centuries, patristic literature began to teem with references to the Church as a mother: She is *fecunda, concipit, generat, parturit*, has miscarriages, nourishes those she has borne at her breast, and experiences pleasure, exaltation, tears, sadness, and sighs in doing so. From her breasts Christians drink the milk of faith. In the fifth century, bishops assumed the function of "educatio prolis," the upbringing of Christians—designating their own function by "educatio," a term that in classical Latin calls for a female subject. See

nal forum." Once a year, the sinner opens the intimate chamber
of his soul to a public, Church-appointed judge who, in absolute
secrecy, listens to the culprit's self-diagnosis. The consecrated male,
the priestly judge, listens each year to a genderless soul, measuring
its transgressions of a written law that defines gendered behavior.
The example of adultery illustrates what occurred. In every
kinship system, fornication means something different; for the
woman it is always a different kind of crime than for the man.
Now, the idea of transgression of Church law turned it into the
same sin. Men and women become equals in sin although, as
members of their respective genders, they committed different
crimes. Sexuality, as a genderless concept, took its first definition
as the set of Church-defined sins against the Sixth Command-
ment: Though shalt not commit adultery. Observing this process,
it would be a mistake to confuse the new ability of the soul to
apply Church decrees to this intimate forum with the sense of
propriety and probity (*honnêteté*) that kept the gender divide
intact. Conscience was refined by the interiorization of a positive
law for *the human*, while probity was the result of growth into
gender. Conscience is the result of education; gender, the result
of education's inverse. Starting in the thirteenth century, the

also Sebastian Tromp, "Ecclesia sponsa, virgo, mater," in *Gregorianum* 18
(1937): 3–29. For the further development of the image, see Karl Dela-
haye, *Ecclesia Mater chez les Pères des trois premiers siècles* (Paris:
Cerf, 1964). In the introduction to this book, Yves Congar refers to the
change in the use of the mother image during the early Middle Ages. The
term is no longer applied to the life-giving characteristics of mutual Christian love, but is now primarily used to justify juridically the authority of
the institutional Church when it controls the fountainheads of life. The
curate is the guardian of the Church's breasts; the Church thus becomes
the model for a social institution pictured as a female whose favors are
monopolized by clerical mediation. No doubt mother goddesses in most
cultures are found symbolized by statues, caves, mountains, and wells.
No doubt the definition of man-as-waif is characteristically Greek: E.
Poehlmann, "Der Mensch—das Mängelwesen? Zum Nachwirken antiker
Anthropologie bei Arnold Gehlen," *Archiv für Kulturgeschichte* 52
(1970): 297–312. Classical antiquity described nature as a stepmother
forced by her stinginess to adopt culture. But the correlation between the
care-providing professional and the service institution in terms of lactation
corresponds to the Westernization of European culture (FN 5).

speculum confessoris developed: By this tool the confessor could probe the penitent's soul, ask the right questions. Through the correct annual responses, the reign of vernacular probity was progressively overshadowed by the dictates of conscience. And while for a millennium women had been muted in a Church ruled by men, they now became equal penitents speaking in a muffled voice to the curate of a sexist regime. Unisex law made co-habitation sexist: It ruled first that adultery makes man and woman equal as sinners, but that even in sin his natural place is on top. The documents that attempt to regulate, by Church rule, frequency, circumstances, and positions of intercourse[114] are in stark contrast with the tradition of Ovid's *ars amatoria* that, ac-

1 1 4   S I N

The sacrament of penance administered in the guise of an obligatory, yearly, secret confession is one of the clear manifestations of the move toward a *caring* society. With the transition from public penance imposed for notorious crimes to the confession of secret sins, the Church obtained the power to regulate private behavior: Jean-Charles Payen, "La pénitence dans le contexte culturel du XIIe et XIIIe siècles," *Revue des Sciences Philosophiques et Théologiques* 61 (1977): 300 ff. This included the im-position of formally legislated rules on genital congress: its times, fre-quencies, circumstances, which up until then had been guided by local probity and constrained by inherited *pané* and taboo. This conflict between vernacular probity and Church law has been particularly well documented during the Christianization of Iceland. Here the missionaries arrived relatively late, when the Church's rules in the matter had already crystal-lized. The Latin text quoted above is from the Fourth Lateran Council, under Innocent III. The most learned and complete guide to the study of the replacement of penance by private confession is Herbert Vorgrimmler "Busse und Krankensalbung," 4, fasc. 3 in *Handbuch der Dogmengeschichte* (Freiburg, 1978), esp. pp. 89–112. The easiest access to the penitential books of the period is still J. Wasserschleben, *Die Bussordnung in der abendländischen Kirche* (Orig. 1851; reprint ed. Graz: Akademische Verlaganstalt, 1958). While liturgical prayers could continue to be recited in Latin, confession made the official use of vernacular language mandatory; see H. Eggers, "Die altdeutschen Beichten," *Beiträge zur Geschichte der deutschen Sprache und Literatur* 77 (Halle: Niemeyer, 1955): 89–123, and 81 (Halle: Niemeyer, 1959): 78–122. Also see Jenny M. Jochens, "The Church and Sexuality in Medieval Iceland," *Journal of Medieval History* 6 (1980): 377–92, and Elizabeth M. Makowski, "The Conjugal Debt and Medieval Canon Law," *Journal of Medieval History* 3 (1977) 99–114. The Church's efforts to teach each follower how to make his yearly confession can be understood both as a first attempt at universal,

cording to court records, Arnaud had lent to a colleague a few days before his trial. As the pastoral Church empowered its missionary clergy to penetrate into the house, the bed, and the soul, it repressed gender by the cultivation of a heterosexual marriage bond, and probity by the education of conscience.

The period between the twelfth and the late eighteenth century in central Europe could well be considered an epoch of probity under the growing shadow of conscience. As would be expected, with conscience penetrating societies formerly regulated by probity alone, the images of "man" and "woman" changed. One way of getting a glimpse of what happened is to study cultural types. Certainly, the lady to whom the troubadour offered his song was a new kind of being: his mistress. She was beyond marriage and kinship for the minstrel; she has been frequently studied, and at best she represents a kind of woman that only a minority could imagine. That this minority was not tiny is evidenced by the ability of some of the simple people of Montaillou to distinguish between women they had loved and those whom they had cherished (*adamari*). But the best proof for an entirely new devotion to *the* woman, which stands above gender and appeals to the most sublime forms of sex, is the spread of a new image of Mary.

The Iconography of Sex

Marina Warner has dipped into the enormous reservoir of images of just one other woman. By studying the pictures and attributes of Mary the Virgin she has tried to see how "woman" was viewed. Clearly, the Virgin during the later Middle Ages was no longer the "blessed *among* women"; she was now the "only one of her sex."

In the changing styles and tempers of her pictorial representations, I find, not only in the Middle Ages but throughout two

---

individual education and as a first attempt to provide each faithful with a yearly medical service, absolutely necessary for his and her soul's survival. The contemporary documents stress *medicina*. The Church's pioneering "medical" care changed the language used by physicians. See J. Agrimi and C. Crisciani, *Medicina del corpoe, medicina dell'anima: Note sul sapere del medico fino all'inizio del secolo XIII* (Milan: Episteme, 1978).

thousand years, a guide to follow the route from the Theotokos in the Greek apsis to the kitsch in a Catholic couple's bedroom. Never has Mary been represented without a strong emphasis on the flesh. From the earliest beginnings of her depiction in the catacombs of Priscilla to the thousands of Romanesque pictures that have been preserved, one thing makes her different from all other women who have been painted or sculpted: the artist's desire to represent an historical woman blessed with a destiny without par. She is the one woman chosen to be the virgin mother, to bear God. Since the fruit of her womb was the source of a new beginning among men, she was the new Eve. But this idea was no longer the most prominent in Gothic, much less later, portraits. Step by step, she became detached from gender and shed both the aura of myth that had been borrowed from the goddess and the series of strong theological epithets with which the Church fathers had adorned her. She turned into a model for "woman," into a type to challenge man, the conscience of genderless man.[115] The idea is clearly formulated by Dante in Canto 33 of the *Paradiso*, when he addresses the Virgin as *"umile ed alta piu che creatura. . . ."*

Stories can tell what history cannot describe; how the mother

Conscience here means the human guide and umpire internalized. As an ideal type, it is opposed to the gendered sense of vernacular probity (FN 82). What has been called the "process of civilization" builds on a process that could be called "conscientization." The term has been coined in Brazil to label a kind of political self-help adult education organized mostly by clergymen popularizing Marxist categories to help the poor discover that they are "humans" (FN 4). It could be used by the historian to describe an enterprise that was decisively shaped by the Church through the institutionalization of the sacrament of Penance in the twelfth century, an enterprise that since then has been followed by other techniques. I would call conscientization all professionally planned and administered rituals that have as their purpose the internalization of a religious or secular ideology. Conscientization consists of the colonization and standardization of vernacular probity and honor through some "catholic" (that is, universally human) set of institutional rules. I would argue that it constituted, during the early Middle Ages, a perversion of the original Christian idea or reform. Reform as the attempt to bring about a renewal of the world by means of one's own personal conversion was conceived by early Christians as the vocation that set them apart. On this, see Gerhart Ladner, *The Idea*

of God became Our Lady is such a tale. When she became the prototype of the "image of woman"—never a goddess, no longer an icon, not yet the sentimental pinup of baroque art—the other figures peopling the Romanesque cathedrals also began to go their own way. Many of these saints and monsters had come into the Church together with their own "nation" when it had been baptized, with their *"gens."* The furry guardians of local gender, upon arriving in the presbytery, were occasionally dressed up in the

of Reform (Sante Fe, NM: Gannon, 1970). Christians gave the term *reform* an original, unprecedented content, equally distant from (1) the hankering after a past paradise, (2) the utopia of a millennium, and (3) a periodic awakening with nature in a "renaissance." These three meanings had been known to antiquity, as had the idea of personal salvation through a mystery cult; none of them correspond to the Christian idea. The new Christian idea of reform found one of its concrete expressions in early penitential practices. These were meant for men, converts or sons of converts, who had slid back into forms of violence pagan decency would have demanded of them, but that were part of "this world" from which they had promised to turn away when they had accepted baptism. By publicly accepting a penitential ritual, they publicly gave expression to their inner reform. In the confessional, this public and precise statement of an attitude was replaced by the intimate, secret commitment to contrition and amendment pastoral care began to inculcate. The "courtroom within" called for a place for quantitative accounting in the beyond. A report on the cultural mutation of afterlife is given by Gilbert Chiffoleau, *La comptabilité de l'Au-delà: Les hommes, la mort et la religion dans la région d'Avignon à la fin du Moyen Age*. (Rome: Ecole Française de Rome; Paris: Boccard, 1980). Jacques LeGoff, *La Naissance du Purgatoire* (Paris: Gallimard, 1981) reports on the discovery of a third territory suited for this purpose, located between heaven and hell, about which dream-travelers (around 1220) brought the first clear reports. On the changes in the pictorial representation of the three-tiered world of the Christian Middle Ages, see J. Baltrusaitis, *Cosmographie chrétienne dans l'art du Moyen Age* (Paris: Gazette des Beaux-Arts 1939). The practice of *confession* introduced the distinction between sin (fault, *culpa*), which would have led to hell unless forgiven sacramentally by the priest, and the punishment for this sin, which would remain untouched by forgiveness. This measurable punishment for a sin already forgiven can be inflicted by God in the form of disease or disaster, or it can be commuted by the Church into crusade, pilgrimage and, later, money donations. If not expiated in this world, since the late twelfth century only, punishment was due in the new locus, purgatory. This, henceforth, made it possible to combine a conscience cleansed in confession with continued fear of the punishment still due. This development further separated the West from the Greek Orthodox Church, which re-

togas of martyrs or decorated with the insignia of clerical saints.[116]
Others found their niche in the carved-stone foliage, with their
horns and scales intact. The young woman who was thrown to
the dragon in the legend was now garbed as St. Margaret and
placed above the altar, keeping the dragon on a leash. The river
gods and satyrs, the kobolds and personified storms, all found
their place, one in a capital, another in the bestiary frieze, and
many as cornerstones or supports for doorways and chairs. Shaggy
northern monsters shared the same column with Sassanian lions,
chimeric peacocks recently lifted from a text in the library, and
biblical figures in abundance. The Church felt confident of embracing heaven, hell, and earth, together with all that could fly or

---

acted against the invention of purgatory: Gilbert Dagron, "La perception
d'une différence: les débuts de la querelle du Purgatoire" *Actes du XVIe
Congrès international d'études byzantines* (Athens, 1979).

1 1 6 THE MADONNA

The transformation of *Mother Church* from a symbol of fertile love to a
symbol for the monopoly of lactation (see FN 113) runs parallel to a shift
in emphasis in the devotion to Mary: a shift from the icon of *theotokos* (in
Greek, "birth-giver of god") to the idol of the Madonna. The transition
from the huge woman on gold ground in the Apsis mosaic to the three-
dimensionally painted lady symbolizes the distance that begins to separate
Europe from the Christian East (see also FNs 112, 115). Like the roads
traveled by "care" (FN 112), heresy (FN 111), and conscience (FN
115), this transition allows us to follow the Westernization (FN 5) of
Europe. It would be a mistake to identify any of these transformations
with a date; they each happened in different centuries, and at different
moments for different milieus. They are less visible in reformed than in
Catholic areas. It would be foolish to say that any of these transformations
led out of a past paradise, or that the twelfth century was a doorway that
led out of the garden; I focus on it because I am more familiar with it.
Finally, it would be a gross error to see in the troubadours' image and ideal
of "womanhood" the renaissance, or in the Victorians' a straight secular
issue, of the Madonna. However, these cautions are only meant to under-
score the importance of the attempt to mirror the evolution of attitudes
toward gender in the representation of Mary made by Marina Warner,
Alone of All Her Sex: The Myth and the Cult of the Virgin Mary (New
York: Knopf, 1976). Warner focuses her attention mainly on high art
under the influence of the religious establishment. A parallel approach
would focus on the image of Mary as it has been produced by popular
religiosity (FN 117).

crawl. For five hundred years, its rule of thumb remained: "*Ecclesia omnia benedicat*"—let the Church bless everything people do, see, or make. In the eleventh century, even the devil had become more of a joke than a threat. Local myths and customs enriched the ritual and made the cathedral a hothouse of old lore. The presence of this host of baptized symbols bore witness to the power of the Church's message, and to the possibility of an infinite variety of vernacular existence under the shield, the aegis, of faith.[117]

This fraternization of barely gentled local spirits, "baptized" imported gods, gorgon heads with new meanings, and "legitimate" prophets and apostles in the Romanesque Church must be clearly seen in order to understand what the exodus of the "re-

1 1 7 RELIGIOSITY

The study of popular religiosity is something other than the study of religion in which religious sciences engage. The distinction parallels that between the study of gendered speech and of sexed language (FN 101). I would reserve the term "religion" for all sides of those phenomena that can be perceived from a central perspective and, therefore, can be the subject of scientific research. I would call "religiosity" all the gendered acts of prayer and devotion, all the concrete gendered rituals, blessings, and songs that express vernacular feeling and attitudes. In the study of religiosity, especially in Europe, I let myself be guided by Lenz Kriss-Rettenbeck, *Bilder und Zeichen Religiösen Volksglaubens* (Munich: Callwey, 1977) and by the same author in collaboration with Liselotte Hansmann, *Amulett und Talisman: Erscheinungsform und Geschichte* (Munich: Callwey, 1976). The author searches for the shape, content and significance of piety (*Frömmigkeit*) by interpreting votive offerings, objects of piety (*Andachtsbilder*), gestures, amulets and talismans. He carefully distinguishes *piety* both from *magic* and from *superstition*. Magic is neither an early form nor a part of religion or science, nor is it central to religiosity: It is an act of symbolic dominance. "Superstition," as used during the Middle Ages, did not mean the "unfounded or silly belief of little old women," but the refusal to serve God and a commitment to his enemy, the devil. On the transformation of *the social reality of superstition* from a medieval perversion of religion into an eighteenth-century perversion of sound reason, see Dieter Harmening, *Superstitio: Überlieferungs und theoriegeschichtliche Untersuchungen zur kirchlich-theologischen Aberglaubensliteratur des Mittelalters* (Berlin: Erich Schmidt, Verlag, 1979). The gothic housecleaning of the cathedral called forth an unusal marriage between magic and superstition. Witch hunting fascinated the Renaissance divine and philosopher for two reasons: (1) The phenomenon itself was

cent" arrivals meant when it inevitably occurred. First, Bernard of Clairvaux, the austere and unbending reformer of monasticism, began to inveigh against monks tolerating in their cloister effigies that might be necessary to lead more simple souls toward the pure light of faith but could only distract the contemplative from the purity of his love. Then, a century later, as the Church

---

new and (2) the combination of a search for power with a search for independence from God was common to witchcraft and the new witch-hunting science. Within the context of my argument, the histories of science and of witchcraft make a contribution to the study of sex, while the attempt to understand popular religiosity provides us with a privileged view of gender. For a study of popular religiosity, see Raoul Manselli, *"Simbolismo e magia nell' Alto Medioevo" in *Simboli e simbologia nell' Alto Medioevo* (Spoleto: Presso la Sede del Centro, 1976): 293–329, as well as the same author's *La religion populaire au Moyen Age: Problèmes de méthode et d'histoire* (Paris: Vrin, 1975) and J. Toussaert, *Le sentiment religieux en Flandre à la fin du Moyen Age* (Paris: Plon, 1963). Useful material (specifically on penance and contrition) can be found in Jean-Charles Payen, *Le Motif du repentir dans la Littérature Française Mediévale des origines à 1230* (Geneva: Droz, 1968). A monumental reference work that often provides unique guidance to the study of religious devotion under the aegis of the Catholic faith is the *Dictionnaire de spiritualité, ascétique et mystique, doctrine et histoire*, launched by Marcel Viller (Paris: Beauchesne, 1932). (Publication has reached volume 10, fasc. 67,3 at the letter M and might be concluded by the end of this century.) The relationship between the curate and the religiosity of his faithful appears best in Etienne Delaruelle, *La piété populaire au Moyen Age*, (Turin: Bottega d'Erasmo, 1975). Two new studies I have not been able to use so far are M. Ménard, *Une histoire des mentalités religieuses aux XVIIe et XVIIIe siècles: Mille retables de l'ancien diocèse du Mans.* (Paris: Beauchesne, 1981) and Marie-Hélène Froeschlé-Chopard, *La religion populaire en Provence Orientale au XVIIIe siècle* (Paris: Beauchesne, 1980). I consider the study of popular religiosity during the nineteenth century of great importance, because religious symbols were used during this period to put the blessings of the Church on a new, sexed world view. This appears, for example, in Gottfried Korff, "Heiligenverehrung und soziale Frage: Zur Ideologisierung der populären Frömmigkeit im späten 19. Jh" in G. Wiegelmann, ed., *Kultureller Wandel im 19. Jh.* (Göttingen: Van den Hoeck, 1973): 102–11 and, by the same author, "Bemerkungen zum politischen Heiligenkult im 19. und 20. Jahrhundert," in Gunther Stephenson, ed., *Der Religionswandel unserer Zeit im Spiegel der Religionswissenschaft* (Darmstadt: Wissenschaftliche Buchgesellschaft, 1976): 217–30. My interest in the penetration of Church-managed ideology into popular religiosity has led me to sponsor a collection of documents on the popular

turned inquisitorial and became more concerned with conscience than with creed, its new pastoral efforts destroyed the milieu for these established guests. The old guardians of probity would no longer fit into the austere arches of Gothic morality. The hunt for all kinds of dissidents dislodged the old gods from the buttresses and niches where for generations they had served to guard parochial propriety under the shelter of the Catholic faith.

The dragons and kobolds, the basilisks and wild men, were squeezed out of the interior as architecture changed from Romanesque to Gothic. There was no room for them on the tightly bundled, narrow and pointed pillars. Like bats, for a century or more they continued to cling to the outside of the church. As gargoyles, they stuck out into the air as if they were about to take flight, meanwhile disgorging water from their mouths or groins. The theologians, wrapped up in conscience, could no longer bless them. As the Renaissance approached, learned men interpreted the memory of this harlequin rabble as emblems, symbols, and cabalistic types. And, as a matter of fact, the gargoyles did take off, roaming around the countryside for the next three centuries as creatures never before seen: defrocked saints, martyrs with club feet, dragons with clipped wings. They behaved like packs of domesticated animals gone wild again, like alley cats in a war-ravaged town. These strange spirits called forth a new kind of priest, generally called a "witch."

Part of the history of gender would be the stories one or the other of these spirits-turned-ghosts-or-devils could tell about their exodus.[118] Squatters, for example, are known around the globe; iconographers call them *obscene* squatters. Some are male, but more are female figures. They forcefully thrust the open vulva out and up in a position that strongly suggests power. "Beset" was the name of this icon in Egypt. She was a goddess from the Sudan

---

religiosity of Latin America since 1820, which is now housed at the Library of the Colegio de México, Camino al Ajusco, Mexico 20 DF and directed by Valentina Borremans. Part of this collection is being made available on microfilm by Inter Documentation Company, Leiden, Holland.

118 THE DEVIL

The inconographic study of the devil, his demons, and zoormorphs during this period is one way of reconstructing its image of women. Sénéfiance 6. *Le diable au moyen âge (doctrine, problèmes moraux, présentations)*. Col-

who came down the Nile to become dominant among her like on all the shores of the Mediterranean during later dynasties. Pliny, in his *Natural History*, testifies that hail will infallibly be averted from a ripening field if a woman in her menses lies in it on her back and uncovers her pubes. Sometimes, the amulet alone will work. He further reports that a woman will serve to frighten and dispel a tempest on the high seas on any day of the month. Beset has come down to us in hundreds of examples. In the late Romanesque churches, she mingles with a sister, also from the Mediterranean: the double-tailed mermaid. And from the northern isles another squatter descends toward France. This one is dressed in the garb of Eve, our common mother. She is Shela-na-gig, a Scot who must have been blessed quite early, when some Irish or Scottish clan came into the Church. She too is by origin a guardian spirit of gender, a powerful antidote to evil. Upon coming into the Christians cosmos, the squatter became the symbol for

---

loque mars 1978. Aix-en-Provence (Paris: Champion, 1979). Still useful on holy and diabolic animals is W. von Blankenburg, *Heilige und dämi-nische Tiere* 10 (Leipzig: Koehler, 1943). See also Dietrich Schmidtke, "Geistliche Tierinterpretation en in der deutschsprachigen Literatur des Mittelalter 1100–1500" (Berlin: Dissertation, 1968): especially 208 ff. For the correlation between animal representations and the fantasy of the age, see J. Baltrusaitis, *Le Moyen Age fantastique: Antiquités et exotismes dans l'art gothique* (Paris: Flammarion, 1981; expanded edition of the 1955 original). On the survival of antique gods as demons, see M.Th. d'Alverny, "Survivance de la magie antique," *Antike und Orient im Mittelalter* (Miscellenea Mediaevalia 1, 1962): 155–78 and, for its bibliography, J. Seznec, *La survivance des dieux antiques* (London: Warburg Inst., 1940), reprinted as *The Survival of the Pagan Gods* (Princeton, NJ: Princeton University Press, 1972). Also A.A. Barb, "The Survival of Magic Arts," *The Conflict Between Paganism and Christianity in the Fourth Century*, ed. A. Momigliano (Oxford: Clarendon Press, 1964): 100–25. On the social status of the animal, see J. Vartier, *Les procès d'animaux du Moyen Age à nos jours* (Paris: Hachette, 1970). A good guide to the medieval image of women is a special issue of *Cahier Civilisation Médiévale* 20 (1977), especially Jean Verdon, "Les sources de l'histoire de la femme en Occident aux Xe-XIIIe siècles." Notice particularly the conclusion of Chiara Frugoni, "L'Iconographie de la femme au cours des Xe-XIIe siècles" (*Ibid.*, pp. 177–87): When looking for the representation of women—not zoomorphs, female spirits, martyrs, or the Virgin Mary . . . "the iconography of women is the iconography of an absence." Specifically on Eve: E. Guldan, *Eva und Maria: Eine Antithese als Bildmotiv* (Cologne: Böhlau, 1966).

all that lives on the earth, and thus came to be Eve, the mother of all life. As Eve, she was carved into the pivot of the central pillar of a church's main western portal. She is enthroned above the zodiac that frames The Last Judgment at the cathedral at Autun. She points her nakedness toward the sunset, the night, the direction from which all harmful spirits and powers threaten the people of God. She alone is powerful enough to protect the crowd of faithful and zoomorphs within the Church. Sometimes, though, two squatters, one of them ithyphallic, guard the west portal, in which case the first human parents always appear in the tympanum above. As Eve, Shela-na-gig can be interpreted as the epitome of traditional hierophany baptized by the Church. All squatters are hierophants, revelations of sacred power and protection. As Eve, the squatter is elevated into the gendered protector of a catholic crowd.

If Shela-na-gig's taking Eve's veil represents the high point of the squatter's power, banning her from the Church despoils her of her sacred nimbus. The squatters that humanistic scholars turn into learned emblems are symbols, not hierophants; no demon would be frightened by the two-tailed sirens teeming in Raphael's loggias. The theologians turn the mermaid into the allegory of carnal lust, which they represent as an attractive vice. As one of the seven deadly sins, she now teases conscience and is painfully removed from the sacredness of the divide she formerly guarded. But much more importantly, removed from Eve's apple, from conversation with the serpent and Adam, having lost the diaphanous transparency by which she had revealed sacred power, the squatter nevertheless survives in spite of being dislodged from the Church. With her gender broken but not yet destroyed, she becomes one of the postures of the witch. As such, she survives in kitchen and cove.[119]

During the half millennium in which they had obediently supported columns and portals and chairs, the squatter, the billy goat, the dragon, the giant, and the dwarf had lost the edge of their sacred gender. The Church's indiscriminate blessings had

---

119 THE WITCH

I use the term "witch" in a narrow sense to designate an historical personage, real or imagined, that appears at the time when the gargoyles disappear from the cathedral spires and that vanishes during the late Enlightenment.

worn it down. Now the new theologians learned to distinguish carefully between the *sacraments*—neither more nor less than seven, universal, necessary for salvation—and the old blessings, which came to form the layer of *sacramentals*, clearly second class. For the new divines, the old spirits of local decency were at best no more than symbols, generally intruders if not vermin. And as they slipped away, taking off from the steeples or being driven from the thicket of the cloister garden, roaming on their own, the ancient goblins were metamorphosed. No longer pagan gods but Christian devils, no longer unredeemed guardians but apostate spirits, no longer ambiguous hierophanies but ghosts smelling of sulphur, they began to wander. They had lost the power to exorcise vernacular fears, but they could still haunt the countryside. Expelled by the Avignon-based Church, the domesticated shades of the past returned to the village square, to the rivers and mountaintops, as pale and crippled demons with Christian names, congealing into a new threat for a clergy now at the service of a novel order.

Delumeau has delineated the new fear characteristic of this

I reserve "witch" to designate the sorceress during the epoch of broken gender (FN 120). A witch can be a herbalist, an abortionist, a magician, shaman, or exorcist—much more often a wretched old woman and occasionally a man—but as a witch she is the epitome of the woman who protests the loss of vernacular gender. She is neither the priestess of a local divinity nor the devotee of an idol but is associated with the Christian devil, who is as Catholic as the one God whom he opposes. Her company are not vernacular spirits untouched by holy water but the exorcised zoomorphs and demons now associated with Satan. Wherever the process of civilization tries to impose a synthetic gender line, there the witch appears. Robert Muchembled, *Culture populaire et culture des élites dans la France moderne, XVe–XVIIIe siècles* (Paris: Flammarion, 1978) establishes the connection between witchcraft and the repression of local subsistence by the rising nation-state. Jean Delumeau, *La peur en Occident, XIVe–XVIIIe siècles* (Paris: Fayard, 1978) examines for this period *who* feared *what* and *when*, and the different expressions fear expressed by a community took. With the loss of vernacular boundaries to experience, a new kind of fear became general; it required abstract symbols, of which *the* woman became the most important. That the witch constitutes a gender-specific reaction against the loss of locally embedded subsistence was first suggested to me by reading Julio Caro Baroja, *World of the Witches* (Chicago: University of Chicago Press, 1965).

peculiar situation as the Middle Ages declined. The confusion, anguish, and horror of people who had simultaneously lost both the tranquility of their Christian faith and the vernacular symbols of propriety they could trust gave rise to a religious situation without precedent. The line of priests and soothsayers who had formerly given ritual sanction to gendered existence had been broken, and the Roman priests who replaced them had turned into pastors charged with the administration and normalization of gendered life. A void was created, one that called for a new rite. Its celebrant was the witch, the priestess of the epoch of broken gender. Perhaps she was indeed as unique as the gendered conjugality characteristic of the period, as new as the homosexual, as strange as her prosecutors claimed.[120] In any case, the struggle against her united the secular and the religious arms of the new state.

120 / THE CIVILIZATION
OF BROKEN GENDER

I follow Ludolf Kuchenbuch in speaking about the civilization of broken gender that dominated the West between the eleventh and the eighteenth centuries. The use of this term allows me to designate the second of four successive stages in the formation of today's sexed couple, and of the couple's economic function within the household. (1) Well into the Middle Ages the marriage tie still did not aim directly at the creation of a couple. The wedding knitted what were often elaborate ties between the members of two kinship groups, their holdings, their status, and their offspring. This kind of marriage took a bewildering variety of forms; it fostered subsistence and strengthened the peasant's ability to resist the demands of king and lord. (2) A new type of marriage that appeared during the eleventh century aimed directly at the creation of a tie between the two gendered co-producers of rent (FN 77). Rent looses its gender even before it is paid in money (FN 73). The Church elevates the mutual agreement (con-sensus) into a sacrament, and the couple becomes a sacred institution. The process of civilization [Norbert Elias, *The Civilizing Process* (New York: Urizen, 1977), esp. chapter 2] progressively imposed conjugal wedlock on the lower classes—while replacing local proprieties with Catholic decencies as the criterion for gendered behavior. The *gendered couple* allowed the European household to function as an historically unique economic enterprise: (a) Broken gender made men and women more adaptable to new and changing techniques and allowed the household to produce a high level of marketable commodities; (b) yet, the household remained relatively independent from marketed consumption goods, because it continued to rely on complex, gendered subsistence; (c) the lone household torn from village and kin has only weak defences against the expropriation of its surplus. The civilization of broken gender ended in the proto-industrial interval (FN 125), which transmogrified the gendered couple into a (3) genderless economic partnership between a wage laborer and a shadow worker. I therefore speak of this third period as the civilization of economic sex. For (4) the present emergence of a de-sexed, synthetic gender line propagated by a variety of true believers and challenged by a bewildering variety of alternative gropings, I dare not coin a name. For literature on the transition from vernacular to broken gender see FN 77; for an introduction to family history, FN 121. On the legal history of the couple during the civilization of broken gender, see esp. Gaudement (*op. cit.* FN 77). Velma Bourgeois Richmond, "Pacience in Adversitee: Chaucer's Presentation of Marriage," *Viator* 10 (1979): 323–54 provides a repertory of the literature that explores the difficulties of the modern critic or historian when he attempts to establish late medieval attitudes toward sex, mutuality, and love. John K. Yost, "The Traditional Western Concept of Marriage and the Family: Rediscovering its Renaissance-Reformation Roots," *Andover Newton Quarterly* 20 (1980) and Alberto Tenenti, "Famille bourgeoise et idéologie au Bas Moyen Age," in G. Duby and J. Le Goff, eds., *Famille et parenté dans l'Occident médiéval.* Actes du Colloque de Paris 1974, Ecole française de Rome edition no. 30 (1977): 431–40 both deal with the discovery, in Florence, that marriage could be conceived of as a life-long enterprise undertaken by a couple, at the time of Dante and of Boccacio (died 1375) and that marriage was the lot of noblemen and peasants—the learned man had to seek a better state. By the time of Leon B. Alberti (born 1404) a citizen, to be respected in Florence, had to live a family life. "The appearance of matrimonial unity was as important as the appearance of corporate unity is today, and for the same reasons," says Mary Carruthers, "The Wife of Bath and the Painting of Lions," *Proceedings of the Modern Language Association* 84 (1979): 212. The *Héptameron* of Marguerite d'Angoulême, Queen of Navarre, is a mine for the study of mid-sixteenth-century attitudes toward the couple. Edward Benson, "Marriage ancestral and conjugal in the Héptameron," *Journal of Medieval and Renaissance Studies* 1, 2 (1975) analyzes this. During the sixteenth century the character of economic life changed in ways that rewarded the trader and artisan whose wife could help directly in his business, so that the abilities and values of the marriage partner became, for the first time in history, economically important. The coupling of two gendered but newly compliant pairs of peasant hands was important for the landlord, who wished to extract higher levels of rent; it was equally important for the artisan for a new kind of enterprise. The *Héptameron* is full of information on the bitterness that this evoked in the relationship between the sexes because neither understood that the couple had been organized as a corporation.

VII. From Broken Gender to Economic Sex

The purpose of this essay is not a history of gender but the elaboration of concepts allowing us to disentangle gender from sex[121] within a history of scarcity. Reflecting on the declining Middle Ages, I have tried to show that a new economic order was instilled in souls through conscience. Conscience then weakened the guardians of vernacular gender several centuries before sex could replace it. A long period of *broken gender* separates the yoking of couples in conjugal wedlock from their industrial polarization into wage and shadow work. This time of broken gender differs greatly from place to place and could be given various names. To call it the *war on subsistence* highlights the rise of the nation-state. To call it the enclosure of *commons* underlines the transformation of common gender domains into genderless productive resources. To do justice to the processes involved, one would also have to call this era the *age of witchcraft*, the period of the birth pangs of sex. It begins when conscience is first fashioned, and ends when sexism becomes trivial.

Gender-blind historians describe it as a "transition to a capitalist mode of production," thereby hiding the fact that an ahistorical *novum* emerged from the mutation: a consumption-dependent producer who is necessarily sexist.

Pre-capitalist societies are based on gender.[121] Subsistence is

121 FAMILY HISTORY

I have drawn heavily on this new discipline to formulate the distinction between gender and sex. The seminal book in the field has been for me Philippe Ariès, *Centuries of Childhood* (New York: Random House,

a neutral term for this gendered survival. The shift to capitalism
coincides anthropologically with the decline from broken gender
into the regime of sex. Societies in which the reign of gender has
broken down *are* capitalist; their genderless subjects are individual
producers. Curiously, this decisive transformation has not yet been

---

1965). Most studies on family history that have appeared since then must
chew on the ideas formulated by Ariès; some of his critics do so in anger
and others, like myself, with relish. On the reception given to Ariès, see
Adrian Wilson, "The Infancy of the History of Childhood: An Appraisal
of Philippe Ariès," *History and Theory* 19, no. 1 (1980): 137–53. I would
have written neither *Deschooling Society* nor the present book without the
guidance I have received from Ariès. So far, however, most studies on
family history are gender-blind. For an orientation to the new discipline, a
good guide is Michael Anderson, *Approaches to the History of the Western Family, 1500–1914* (Bristol: Macmillan & Co., Economic History
Society, 1980). The author dedicates each of the three chapters of his
book to one of the major currents that have developed within the discipline: (1) the quantitative demographic study of age at marriage, patterns
of childbearing, and patterns of contraception; (2) the changing attitudes
toward domesticity, privacy, sentimentality, and community control over
the family, as well as different forms of childbearing; and (3) new approaches to the economic history of the modernizing household. As a
general introduction to the field, I recommend to the beginner J.-L. Flandrin (*op. cit.* FN 85). The author interrelates with great competence demography, the study of mentalities and of behavior, and the typology of
household structures. Good access to the studies on family history published in the French journal *Les Annales: Economie, Société, et Civilisation*
[elsewhere, *Annales, ESC*] is now available to English speakers through an
anthology: R. Forster and O. Ranum, eds., *Family and Society*, trans.
Patricia Ranum (Baltimore: Johns Hopkins University Press, 1976). The
correlation between demography and attitudes, as these differ by class, can
be found in various contributions to C. Tilly, ed., *Historical Studies of
Changing Fertility* (Princeton, NJ: Princeton University Press, 1978).
Exemplary local studies of the nineteenth-century family in England are:
D. Levine, *Family Formation in an Age of Nascent Capitalism* (Chats-
worth, CA: Academy Press, 1977) and, for the United States, P.J. Greven,
*Four Generations: Population, Land and Family in Colonial Andover,
Massachusetts* (Ithaca, NY: Cornell University Press, 1970). The diversity
of family forms that can prevail at the same time within the same area is
highlighted by P.J. Greven, *The Protestant Temperament: Patterns of
Childbearing, Religious Experience and the Self in Early America* (New
York: Knopf, 1977). The process by which the proto-industrial mill
and the police converge to break down the gendered couple and replace

identified as the crucial anthropological condition that accounts for the transition from pre-capitalist economies to the growing commodity dependence for everyday needs called "capitalism." Capitalism is a curious term.[122] It was unknown to Marx when Engels first used it in 1870. Proudhon had occasionally

---

it with the model of the sexual polarization of functions is described by Jacques Donzelot, *The Policing of Families*, with a foreword by Gilles Deleuze, trans. Robert Hurley (New York: Pantheon, 1979). On the impact of women's work (wage and shadow), see FNs 31, 67–69. A good bibliography of the social and cultural history of marriage: Natalie Zemon Davis, "La storia delle donne in trasizione: il caso europeo," *Donnawomanfemme* 3 (1977): 7–33. Collections on the same subject are James Wallace Milden, *The Family in Past Time: A Guide to the Literature* (New York: Garland, 1977): and Gerard Soliday, ed., *History of the Family and Kinship: A Select International Bibliography* (New York: Kraus, 1980).

122 CAPITALISM

I use the term pre-capitalist with more confidence than the term capitalist, and I use both terms *faute de mieux*. On the use of these terms, see above all Edwin Deschepper, "L'histoire du mot 'capital' at dérivés" (Brussels: Dissertation at the Université Libre de Bruxelles, 1964) as well as Edgar Salin, "Kapitalbegriff und Kapitallehre von der Antike bis zu den Physiokraten," *Vierteljahrschrift für Sozial- und Wirtschaftsgeschichte* 23 (1930); Jean Dubois, "Le vocabulaire politique et social en France de 1869 à 1872 à travers les oeuvres des écrivains, les revues et les journaux" (Paris: Larousse, 1963) as well as the much simpler article by Bert Hoselitz, "Zur Begriffsgeschichte des Kapitalismus," *Saeculum* 18 (1967): 146–63. The opposition for pre-capitalist/capitalist societies is significant for me, because it is the most common way to designate a social transformation that in fact coincides with the transition from the reign of gender to the regime of sex. Further, the distinction I make within the reign of gender between vernacular life-styles and the epoch of broken gender allows me to distinguish in pre-capitalist Europe two successive stages: the stage of subsistence based on the complementarity of vernacular gender, in which commodities play a decidedly secondary role; and the stage of broken gender, in which the enhanced productivity that resulted from economic wedlock greatly increased the level of simple commodity production. What has been called simple commodity production thus turns out to be mainly that surplus that can be extracted from gendered wedlock (FN 77). In contrast to these two, in the next stage capitalist commodities are the product of a society based on an entirely different household; they are the product of economic—which means genderless—work. This work was

inserted it in a text, but only Sombart gave it familiar currency.
Fernand Braudel[123] still finds it necessary to apologize for its use
in the title of *Material Civilization, Economy and Capitalism
from the 15th to the 18th Century*, a magnificent portrait of
economic life after the Reformation and before the French Revolution. An economic Breughel, he depicts a vast canvas of material, institutional, and political life during those centuries. He
brings to life a post-medieval Europe, teeming with fairs, markets, and workshops, expanding trade routes and associations.
Throughout, he underscores the fact that what he calls capital,
capitalist, capitalism only very slowly penetrates into the pro-
curement, production, and exchange of primary necessities. He
carefully searches for the changes that might explain this penetra-

---

imposed because the household's dependence on capitalist commodities
during a first stage of industrialism was principally conceived of as depending on wage labor: by the end of the twentieth century, it is comprised
overwhelmingly of a dependence on shadow work (FN 30). Gender analysis thus allows me to add a further category to the two distinguished by
Karl Polanyi, *Trade and Market in the Early Empire* (chapter 5, *op. cit.*,
pp. 64–96, FN 33) and also in "The Semantics of Money Use," *Essays by
Polanyi* (*op. cit.*, pp. 175–203, FN 11). Polanyi makes a distinction between trade goods and the commodities offered by merchants. On the
reception of Polanyi's categories, see Humphreys (*op. cit.* FN 5). I accept
this distinction in a general way and do not here relate it to gender. However, the simple commodity, which Aristotle "discovered," I contrast to
the capitalist commodity, the industrial good or service, because the former
is of gender origin while the latter is not.

1 2 3   T H E   I N D U S T R I A L   R E V O L U T I O N

Fernand Braudel, *Civilisation matérielle, économie et capitalisme*, XIe-
XVIIIe siècles, 3 vols. (Paris: Colin, 1979) is soon to be translated into
English. By the same author, at present available in English, *Capitalism
and Material Life, 1400–1800* (New York: Harper and Row, 1974) is a
first draft of the first volume of the major work. Also see *Afterthoughts on
Material Civilization and Capitalism* (Baltimore: Johns Hopkins University Press, 1977). R.M. Hartwell, ed., *Causes of the Industrial Revolution in
England* (orig. London, 1967; now a Barnes and Nobles paperback) succinctly summarizes the major explanations given by historians for the onset
of industrialization, and the objections to each of these. This survey confirms the blindness to the anthropologically decisive transformation: the
loss of vernacular gender.

tion, and the reasons exponential capital accumulation became a factor affecting the everyday existence for most people before the beginning of the nineteenth century. He identifies growing market dependence, legal conditions protecting long-range accumulation, and overseas expansion of economic space as the converging conditions without which capitalist/industrial production could not have become dominant. But throughout the three volumes he consistently overlooks the universality of gendered existence in pre-capitalist societies and the loss of gender in the transition to capitalism. For him, gender is not a crucial historical factor.

To write the history of the foundations on which our world stands is quite different from the attempt to tell the story of what has been lost. For the historian who looks at the past in a rearview mirror, sickle and scythe are but local farm tools once used in the harvest, replaced by *techniques* when modernization occurs. If such history pays any attention to mentalities and sentiments, it tends to focus on the characteristic alienation, loneliness, and exploitation that grow apace with the new techniques. It examines the pain inflicted on people by the new market economy, mechanization, or hunger. The other injury resulting from the loss of traditional gender, now washed away through the new plumbing, remains the hidden side of the sorry story. What did *she* lose with the sickle? What else went with the scythe *he* had to give up? To write the story of the motley losses, one has to rummage around and ferret out the specific vernacular feelings, which have barely left a trace. The historian has to describe the death of a gendered reality that, despite its existence through millennia, has eluded his colleagues.

To prepare for such a task, I have tried to provide a background for my theoretical reflections with a stage outline marked by an occasional charcoal sketch. In several of these, I wanted to illustrate societies' housebreaking that precedes wedlock. Now one story only must suffice to enliven my description of the birth pangs of economic sex: A Lutheran village in Württemberg bears witness to the reactions of men and women faced with the first imposition of genderless work.

Between 1800 and 1850, the unusual number of four dozen divorce proceedings were recorded in Württemberg. David Sabean has tried to interpret the grounds given for the dissolutions, grounds unlike any adduced in earlier times.[124] To understand what had occurred, he had to consider the economic transformation of the region during this period. A railroad was being built, tenancy was being altered, and most of the families were being forced from homesteading toward producing cash crops from fruit trees. Plum and apple orchards, together with the large-scale production of sugar beets, replaced diversified farms and kitchen gardens. Putting in and harvesting the cash crops proved to be more labor-intensive than homesteading had been. And the change occurred in one generation. Women were suddenly forced to join men in men's work in order to earn enough family income to buy what had formerly been grown in the garden plot. They were also forced to work more and faster in the kitchen. The divorce proceedings reflect how deeply disturbing these innovations were for both men and women, how helpless each felt, how unable to understand the implications of their seemingly rational decisions. Women complained that men suddenly ordered them around at work, a totally new experience for them. No matter how much the gender-defined work of women might seem subordinated to that of men, the notion that men could direct women in the work itself had so far been unimaginable. Women resented the loss of domain. Women also complained that, while men had time after working at the rhythm of the plow to relax at the inn, *they* had to hurry back and forth between the hoe and the kitchen. Envy of a new kind, envy for the other gender's schedule and rhythm, thus appeared, an envy destined to remain as a central characteristic of modern life, an envy fully "justified" under the assumptions of unisex work but unthinkable under the shield of gender. The men, on the other hand, regularly complained that their women were inferior to their mothers: Formerly their diet had been rich and varied; now they had to eat *spaezli* day after day. The curtain closed on the epoch

124 THE LOSS OF RURAL GENDER

See David Sabean, *"Intensivierung der Arbeit und Alltagserfahrung auf dem Lande—ein Beispiel aus Württemberg," *Sozialwissenschaftliche Informationen* 6 (1977): 148–152. For comparison with the eighteenth century, albeit in France: Alain Lottin, "Vie et mort du couple: difficultés conjugales et divorces dans le Nord de la France aux 17e et 18e siècles," *Le XVIIe Siècle*: 1974): 59–78.

of broken gender and conjugal coproduction. In this microcosm, we see vividly how the new script for the industrial age was to be written. For the drama to live and move, the stage had to be peopled with heterosexual actors who were also economically neutered workers.

In most versions of the modern drama, a short intermission separates gender from sex—the reign of gender (where the household obtains its subsistence from the apportioned tasks ac-complished by the sets of non-interchangeable hands) from the régime of industrial economics (where genderless hands produce commodities in exchange for pay). During this proto-industrial intermezzo, unisex work, to be performed in the home, is forced on the household.[125] Thus, the household is transformed into a mill where gender is ground down until only sex is left. The sufferings this crushing of gender caused both men and women have gone largely unreported. Two reasons can be offered to explain this blind spot. On the one hand, the *new* experience of economic misery became the glue of proletarian unity. Wage labor brought a new kind of pain that annihilated women and men. All wage laborers suffered from the very same epidemic of disorientation, loneliness, and dependence. These feelings brought forth political interpreters and an elite of a new class. The diagnosis of the universal woe became the career field for new professions— educators, physicians, and other social engineers—which thrived on the production of policies, guidance, and therapies. The self-interest of both the revolutionary leader and the socialization merchant precluded any attempt to *understand* the gender-specific pain of loss. On the other hand, the pain of impoverishment, due to the obliteration of gender, constituted something quite different in each region; few possessed a language suitable for translating the subtle vernacular varieties of this pain of loss.

While the stage for factory labor was being hammered to-

125 THE PROTO-INDUSTRIAL INTERSTICE

Social historians use the term "proto-industrial" to highlight the unique patterns of popular culture in the transition from simple commodity production to the capitalist mode of production in nineteenth-century Europe. See P. Kriedte, H. Medick, J. Schlumbohm, *Industrialisierung vor der Industrialisierung* (Göttingen: Vandenhoeck und Ruprecht, 1978), especially Medick, pp. 90–154.

gether and a modern economic set was being constructed, but before the script was rewritten for the new and unfamiliar sex roles, novel critical theories were conjured up for the avant-garde theater. The genius of Marx and Freud can be appreciated only by those who see how early in the development of the modern drama they defined its rules. They forged the definitive concepts that would be used to describe *and* orchestrate the new kind of actor, industrialized "man." Seven hundred years earlier, the Church had imputed genderless sin to genderless souls. Now the genderless power of genderless humans in a genderless cosmos became the key transcendental characteristic of the categories used in a new kind of metaphysics. Around the middle of the nineteenth century, a dozen natural scientists, simultaneously though independently, redefined the *vis viva universi* (the living force of the universe) as energy, sometimes bound, sometimes free. Helmholz is usually credited with the feat of having formulated the laws by which physical energy henceforth fit the assumptions of scarcity that are constitutive of formal economics. During the same decade, the labor force was made into a key concept, by which the human contribution to human existence could be treated as a scarce resource. Finally, a generation later, Freud, textually repeating sentences from Helmholz, attributed psychic energy in the form of libido—sometimes bound, sometimes free—to the human. The new canonists fabricated their theory of secular man and his salvation on assumptions derived from chemistry and fluid mechanics. They claimed to find a genderless power that, as capital, circulates through social conduits and, as libido, through psychological channels. Thus, during the first three-quarters of our century, we have had to live with energy, labor, and sexuality as "the facts of life." Now that the code word "crisis" is abroad, perhaps we can publicly question their reality.

Society needs a past. To have a sense of the present, the living require a past that fits them. There is no first person plural, no "we," without its myth of creation. The two-gendered "we" of all times was kept alive by each society's rituals, feasts, and taboos. Industrial society, too, needed a myth of creation; it could not exist without one. So it created a special institution to provide each household with "news" and a constant sense of a "past." The past became an industrial enterprise.

From Broken Gender to Economic Sex

The scheme through which industrial society churns out its past has been called history. For one hundred years, history has fabricated a continuity between the genderless present and the gendered past, legitimating the descent of sex from gender. With an increasingly refined methodology, the new science has interpreted the story in sexist categories to give a past to our economic world. Without such economic reconstruction of a gendered past, the contemporary world of sexist economics could not have been made attractive, especially to those against whom it has consistently discriminated. History has joined myriad synthetic ties of sentimentality to a realm of gender that the contemporary world had in fact abandoned to begin its frenzied journey. Historians have woven a tapestry to make us feel comfortable in our sexist environment, but the fabric has been manufactured out of industrial fibers. Powerful enterprises attempted to make the past appear as seed, a primitive form of the present; its languages, customs, and institutions being the genuine ancestors, the embryonic forms, of those that are contemporary and familiar. Our library shelves are crowded with books that attribute a class structure to Greek city-states, which call the Sophist peddling his tricks a forerunner of modern educators, which report on the sex life (*Sic!*) of Mesopotamia. I write this essay to counter such a *centralist* perspective on history. And I reject the label of scientific historian, for I will not reconstruct the past with key words, nor with concepts mined in utopia, yet I believe in honoring the dead by research that is public, disciplined, documented, and critical.

I have tried to direct attention to the break between gender and sex, to bring into view the chasm that divides the present from the past. I have tried to expose the counterfeit genealogy of sex that underlies economic history. It is a fiction needed by a sexist society that cannot face its lack of legitimate ancestry. The grounding of sex in gender is spurious. Both sex and gender have social origins, but they stem from unrelated matrices. The matrix of sex is Alma Mater; the matrix of gender can only be found beyond "the cavern of the seven sleepers," "lodged in rock-clefts on the branches of enormous hollow yews." (Robert Graves, *White Goddess: A Historical Grammar of Poetic Myth* [New York: Farrar, Straus, and Giroux, 1948], p. 13).

Whether they are born outside the matrix of gender or first

delivered from and then educated into the matrix of sex, women must face men. Each matrix, however, endows them with a different relative power. Under the reign of gender, men and women collectively depend on each other; their mutual dependence sets limits to struggle, exploitation, defeat. Vernacular culture is a truce between genders, and sometimes a cruel one. Where men mutilate women's bodies, the gynaeceum often knows excruciating ways to get back at men's feelings. In contrast to this truce, the regime of scarcity imposes continued war and ever new kinds of defeat on each woman. While under the reign of gender women might be subordinate, under *any* economic regime they are *only* the second sex. They are forever handicapped in games where you play for genderless stakes and either win or lose. Here, both genders are stripped and, neutered, the man ends up on top. No wonder that it is the woman who now "discovers" the transmogrification of gender by economics. Typically, she complains that "she" is invisible to others and to herself. She can neither perceive herself in the regime of economics as an equal partner, nor can she recognize herself in a gender. The turgid scenarios of political science, constructed with a set of assumptions about the equality of all men, do not apply to her. The sexist utopia of Herland fails to provide the rank consolations of the locker room, and attempts to reconstruct women's past with key words only caricature the enterprise of scientific history, as such. Now, by their passionate inquiries within this double bind, women's studies have cemented the pivot to upset the scientific applecart.

In this essay I have not tried to explain why society places the man on top and the handicap on the woman. I have controlled my curiosity in order to be free to listen more attentively to the report of the losers, to learn not about them but about the battlefield that is the economy. Industrial society creates two myths—one about the society's sexual ancestry and another about the movement toward ever greater equality. Both myths are unmasked as lies in the personal experience of the neuter of the second sex.

I set out to argue that the fight against sexism converges with efforts to reduce environmental destruction and endeavors to challenge the radical monopoly of goods and services over needs. I have argued that these three contemporary movements converge because economic shrinkage is the common condition for all three. And the recognition that economic cutback, for reasons specific to each movement, is for each not just a negative necessity but a positive condition for a better life can lead from theoretical convergence to concerted public action. I have further argued that these three movements represent three aspects of an attempt to recover the commons, the commons in that sense in which the term designates the precise inverse of an economic resource. For this undertaking I wished to suggest a theory to clarify the concepts necessary for a history of scarcity.

The historical transition from gendered subsistence to dependence on scarce products establishes my argument. Scarcity is historical, as historical as gender or sex. The era of scarcity could come to be only on the assumption that "man" is individual, possessive, and, in the matter of material survival, genderless—a rapacious *neutrum oeconomicum*. And this assumption, incarnate in institutions from wedlock to schools, transforms the subject of history. That subject is no longer the *gens*, or the *lares*, which designate the ambiguous and asymmetric match of a self-limiting set of women and men. Rather, the subject becomes a construct of ideology fashioned into a spurious "we," a construct like class, nation, corporation, or partnerly couple. For a theory on the action necessary for the recovery of the commons, I think it important to explore the etiology of this transmogrification of history's subject.

I have no strategy to offer. I refuse to speculate on the probabilities of any cure. I shall not allow the shadow of the future to fall on the concepts with which I try to grasp what is and what has been. As the ascetic and the poet meditate on death and thus gratefully *enjoy* the exquisite aliveness of the present, so we must face the sad loss of gender. I strongly suspect that a contemporary art of living *can* be recovered, so long as our austere and clear-sighted acceptance of the double ghetto of economic neuters then moves us to renounce the comforts of economic sex. The hope for such a life rests upon the rejection of sentimentality and on openness to surprise.

INDEX

Editor's note: Page numbers in the index refer to both text and footnotes.

Index

Baulant, Micheline, 67
Bazin, N. T., 73
beauty, social, 82
Becker, Gary S., 40
behavior, 69, 80, 84
  feminists and, 76, 77
  Linton on, 86, 87
Benedict XII, Pope, 115–17, 150
Benson, Edward, 168
Bentham, Jeremy, 10
Benveniste, Emile, 103, 120
Benz, Ernst, 152
Berbers, gendered space of, 105, 106
Berger, Peter, 5
Berk, Richard, 40–41
Bernard of Clairvaux, 162
Beset, 163–64
Bestor, Arthur E., Jr., 23
Bickner, Mei Liang, 25
Bidlingmaier, Maria, 92, 107, 108
birth control, 51, 125–26
Blacking, John, 109
Blankenburg, W. von, 164
Bledstein, Burton S., 79, 125
Bock, Gisela, 46
Bogumils, 150
Borneman, Ernest, 19
Borremans, Valentina, 18, 55, 64, 163
Boserup, Esther, 63
Bosl, Karl, 62
Bossen, Laurel, 63
Boswell, John, 148
Bouda, Karl, 135
Boughey, Howard J., 121
Bourdieu, Pierre, 106, 112
Boyte, Harry, 18
Bradshaw, John, 28
Branca, B., 150
Braudel, Fernand, 172
Brown, Judith C., 23–24
Brownmiller, Susan, 32
Buck, Carl Darling, 8, 112, 120
bugger, buggery, 148, 150–53
Bulgarians, as Christians, 150
Bullough, Vern, 147
Burman, Sandra M., 46–47
Burns, Scott, 36, 40
Buvinic, Mary, 64

calamity, disregard for gender in, 143–44
Canada, 25, 49–50, 91
Canguilhem, G., 110
Cannon, H. Graham, 141
capital, human, 54–55
capital intensive, 55
  housework as, 49–50, 51–52
capitalism, 3, 64
  transition to, 169–73
care:
  pastoral, 151
  professional and clerical, 151–52, 153, 154, 155
caring society, 54, 156
carnivals, 113, 145, 146
Caro Baroja, Julio, 166
Carruthers, Mary, 168
cash nexus, 17, 55, 63–64
Castan, Nicole, 113
Castan, Yves, 112–14
Cathars, 152
Catholic Church, 95, 101, 102, 149–67
  economic wedlock and, 103–4
  heresy and, 149–53
Chaff, Sandra L., 28
Chaney, Elsa M., 64
Chaucer, Geoffrey, 114
Chiffoleau, Gilbert, 159
childbirth, 122–25, 170
childcare, 51, 53–55, 58, 97, 123
childhood, creation of, 70
China, left- vs. right-handedness in, 72
Chinas, B., 97
Christianity:
  envy as viewed in, 13
  see also Catholic Church
civilization of broken gender, 167–68
Clark, C. E., 47
classical antiquity, perception of envy in, 13
Clastres, Pierre, 90, 145
cognitive development, 127
Collomp, Alain, 107
colonialism, 37, 55, 63, 76, 158
commodities, 3, 17, 19, 40, 63, 81, 167
  production vs. use of, 65

Index

commodities *(continued)*
 radical monopoly of, 16, 18, 151,
  178–79
 shadow work and, 48–49, 50, 52,
  56–57
 vernacular as inverse of, 68
commodity intensive, 48, 52, 56, 94,
 151
commons, 15, 16, 19, 169
 recovery of, 17–18, 179
community, 81, 82
 household in relation to, 109–10
commuting, as shadow work, 53,
 55–56
compensatory research, 61
competition:
 of men vs. women, 10–11, 34–35,
  58–59
 among women, 33, 64, 114
complementarity, 4, 14, 20, 33, 63,
 82, 90
 ambiguous, 70–76, 81, 106, 116
 role, 86–87
 social sciences and, 69, 129
 in speech, 133–34
complementary research, 61
Condorcet, Marquis de, 130
confession, 153–57, 159
Congar, Yves, 155
conjugal couple, 100–104, 167, 169
Conklin, Nancy Faires, 133, 135
conscience, 153, 155–56, 158–60,
 163, 169
conscientization, 158
consumers, consumption, 6
 counterproductivity and, 15–16
 medieval tenants and, 95–96
 of services, 79
 shadow work and, 44, 45, 48–49,
  53, 56–57
contrasting research, 61
conviviality, 18, 55
Corbin, Alain, 33
Corominas, J., 7–8
Coult, A. D., 86
counterproductivity, 15–16, 28–29
courtly love, 157
Couvreur, G., 23
crafts, gender and, 96–98
Crano, William D., 86

Crawford, Patricia, 126
culture, 130–31
 biological determinism and, 76
 evolution of, 140–42
 perception of, 70
 vernacular, 3, 69–70, 90–104,
  134, 178
Cunningham, Clark E., 106
curate, 151–52, 156
customary law, 18, 29
Cutliff, S. H., 55

Dagron, Gilbert, 160
Dalla Costa, Mariarosa, 40
Dalton, George, 48
d'Alverny, M. Th., 164
Daly, Mary, 35
Danckert, Werner, 98
Dante Alighieri, 158, 168
Darmon, Pierre, 109–10
Darwin, Charles, 15, 84
Davidoff, I., 26
Davis, Natalie Zemon, 146, 171
de Benoist, A., 76
Delaruelle, Etienne, 162
Delatour, Jean-Marie, 37
Delcourt, Marie, 147
Delumeau, Jean, 166
dependence, 50–51, 76, 97, 129, 179
de Rocchi Storai, Tina, 121
Desaive, J. P., 109
Deschepper, Edwin, 171
determinism, 73, 76–79
development, 6, 151
 economic, 31–32, 53, 55, 62,
  63–64, 65
deviance, 69, 134, 145, 148–49, 152
devil, 161, 163–64
Dexter, Elisabeth Anthony, 24
Dézalay, Yves, 29
de Zouche Hall, Robert, 121
Diderot, Denis, 14
Didier, B., 85
Dietmaringen, Ursula, 71
discrimination, economic, 22–66
 in self-help, 58
 statistics on, 26–27
 types of, 22

Index

Haas, Harry R., 139
Habermas, Jürgen, 132
Haecker, E., 15
Haiding, Karl, 137
Haldane, J. B. S., 82
Halevy, Elie, 10
Handlin, David, 121
Haraway, Donna, 78
Harding, S., 137
Hardmann, Charlotte, 130
Harmening, Dieter, 161
Harris, J., 115
Harrison, Cynthia E., 59
Hartmann, Heidi I., 35–36
Hausen, Karin, 85
Haviland, John B., 113–14
Hawken, Paul, 45
Heilbrun, Carolyn G., 71
Heitlinger, A., 30
Heller, Agnes, 35
Helmholz, Hermann, 176
Héptameron, 168
heresy, 149–53
Herlihy, David, 104
Herskovits, Melville J., 83, 84
Hertz, Robert, 75
Hess, Luise, 98
heterosexuals, heterosexuality, 32
    history of, 148–49
    rise of, 147–57
hierarchy, 76
    of milieus, 106
    of power, 116
    right to rank and, 78, 79
Higgins, M., 38
Hilton, Rodney H., 97
history:
    family, 168, 169–71
    of heterosexual, 148–49
    in industrial society, 177
    subject of, 117–18, 179
holidays, 95, 96
home, gender and, 117–26
home births, 123
homeomorphic equivalent, 73
Homo oeconomicus, 10–11, 14, 54,
    66, 84, 144
homosexuals, homosexuality, 83,
    146, 147–50
honor, 34, 112–13, 116, 158

Hopi culture, interdependence of
    domains in, 115
Hoselitz, Bert, 171
hospital births, 123, 124
household, 152, 167–68, 175
    conjugal, 151
    as "consuming unit," 116
    importance of, 109–10
    types of, 117–18
household machinery, 49, 51–52
housewives, 32, 47–48
    male, 37
    underdeveloped world as, 65
    value of, 41–42, 44, 46
housework, 41–44, 46–51
    international, development of, 65
    paid, 25, 64
    time requirements of, 52
housing, 120–21
Hubeny, Frank, 65–66
Hughes, Diane Owen, 104
Hughes, Marija Matich, 28
human, the, 4, 9,
Humphreys, S. C., 10, 172

iconography, 13
    of sex, 157–68
ideal types, 14, 44, 45, 158
individual, possessive, 11, 19, 179
individualism:
    genderless, 9–11
    invidious, 12–13, 19
industrialization, 18, 50–51, 58, 114
Industrial Revolution, 172
Ingham, John, 90
intelligence, 4, 77, 78, 83
Internal Revenue Service (IRS),
    38–39
Irigaray, Luce, 74
Italy:
    domus and *lares* in, 117–18
    economy of, 39, 56, 60

James, Selma, 40
Japan, 60
    male vs. female speech in, 136,
    137
    wages in, 25, 36

Index

Jelin, Elisabeth, 26
Jespersen, Otto, 134–35, 138
Jochens, Jenny M., 156
Johnson, Allan G., 32
justice, 17
 popular, 110–11

Karberry, P. M., 88
Karnoch, C., 106–7
Katzman, David, 25–26
Keenan, Elionor, 138
Kendé, Pierre, 44
Kendrick, John W., 40
Kessler-Harris, Alice, 24
key words, 5–8, 14, 23, 62, 72,
 101, 178
kinship, 5, 18, 70, 82, 99–100, 111,
 152, 155
 decline of, 103
 household based on, 118, 167
 household vs., 109–10
Klapisch-Zuber, Christiane, 111
Klatzman, Rosine, 37
Klein, Melanie, 13
Kleinberg, Susan J., 47
Knibiehler, Yvonne, 110
Kohr, Leopold, 82
Kolakowski, Leszek, 10–11
Korbin, Frances E., 126
Korff, Gottfried, 162
Krichmar, Albert, 29
Kriedte, P., 175
Kriss-Rettenbeck, Lenz, 15, 161
Kuchenbuch, Ludolf, 96, 103, 167

labor, division of, 24, 46, 63–64,
 83–84, 86, 94
labor, wage, *see* wage labor, wage
 laborers
labor force, number of women in, 23
labor unions, 33, 55–56
La Cecla, Franco, 120
Ladner, Gerhart, 62, 158–59
Ladurie, Le Roy, 115–17
Laitner, Skip, 43
Lambert, Helen H., 77

Landmann, Michael, 9
language, 6, 8
 key words in, 5–8, 14, 23, 62, 72,
 101, 178
 of men, 135–39
 role in, 136
 scientific, 71–72
 sex difference in, 132–33
 of sex vs. gender, 4
 of travesty, 147
 vernacular, 73, 134, 156
 of women, 133–39
 see also speech
lares, 118, 179
Lasch, Christopher, 79
law, 68
 childbirth and, 123–24
 Church, 95, 101, 153–57
 customary, 18, 29
 family life and, 112
 women and, 29–30, 113
Leach, 100
LeGates, Marlene, 85
LeGoff, Jacques, 159
Leibowitz, A., 54
Lepage, H., 40
Leroi-Gourhan, André, 106
lesbians, 148–49
Levine, D., 170
Lévi-Strauss, Claude, 75, 100
liberal establishment, 76
libido, 4, 14, 81, 147, 176
life expectancy, 27–28, 30
light, as *lux* vs. *lumen*, 69
Lindemann, Ferdinand, 66
Linehan, Peter, 148
Linton, Ralph, 80, 86, 87
literacy, 83–84
Little, Lester K., 13
Locke, John, 11
Löefgren, O., 92–93
Lomax, Alain, 86
Lottin, Alain, 174
Loux, Françoise, 109
love:
 Christian, 151, 152, 154, 155,
 162
 courtly, 157
Luhman, Niklas, 19
Luther, Martin, 23

Index

McAuley, Alastair, 27, 30
Maccoby, Eleanor E., 83
McIntosh, Robert P., 15
McKnight, John L., 79, 151
Macoby, Michael, 85–86
MacPherson, C. B., 11
McRobie, George, 18
Madagascar, men's language in, 138
Madonna, the, 160
magic, 61, 74, 161
Makovski, Elisabeth M., 156
Man, Ingeborg, 92
Mandeville, Bernard, 11
Manselli, Raoul, 162
Marcion, 154
Marguerite d'Angoulême, Queen of
   Navarre, 168
Marquard, O., 132
marriage, 29, 33, 58, 100–104
   economic, 102–4, 118, 149, 167–
      68, 171–72, 173–75
   as sacrament, 151
   working women and, 23–24
Marshall, Gloria, 97
Marx, Karl, 11, 34, 35, 86, 171, 176
Marxism, 11, 35, 36–37, 49, 76, 88,
   100, 158
Mary, Virgin, 157–59, 160
mathematics, 66, 69
Mathieu, Nicole-Claude, 130
Mauss, Marcel, 9–10, 75
Mead, Margaret, 85–86, 87
Medici Florence, attitudes toward
   wage labor in, 23–24
medicine, 6, 27–28, 30, 44, 79, 157
   counterproductivity and, 15–16,
      28
   in regulation of childbirth, 123,
      124–25
   sexed body and, 109–10
   sex-specific, 50
Medick, Hans, 103, 111
Ménard, M., 162
Mencken, H. L., 7, 23, 47
mercantilism, 102, 103
metaphors, 4, 62, 73, 75–76, 81–82
   for the other, 73–74
Métral, Marie-Odile, 104
Mexican National Museum, 141
Mexico, 67

gossip in, 113–14
Meyer, H. B., 152
Michaelson, Evelyn Jacobson, 88
Middle Ages, 13, 23, 143, 150–68
   guilds in, 97–98
   poverty in, 23, 62–63
   rent in, 95, 96–97
Middleton, Christopher, 96–97
midwives, 124, 126
Milden, James Wallace, 171
milieu, vernacular, 82, 105–39
military sector, shadow work in, 56
Miller, Roy, 137
Mintz, Sidney W., 97, 107
Mitterauer, Michael, 98, 118
Moholy-Nagy, Sibyl, 120
Molin, Jean-Baptiste, 104
Mollat, Michel, 13, 23, 62
moral economy, 111–12, 145, 146
moral sexism, 71–72
Morgan, Henry, 99
Moser-Rath, E., 114
Mother Church, 154–55, 160
mother tongue, taught, 7–8, 81, 105,
   133, 139
Muchembled, Robert, 166
Murdock, George, 86–87
Myrdal, Gunnar, 77
myths, 3, 28, 35, 70, 73
   of creation, 176
   of equality, 3, 20, 24–26, 28–29,
      178
   of male dominance, 109, 114–15
   socio-biological, 77

Nag, Moni, 41
Nannei, Alessandra, 37
Nash, June, 61
Nathanson, Constance, 50
nation-state, 36, 169
nature, women as, 84, 110, 125,
   129–31
nature/culture paradigm, 130–31
Needham, Rodney, 130
needs, 9, 10, 40, 81, 178–79
   education as, 11
   envy as basis of, 12–13
   key words and, 5
   social services as creators of, 78–79

Index

Index

racism, socio-biology and, 76, 77,
    78–79
Radke, G., 118
Ranulf, Svend, 13
Ranwez, Edouard, 13
rape, 31–32
Rapp, Rayna, 59
Ratner, Ronnie Steinberg, 25
reality, 9
    gender and grasp of, 127–32
    key words and, 6, 8
    vernacular, 69, 74
recession, women and, 30–31
reform, Christian idea of, 158–59
Reifenberg, H., 152
Reiter, Rayna, 115
religiosity, 160, 161–63
Renaissance, 23–24, 103, 163
rent, gender and, 95, 96–97, 102,
    167, 168
reported economy, 22–36, 48
    unreported economy vs., 39, 40,
        44, 56, 57–58
reproduction, 34–36, 49
    "social," 36, 37
research, 79
    by vs. for women, 64
    see also feminism, feminists;
        women's studies
resources, 62
    equal access to, 17
    productive, 15, 18, 19
    women as, 34
Riandey, B., 52
Richards, Audrey, 88, 107, 127,
    145
Richmond, Velma Bourgeois, 168
rights, 111, 115
rituals, 28, 111, 158, 176
    egalitarian, 28–29
    transgression as, 145–46
Robert, Jean, 16, 56, 120
Robert, Paul, 7
Roberts, Michael, 92
Roe, Jill, 85
Rogers, Susan Carol, 88, 114–15
role, 6, 69, 75, 80, 86, 100
    complementarity of, 86–87
    sex, 80–81, 83–89
    in speech and language, 136

Romanesque style, 158, 159–63
Rosen, Harvey S., 41
Rossi, Alice, 77
Rossiaud, Jacques, 32
Roubin, Lucienne A., 108
rough music, 110–11, 113, 145
Royen, Gerlach, 138–39
Rubin, Gayle, 15, 35, 69, 100
Rudofsky, Bernard, 120
Ruoff, Arno, 132
Rysman, Alexander, 114

Sabean, David, 103, 108, 173–74
Sachs, Wolfgang, 16
Sacks, M. P., 30
Sahlins, Marshall, 10, 144
Salin, Edgar, 171
scarcity, 18, 81
    dearth vs., 144
    as economic assumption, 4, 10–12,
        18–19, 45, 84
    history of, 18, 19, 169
    poverty and, 62
    regime of, 3, 18, 19, 28, 144, 178
Schmidt, Leopold, 93
Schmidtke, Dietrich, 164
Schneider, Jane, 33–34
Schneider, P., 112
Schoeck, Helmut, 13
scholasticism, 74
Schreiner, Olive, 61
Schulte, Regina, 126
Schumacher, E. F., 82
Schwartz Cowan, Ruth, 51, 52
science:
    monocular, 61–62, 69
    nature/culture paradigm in,
        130–31
    sexism and, 71–72, 128–29
    stereoscopic, 61–62, 69, 129
Scott, Robert A., 63
Scott, Sir Gilbert, 120
Segalen, Martine, 107, 108–10, 117
self-help, 57–58, 158
self-service economy, 57–58
Semyonov, Moshe, 27
Senegal, traders in, 96
service sector, employment in, 53
servile work, 95, 96

Index